Route 66

Center Books on American Places
George F. Thompson,
series founder and director

Route 66

-- -- -- -- -- -- -- -- -- -- --

Iconography of the American Highway

by Arthur Krim

edited by Denis Wood

Center for American Places

Santa Fe, New Mexico,
and Staunton, Virginia

PUBLISHER'S NOTES: *Route 66: Iconography of the American Highway* is the third volume in the series *Center Books on American Places*, created and directed by the Center for American Places. The book was issued in a hardcover edition of 2,200 copies, with the generous financial support of the Friends of the Center for American Places. For more information about the Center and the publication of *Route 66*, please see page 220.

Center for American Places, Inc.
P.O. Box 23225
Santa Fe, New Mexico 87502, U.S.A.
www.americanplaces.org

Distributed by the University of Chicago Press
www.press.uchicago.edu

9 8 7 6 5 4 3 2 1

Library of Congress Cataloging-in-Publication Data is available from the publisher upon request.

ISBN 1-930066-35-X

Frontispiece: K-Mart's Route 66 logo for its nationally distributed brand of jeans, featuring the Route 66 shield with a diner image. Author's collection.

In memory of Bobby Troup

1917–1999

a good friend of the highway

Afoot and light-hearted I take to the open road,
Healthy, free, the world before me,
The long brown path before me leading wherever I choose.

—Walt Whitman
  "Song of the Open Road"
  Leaves of Grass (1856)

Contents

List of Figures

Preface and Acknowledgments

MY ROUTE 66 JOURNEY began in the spring of 1964 in Worcester, Massachusetts, when I first heard the fast, rhymed lyrics of "Route 66" being sung by the Rolling Stones on their new American album. As a geography major at Clark University, my imagination was captured by the town names and western highway adventure, although the only western highway I knew at the time was Route 9 from Boston.

Later, on holiday trips from my graduate work at the University of Chicago to St. Louis for Thanksgiving, I became familiar with the U.S. 66 shields. Still later, work on my dissertation on Los Angeles gave me a taste of the highway in California.

The present study of Route 66 began when Mike Jackson asked me to give a mapping history of the highway at the Henry Ford Museum in 1988. Mike was then president of the Society of Commerical Archeology, of which I had been a founding board member. My "cultural cartography" received national attention, thanks to Patricia Leigh Brown of *The New York Times*. On this basis Katherine Mahar of the Helen Reese Agency in Boston asked me for a book proposal.

From that point forward a series of potential chapters on the Dust Bowl and the "Route 66" song put me in touch with Susan Shillinglaw of the Steinbeck Research Center at San Jose State University, and with songwriter Bobby Troup in Los Angeles, who over the course of years became a dear friend. Further research on Route 66 connected me with author Michael Wallis in Tulsa and with David Lopez at the Department of Transportation in Oklahoma City, both of whom provided valuable resources on the Oklahoma origins of the highway. Richard F. Weingroff at the Federal Highway Department in Washington, D.C., unlocked the history of auto trails and route numbers, and Tom Snyder in California provided a national perspective on early route locations. In January 1990, my close colleague in symbolic geography, Denis Wood, put me in touch with George F. Thompson, president and publisher of the Center for American Places. The result is this fully illustrated iconography of Route 66, produced for and by the Center under the editorial guidance of George and his colleague Randall B. Jones.

I extend my heartfelt thanks to all those mentioned above and others who have made this book possible. Over the past decade numerous people have contributed their valuable time to this comprehensive history of Route 66. Teri Cleeland (with the National Park Service), Richard J. Pike (with the U.S. Geological Survey), and Robert DeMott (at Ohio State University), among others, read early drafts. Other providers of historical data included Jim Ross of Ghost Town Press in Oklahoma, and Keith Sculle at the Illinois State Historic Preservation Agency. A network of close friends gave time and advice along the road, including Marsha Peters, Tom Koch, Jeff and Eleanor Blumberg, Linda Graetz, Roberta Saperstein, Kate Eastment, Jeff Brewer, Julia Collins, Joan Berzoff, Jane Pellouchoud, David Lightbourne, Michael Conzen, and my brothers Robert and Donald Krim.

The manuscript also benefitted from the peer reviews secured by the Center for American Places. The Center and the author and editor extend heartfelt thanks to Drake Hokanson, John Jakle, and Karl Raitz, whose suggestions for improvement were considered carefully and, as they will note, widely implemented.

ORIGINAL SOURCES

This book attempts to unfold a process of iconization, trac-ing a series of images back to their original sources. Following an introduction to the highway as icon and an overview of the original setting, of fundamental importance in the iconography of a highway, the book is divided into three parts. The first pursues the *idea* of the highway, its logic, in the behaviors of Native Americans, European colonists and settlers, and the creators of the nineteenth-century wagon trails. A second chapter tackles the idea of the Pacific Railroad project that emerged during the Gold Rush. A third chapter looks at the way this railroad evolved under pressure from both the chartered companies and the landscape. The second part, chapters four through seven, treats the road as a *fact*: U.S. Highway 66. Chapter four examines the immediate antecedents of U.S. 66 in the named auto trails of the early twentieth century; the fifth chapter tries to make sense of the dramatic events that led to the numbering of the route; and chapter six examines the booster associations created to promote the new highway. Chapter seven looks at its transformation during the Dust Bowl of the 1930s. The third part, chapters eight through fourteen, is concerned with the development of U.S. 66 as a *symbol*. Chapter eight is devoted to John Steinbeck's creation of the "mother road" in *The Grapes of Wrath*, and nine to its transformation into John Ford's film of the same name. The tenth chapter follows Bobby and Cynthia Troup from Lancaster, Pennsylvania, to Los Angeles and their creation of "(Get Your Kicks on) Route 66!" The eleventh chapter reverts to matters of fact and the creation of the Interstate Highway System, but the twelfth returns to the increasingly abstracted symbol of Route 66 in the rock and roll renditions of the Troups' song. The thirteenth chapter is devoted to the symbol's fate at the hands of pop and other artists, while the fourteenth mixes matters of symbol and fact in the decommissioning of the highway by 1985. A concluding chapter briefly recapitulates the 150-year trajectory followed by the original idea to its recent apotheosis in Times Square.

In order to understand its development, each image element is traced to its original sources. For example, the genesis of *The Grapes of Wrath* and the lyrics of "(Get Your Kicks on) Route 66!" are tracked from their first appearance in period references. This way each of the image elements can be appreciated as a development made by real people addressing real issues in real time and space. Each is presented here in period photographs, maps, and advertisements, in an effort to flesh out the context in which it arose and matured.

The present iconography of Route 66 is focused on the *symbolic* history of the highway. Many recent studies have detailed the state-by-state location of original Route 66 segments and paid careful attention to surviving features. This study is intended as *a gazatteer of symbolic sources*, a chronological guide to the imagery of U.S. 66, from its earliest conceptions to the very recent past. The development of nostalgia for the highway since its decommissioning in 1985 is not a part of this project. It is hoped that the reader will be sufficiently rewarded by the iconography itself, and by the parallel stories of the road on the ground and in the mind.

Route 66

I.1. K-Mart billboard, Times Square, New York, March 2001. The Route 66 shield is shown in a Southwest setting. Author's photo.

Introduction:

Highway Icon

In the beginning Route 66 was simply an idea. Then it was a highway. Now it is a universal symbol that anyone can appropriate for any purpose. In March 2001, a giant billboard advertising K-Mart's "Route 66" blue jeans wrapped around the corner of Seventh Avenue and West 49th Street in New York's Times Square (Fig. 1.1). A guy on the Seventh Avenue side leans toward a girl on the 49th Street side who leans toward the guy. When they reach the corner, they will kiss. They are supposed to be in back-to-back booths in a roadside diner through whose windows we can see a highway, the characteristic desert forms of the American Southwest, and a big DINER sign. Hovering in the corners are red and yellow Route 66 highway shields. To see Route 66 projected across Times Square as an image of escape to the open spaces of the West from the urban realities of Manhattan is to understand just how abstract the highway has become, and what an icon it has become, reformed, reshaped, and recolored, as here, to promote consumption of a popular commercial product.

Designed by New York's TBWA/Chiat-Day, the advertisement had been erected by Infinity Outdoor Advertising in November 2000, as part of K-Mart's national campaign for its "Route 66" clothing line.[1] The idea for the brand had been developed in 1995 by K-Mart in Troy, Michigan, in recognition of the fact that the Route 66 shield retained its attractiveness as a symbol of youth and adventure, and so could be used to promote the youth-oriented clothing line.[2] By 1998 the Minneapolis firm of Campbell & Mithun had designed the logo for the brand, "mind mapping" Route 66 in red numbers onto a yellow background to distinguish it from the federal highway markers which had been black on white (frontispiece, page ii). The change, among others, allowed K-Mart to register "Route 66" as a brand of The Original Clothing Company, and thus to appropriate a public symbol for private commercial use.[3]

ICONOGRAPHY

There was nothing new in this for Route 66. Route 66

3

imagery played a part in the imagination of New Yorkers throughout the highway's history. In 1928, Andy Payne, winner of the transcontinental "Bunion Derby" footrace that followed U.S. 66 from Los Angeles to Chicago, took his victory lap around Madison Square Garden in New York. In 1939, New York's Viking Press published John Steinbeck's novel, *The Grapes of Wrath*, about the Dust Bowl exodus along Highway 66. And, in 1959, Sterling Silliphant and Bert Leonard met on New York's Upper West Side to develop the CBS television series, *Route 66*. Nor was the transformation of Route 66 to private commercial use new: in 1930 Phillips Petroleum adopted the red and black "66" shield sign to advertise its gasoline, and in 1946 Bobby and Cynthia Troup exploited the name, indeed the whole road, to create "(Get Your Kicks on) Route 66!", the popular song that made their fortune.

There is nothing random or haphazard about the process by which powerful symbols such as Route 66 arise from the background noise of human activity and communication, to generate novels and movies, songs and television shows, Pop Art and advertising. Such things can be collected and put in order to create an historic iconography, following a scholarly tradition that dates back to the Renaissance.[4] Iconographies of Italian saints and Netherlands artists alike observe an established methodology in which distinctive visual elements are catalogued, their sources tracked down, and the development of their themes traced.[5] In the twentieth century iconographic research embraced the city as a subject, generating rewarding work from the very first volume, in 1915, of I. N. Phelps Stokes's *An Iconography of Manhattan Island*, through John A. Kouwenhoven's 1953 *The Columbia Historical Portrait of New York*, to the author's own 1980 *Imagery in Search of a City: The Geosophy of Los Angeles*.[6]

Among the most important of these iconographies is Alan Trachtenberg's *Brooklyn Bridge, Fact and Symbol* of 1965. Trachtenberg develops a thesis about what might be called the "iconographic arc." Under its aegis Trachtenberg first studied the bridge as a projected idea, then as a realized structure, and finally as an abstracted symbol. Here is Trachtenberg describing this three-stage process in the context of Hart Crane's epic poem, *The Bridge*, of 1930:

> Hart Crane completed the passage of Brooklyn Bridge from fact to symbol. Such a passage was implicit in the earliest ideas of an East River bridge in Thomas Pope's conception as well as John Roebling's. In the transformation, Crane eliminated the bridge's function as 'an economical approach to shorter hours, quicker lunches, behaviorism and toothpicks.' He imagined an ideal function: a leap into a new consciousness. He refused to, or could not, acknowledge the social reality of his symbol, its concrete relations to its culture.[7]

Route 66 appears to have followed a similar iconographic arc. First came the functional conception of a Pacific Railroad projected along the 35° parallel during the California Gold Rush of 1853, then the construction of a "transcontinental" auto highway with the Ozark Trails of 1917 and the federal numbering of the Chicago-to-Los Angeles U.S. Highway 66 route in 1926. Soon, Route 66 became an abstraction: the Mother Road of Steinbeck's *The Grapes of Wrath* in 1938, the song-map lyrics of the Troups' "(Get Your Kicks on) Route 66!" in 1946, the television series *Route 66* in 1960, the work of Pop and other artists in the 1970s, and the K-Mart logo of 2000. At each step the evolving icon fused all the accumulated imagery existing at the previous stage with new purpose, melding *idea* (Part I), *fact* (Part II), and *symbol* (Part III) into an increasingly powerful image, "a leap into a new consciousness," iconic Route 66, the "Open Road," the one Walt Whitman had first offered American readers in 1856.[8] The diagram, "Route 66 Iconography," summarizes the evolution of this complex, and it therefore functions as a guide to the text and as a graphic table of contents tracking the elements of the image over time (Fig. 1.2).

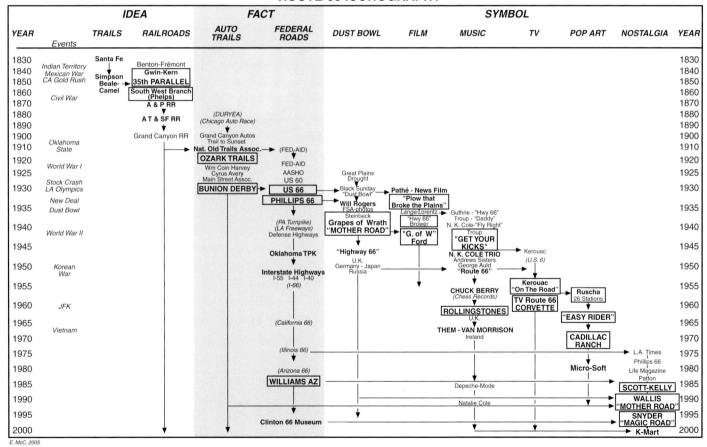

I.2 Route 66 iconography, 1830–2000. Diagram showing Route 66 image elements transformed from *idea* to *fact* to *symbol*. By the author.

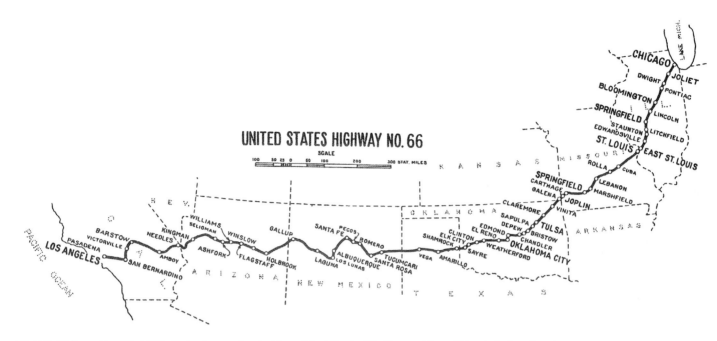

UNITED STATES HIGHWAY NO. 66

SCALE

I.3. U.S. Highway No. 66, 1931. Federal map showing the original Route 66 alignment from Chicago to Los Angeles through Santa Fe, New Mexico. By permission of the Bureau of Public Roads.

PHYSICAL SETTING

Route 66 traversed nearly two-thirds of the United States from the Great Lakes to the Pacific Ocean, in a pronounced diagonal from the Midwest through the Southwest to California (Fig. 1.3). Its logic was physical. It was the route to the Pacific with the least grade and the least adverse climate. Put simply, Route 66 was a frontier road that went southwest from Chicago across the Heartland and Great Plains, around the Rocky Mountains at Santa Fe, across the Colorado Plateau, and over the Mojave Desert to Los Angeles. If high mountain passes were avoided, the skills of early auto travelers were nonetheless challenged by dangerous, steep grades in the Sandia Mountains of New Mexico, the Black Mountains of Arizona, and the twisting Cajon Pass down to San Bernardino and the Los Angeles Basin. The highway's original 2,430 miles encompassed a variety of landforms and climates that gave the highway a distinctive, Western character (Fig. 1.4).

Route 66 passed through a land hardly known to Americans before 1850, and not fully incorporated into the U.S. until after 1900. When in 1925 the highway was designated a federal route, living memories still harbored tales of Indian raids, emigrant wagon trains, and early railroads that

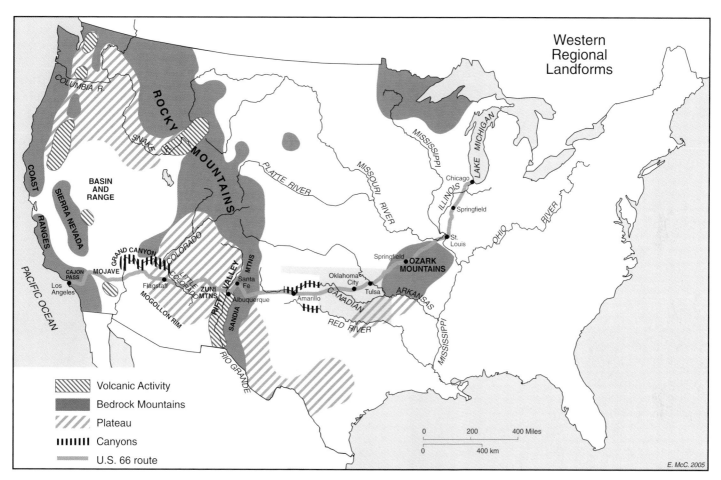

I.4. Western regional landforms. Map of the basic geologic regions along the Route 66 corridor from Chicago, through Oklahoma (shaded), to Los Angeles. By the author.

recalled the frontier traditions of the American West. In the period following the Second World War, the rugged landscape gave Route 66 a tourist appeal that endured until it was supplanted by high-speed interstates and the decommissioning of the route in 1985. The sixty-year history of Route 66 spanned the final demise of the Western frontier, the rise

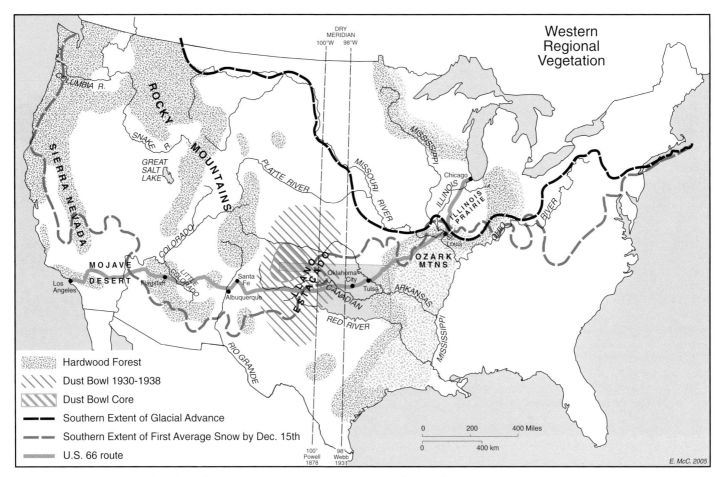

I.5. Western regional vegetation. Map of the natural vegetation regions along the Route 66 corridor from Chicago, through Oklahoma (shaded), to Los Angeles. By the author.

of the suburban culture of the Sunbelt, and the emergence of California as the *new* American frontier.

If the basic topography of Route 66 provided a fantastic landscape of rugged forms, a distinctly dry climate further defined the experience as Western. After the prairie grasslands of Illinois and the wooded uplands of Missouri, Route 66 crossed the 100° meridian in Oklahoma, the line of less rain that the Western explorer, John Wesley Powell, had proposed in 1878 as the division between the humid lands of the East and the semi-arid and desert lands of the West.[9] Only in the mountain uplands of Missouri and New Mexico, and the high plateaus of Arizona, was moisture sufficient to maintain the full-growth forests familiar to Eastern travelers. On the eve of the Dust Bowl, the historian Walter Prescott Webb shifted the dry desert divide eastward to the 98° meridian.[10] On Route 66 this new dryland boundary was passed at El Reno, Oklahoma, near the Canadian River crossing where Eastern broadleaf forests gave way to the prairie grasses of the High Plains (Fig. 1.5).

Dryland grasses, however, reached even as far east as Chicago, where at the 88° meridian average rainfall along the shores of Lake Michigan often fell below thirty-five inches a year.[11] Indeed *much* of Illinois had been prairie, a natural grassland on fertile glacial soils that made possible the rich farm lands of the Corn Belt through which Route 66 passed on its way from Chicago to St. Louis.[12] Southwest from Chicago (elevation 660 feet), Route 66 crossed the level plains of the Illinois prairie on the fertile glacial tills laid down in the last retreat of Ice Age glaciers some 10,000 years ago. The gentle glacial moraines were barely noticed by the traveler passing through the endless farmlands south to St. Louis and the Mississippi River.[13] Here the great river joined with the Missouri just above the city in a broad floodplain (445 feet above sea level) marked by steep banks where the great steel bridges spanning the muddy channel stood as gateways to the trans-Mississippi West.

From the Mississippi, Route 66 quickly gained elevation on the rocky uplands of the Ozark Plateau. This was a western outlier of the Appalachian Mountains with ancient rocks of Devonian Age, containing valuable lead and silver deposits amid pockets of limestone with hidden caves such as the Meramec Caverns in central Missouri, which became tourist destinations.[14] With broadleaf forests on the uplands, the landscape would again have been familiar to Easterners. The dense woodland growth was the consequence of the elevation and the proximity to tropical moisture from the Gulf of Mexico that brought warm rains into southern Missouri.[15] Route 66 followed the crest of the Ozark Plateau (elevation 1,200 feet) until it graded down to the edge of the Great Plains at Springfield in southwest Missouri. Here, where the annual rainfall hardly reached thirty inches, the highway roadside again turned to grasslands.[16] Here as well a second outlier of Devonian rocks created a rich lead and zinc mining district that ran from Joplin, Missouri, to Galena, Kansas.[17]

Across the state line in Oklahoma the lead gave way to rich traps of Pennsylvania Period oil domes that extended beneath Tulsa (elevation 700 feet) to the Permian Basin under Oklahoma City, with its working wells on the state capitol grounds.[18] For many travelers on Route 66, Oklahoma City was the beginning of the Western landscape which turned dry and parched at the silent line of Webb's 98° meridian. Beyond Oklahoma City lay the heart of the Dust Bowl and the realm of the Great American Desert that explorers in the early nineteenth century described. This region was prone to cycles of extended drought, and in the 1930s just such a calamity forced the mass migration of rural families from Missouri, Kansas, and Oklahoma onto Route 66 and out to California.[19]

From the gently rolling landscape of eastern Oklahoma, Route 66 gradually rose westward at the Canadian River channel to the High Plains of the Texas panhandle.[20]

Beyond the Canadian River and in the parched panhandle of Texas rainfall hardly reached ten inches a year. Here the prairie was so dry that early Spanish explorers had named the region the *llano estacado*, the "Staked Plains," where wooden posts had to be driven into the hard sod to mark the trail.[21] This was the classic cowboy country of large grazing ranches with hot, dusty summers and cold winter blizzards that swept down on drivers, often blinding them, between Amarillo and Tucumcari. Beneath the level land, the rich oil fields of the Cimarron Uplift at Amarillo (elevation 3,675 feet) held rare helium gas deposits that provided a strategic reserve for the great dirigible airships of the 1920s and later the U.S. Navy surveillance blimps of the Second World War.[22]

From the flat plains of the Texas panhandle Route 66 followed the edge of the Canadian River canyon to the upper valley of the Pecos River in New Mexico. Here the highway first encountered the rise of the Rocky Mountains, which provided a green refuge from the desert plains below. This was the edge of the Rio Grande Valley, watered by the snow peaks in Colorado and the summer monsoons from Mexico. Along Route 66 the hills were dotted with pine (piñon) and juniper, spruce, and aspen.[23] Originally the highway was routed north along the Pecos River from Santa Rosa through the Glorieta Pass to Santa Fe (elevation 7,000 feet), then south to Albuquerque to avoid the steep grades of the Sangre de Cristo Range, the southernmost extension of the Rockies at Santa Fe. During the Dust Bowl era a direct line for Route 66 was opened from Santa Rosa west to Albuquerque with dramatic road cuts through Tijeras Canyon in the Sandia Mountains into the Rio Grande Valley.[24] The valley was a deeply rifted block whose sharp edges mark a recent tectonic tear in the North American continent with volcanic lava fields on the western edge of Albuquerque.[25] In the lower elevations between Santa Fe and Albuquerque, the Rio Grande remained a dry stream except in spring flood season.

At Albuquerque (elevation 4,900 feet) Route 66 crossed the Rio Grande and began the long climb onto the Colorado Plateau. The original grade followed the Rio Grande south to Isleta Pueblo and Los Lunas and turned west up the valley of the Rio Puerco and Rio San Jose to Laguna Pueblo, while a later routing struck directly west across the plateau to the Rio San Jose. During the Second World War large deposits of uranium were mined from the Permian rocks north of Grants to provide fuel for the nuclear fission of the atomic bomb at the secret government laboratories at Los Alamos near Santa Fe.[26] The highway ascended the high valley of the Rio San Jose to reach the continental divide at Thoreau (elevation 7,200 feet) and pass over the volcanic lava fields marking the western edge of the Rio Grande Rift block. As Route 66 rose up to the Zuñi Mountains at Gallup, the flat mesa summits were capped by pine (piñon) forests that captured the summer rains and winter snows.[27]

Gallup marked the gateway into Arizona. There the highway once again dipped below the moisture elevations to the Painted Desert and the dramatic landscape of the canyon lands of the Little Colorado River. The road followed the Puerco River through a variety of fascinating natural features, including the Petrified Forest to the Little Colorado at Holbrook (elevation 5,080 feet). Near Winslow was the unique Meteor Crater, an impacted depression a half mile across formed 22,000 years ago by a large primal fragment from outer space, the largest of its type in the U.S.[28] From Winslow, Route 66 ran west over the Mogollon Rim, crossing the deeply entrenched Canyon Diablo and Canyon Padre as the land rose towards the 12,000-foot summits of the San Francisco Peaks, a volcanic cone active a mere half-million years ago whose steaming vents still scar the landscape at Sunset Crater north of Winona. In the foothills lay Flagstaff (elevation 7,000 feet) and further west the former volcanic peak of Bill Williams Mountain at Williams, gateway town to the Grand Canyon.[29] As Route 66 regained altitude, evergreen forests appeared that attracted loggers and reclaimed the mountain slopes.[30] Route 66 avoided the deep Colorado River chasm by running south to the Aubrey and Haulapai valleys down the Grand Wash cliffs to the base of the Black Mountains at Kingman (elevation 3,300 feet). These steep-faced hills were part of the Basin and Range Province, that fractured interior region between the Rocky Mountains and the Sierra Nevada containing pockets of great mineral wealth that lured miners to the desolate peaks at the turn of the twentieth century.[31] As the road dropped below the peaks, desert lands returned, supporting only dry creosote bush.[32] The early Route 66 followed the Gold Road up from Kingman through the treacherous Sitgreaves Pass (elevation 3,500 feet) to Oatman where the highway twisted down again to the Colorado River at Topock (elevation 475 feet), perhaps the most dangerous section of the original Route 66 driving experience.[33] In later years the highway was relocated south around the Black Mountains, exchanging the switchback grades for a level route beside the Santa Fe Railroad from Kingman.

Crossing the Colorado channel provided Route 66 with the gateway to California. Here the highway traveler faced the fantastic formation of the Needles that signaled the stark reality of the Mojave Desert. Before the completion of Boulder (Hoover) Dam in 1935, the Colorado often flooded over its channel near Needles, washing out railroad bridges and cottonwoods.[34] From the Colorado, Route 66 rose toward the Piute Mountains at Goffs (elevation 2,600 feet) with a gradual grade down to Cadiz Valley and the Bristol Dry Lake (elevation 614 feet). Along the way stood the landmark cone of the Amboy Crater, a recent volcanic feature amid the fragmented blocks of the Basin and Range mountains.[35] All the way from Needles, Route 66 ran along the route of the Santa Fe Railroad through the Mojave, 150 miles without water.[36] This was the dreaded "danger zone" during the years of the Dust Bowl migration, often driven at night to avoid the searing heat on the road to Barstow.[37] Only in the hidden peaks of the Providence Mountains did springs, which early Spanish explorers learned about from the native Indian peoples, provide travelers a safe haven.[38] At Barstow (elevation 2,100 feet), Route 66 turned south to pursue the reliable course of the Mojave River, a desert stream whose source lay in the 10,000-foot snow peaks of the San Gabriel Mountains on the edge of the Los Angeles Basin. The road passed the old silver mines at Victorville on its way to the crest of the Cajon Pass (elevation 4,300 feet) on the fault-rifted San Gabriels.[39]

Cajon Pass was the gateway into the seemingly eternal spring of Southern California, whose orange and lemon groves were irrigated by moisture dumped on the San Gabriels by winter storms.[40] From its summit Route 66 wound down Cajon Wash into the Los Angeles Basin at San Bernardino (elevation 1,100 feet). In the valley the highway ran west along the alluvial fans of the foothills to Pasadena where it turned south into Los Angeles (elevation 250 feet) along the Arroyo Seco. A later extension linked Route 66 directly to the seashore at Santa Monica, to complete the connection between the Great Lakes and the Pacific Ocean. Although itself a dry climate, the irrigated Los Angeles Basin seemed a land of milk and honey to travelers weary of the Mojave Desert. Indeed the parallel to the biblical lands of the Mediterranean were matched by California's Pacific shoreline and its classic sun-kissed climate of warm winters and hot, dry summers.[41] It was this wondrous climate that drew people out Route 66 to Los Angeles, from the Jazz Age boosters through the Dust Bowl migrants, and in the post-World War II prosperity helped create a major Sunbelt metropolis along the Pacific Rim.

Part 1

Before the Fact:
The Route in the Mind

Chapter One
Prefigured Pathway

BEFORE THE ACQUISITION of the Louisiana Territory and New Mexico, and well before Route 66, a series of ancient pathways and explorers' trails traversed the vast region between the Mississippi and the Pacific. An ongoing belief holds that much of Route 66 followed the tracks of ancient Indian trails. In fact only small trail segments survived into the auto era, and even these sections remain open to debate regarding their precise location. Nevertheless, in the trail systems they did articulate and, as importantly, in their failure to reach across the Southern High Plains, the prehistoric cultures that occupied the valleys of the Mississippi and the Rio Grande not only prefigured isolated road segments, but anticipated the core historic problem of Route 66, namely, the apparent void constituting the Southern High Plains, the *llano estacado*, the Great American Desert, Indian Territory, or Oklahoma, as it was variously known. It is not too much to say that the route segments these peoples developed, together with the problems they faced in the

Southern High Plains, constitute the earliest prefiguration of what ultimately evolved into the icon we know as Route 66.

CLOVIS AND FOLSOM OCCUPATION OF THE SOUTHERN HIGH PLAINS

To understand the history of Route 66 is to appreciate the fact that the Great Plains, especially the High Plains, which stretched west from Oklahoma along the corridor of the Canadian River across the Texas panhandle into New Mexico, was by and large a prehistoric void. Paradoxically, this was not initially the case. Here, as Route 66 was first being marked across eastern New Mexico, the discovery of carefully crafted stone spear points along with extinct mammoth bones in dry stream sediments at Folsom in 1927, and again near Clovis in 1932, confirmed that ancient Ice Age peoples had occupied the High Plains of the upper Canadian River at a very early time.[1] When radiocarbon dating was finally applied to the Clovis point sites, they showed an age of some 11,000 years, with mammoth kill sites as far east as the

Mississippi River at Kimmswick, south of St. Louis.[2] The Clovis sites showed that, in the centuries of the Late Pleistocene, the Southern High Plains were among the most desirable of all North American locations for the Ice Age hunters who followed the big game animals down between the mountain glaciers. These are the oldest known human hunting sites in the continental U.S. and demonstrate that the dry lands of the Dust Bowl period had at one time been the most advanced region of cultural economy along the Route 66 corridor (Fig. 1.1). The hunting trails of these Clovis and Folsom peoples have long since disappeared under the sediments of prairie soils, but the course of the Canadian River likely served the best watered way across the Southern High Plains as the hunters followed the mammoth herds from west to east and back again between the Rio Grande and the Mississippi.

CHACO AND CAHOKIA

As the grasslands of the High Plains gradually dried out following the climate adjustments of the postglacial period, the great mammoth herds disappeared, to be replaced by bison and antelope. The hunting peoples now turned to the well-watered shelter of the Rocky Mountains and the fertile flood plains of the Mississippi Valley. In these two locations, distinct and creative cultures developed sedentary agriculture over the next several millennia. What resulted were two complex, settled societies, one centered in the upper Rio Grande north of Santa Fe, the other around the junction of the Missouri and Mississippi rivers near St. Louis (Fig. 1.2).[3] Rather than being an area of an advanced society, the Southern High Plains *now* became a backwater of older

nomadic culture, as the planting peoples developed agricultural innovations in the leisure time permitted by their settled village life. Once established, these core cultures defined patterns of development which persisted into the modern period, remaining visible in the Route 66 corridor in the cities of the Mississippi Valley and the Rio Grande, and the ranch lands of Oklahoma and Texas.

Along Route 66 between Santa Fe and Flagstaff, in the mountain foothills of the Rockies where the Rio Grande and Colorado River find their sources, prehistoric peoples found a rich harvest of piñon nuts, which they collected in baskets constructed by coiling reeds they collected along the river bottoms. These peoples evolved advanced societies ancestral to the present Navaho and Zuñi peoples. In the dry caves of Nevada, traces of these ancient basket makers have been preserved from as long ago as 7000 B.C.[4] Around 1500 B.C. peoples in the area adopted corn planting from Mexico, and by A.D. 500 they had developed a unique coiled clay pottery for storing the harvest. The Anasazi peoples expanded the system, flourishing in the Four Corners region.[5] In Chaco Canyon at Pueblo Bonito, they built an impressive five-storied ceremonial center with beautifully cut stone walls. The Anasazi grew wealthy trading turquoise from the Cerillos mines in the Rio Grande Valley with Aztecs in distant Mexico.[6]

Chaco Canyon reached its climax about A.D. 1250 when a network of great radial roads was built. These stone ways extended like spokes of a wheel with a fifty-mile radius, reaching as far south as the Puerco Valley near Gallup and the Rio San Juan at Grants.[7] These are the oldest known highways constructed along the Route 66 corridor, and

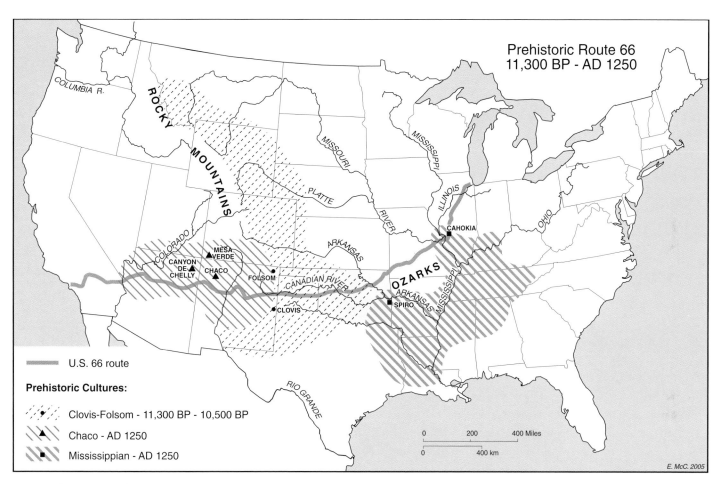

Prehistoric Route 66
11,300 BP - AD 1250

Prehistoric Cultures:

Clovis-Folsom - 11,300 BP - 10,500 BP

Chaco - AD 1250

Mississippian - AD 1250

U.S. 66 route

E. McC. 2005

1.1. Prehistoric Route 66, 11300 B.C. to A.D. 1250. Map of the prehistoric Clovis-Folsom hunting culture of the Great Plains; the urban cultures at Chaco in the Rio Grande Valley and Cahokia in the Mississippi Valley; and the site of the Canadian River corridor of buffalo hunting culture in what is today Oklahoma (shaded). By the author.

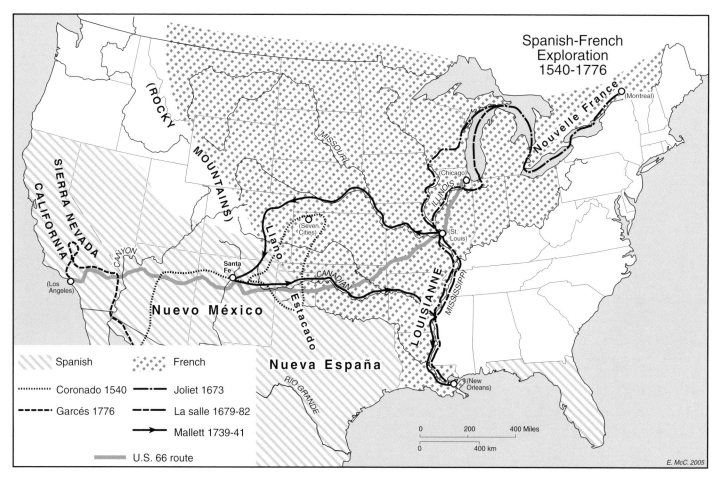

1.2. Spanish-French exploration, 1540 to 1776. Map of early Spanish and French territories, showing the Spanish *entradas* around the Grand Canyon between Santa Fe and Los Angeles, and the routes of French voyageurs from Montreal to the Mississippi and from St. Louis along the Canadian River. By the author.

mark the significance of the culture achieved here along the continental divide before drought forced abandonment of the fields around A.D. 1300. The Anasazi then migrated into the Puerco and Rio San Juan valleys to reconstruct themselves as the Pueblo culture encountered by the Spanish on their arrival in the area in the sixteenth century.[8] Even though reduced in circumstance, the Pueblo culture did reach out to the buffalo hunters of the High Plains. Stone foundations built by Pueblo peoples have been found along the corridor of the Canadian River in the panhandles of Texas and Oklahoma, where white shells from the Pacific foreshadow the trade that would later roll along Route 66.[9]

Contemporary with the Chaco culture in New Mexico was the great ceremonial center of Cahokia, now in East St. Louis, Illinois, where monumental mounds rise forty feet above the Mississippi flood plain. In A.D. 1250, at the time of its zenith, the Cahokia center was the largest settlement in North America, estimated at some 40,000 people.[10] As with the Anasazi, the Cahokia culture can be traced back to earlier post-Pleistocene settlements along the Mississippi, Missouri, and Ohio rivers, with an early agricultural village at Koster on the Illinois River dated to 5000 B.C.[11] Again, the introduction of corn by way of Mexico after 1500 B.C. set in motion the development of Cahokia, which began as an Aztec-styled pyramid center about A.D. 900, linked by trade routes along the Gulf of Mexico.[12]

More immediate to the history of Route 66, the Cahokia Mississippi culture extended its influence to such secondary centers as Spiro Mound on the Arkansas River in eastern Oklahoma, southwest over the Missouri Ozarks, and along a diagonal that would later be followed by Route 66 from St. Louis, with exotic trade goods from the furthest reaches of the Mississippi realm. These included sea shells from Florida and copper ingots that had moved from Lake Superior down the Illinois River along the very corridor Route 66 would follow from Chicago.[13]

Yet these Cahokia copper trade routes never reached west across the prairie to the Pueblo culture at Chaco Canyon, nor did Pueblo turquoise ever reach the Mississippi. Separating the Mississippi and Rio Grande realms was a void, the great prairie plains that in the American period would become the Indian Territory of Oklahoma.[14] Curiously, following the climate change of A.D. 1300, when the Mississippi mound settlements were abandoned, some turquoise from the Pueblo peoples did make its way over the High Plains along the Canadian River to Spiro Mound through exchange with the buffalo hunters.[15]

After the collapse of Cahokia in A.D. 1350, its peoples were absorbed into the local tribal groups along the Missouri and Mississippi rivers so that no trace of the great civilization was evident to the Spanish explorers of the sixteenth century, save for a stray turquoise pendant they found in an Arkansas River village.[16] Once again the buffalo hunters became the dominant culture in the vast area between the Ozarks and the Rockies along the Canadian River corridor that would become Route 66.

SPANISH AND FRENCH

When the Europeans arrived in the trans-Mississippi region of the American Southwest, Chaco and Cahokia had been deserted for some 300 years. Both the Spanish and French explored the unknown lands along modern Route 66 from their respective realms in Mexico and Quebec, generally following established native trails and riverways. As the Anasazi and Mississippi cultures never connected across the Southern High Plains, so too did the Spanish and French remain isolated from each other in their colonial outposts at Santa Fe and St. Louis.

The Spanish were the first Europeans to explore the Route 66 region with the entrance of Francisco Coronado in 1540. His expedition searched for the seven cities of gold, which took him north from Sonora across the Gila River in Arizona to the edge of the vast canyon lands of the Colorado River, before turning east to the Zuñi Pueblo at Cibola.[17] Finding only mud brick houses, Coronado followed the old trail along the Rio Pescado over the continental divide to El Moro Rock and down to the Rio Grande.[18] Still in search of gold, Coronado marched further east into the buffalo country along the Canadian River to the mythical site of Quivira in Kansas, only to return disappointed in 1542.[19]

A succeeding generation of Spanish explorers, including Juan de Oñate (from 1601 to 1605), also searched for the seven cities, again reaching the Grand Canyon lands of the Colorado, the Zuñi pueblos, and the Rio Grande, and even as far east as the buffalo lands of the upper Canadian River.[20] After Santa Fe was established in 1610 as the capital of Nuevo Mexico, Father Francisco Garcés explored the Colorado River canyon lands in 1776 as a way to California. When he asked local Indians about further trails, he noted in his diary: "They drew on the ground a sort of map, pointing out all the surrounding nations and the ways to them. They were pleased and astonished when on the same map I outlined my journey. Thus we understood each other, and thus gained information about all these nations."[21]

From this "sand" map Father Garcés learned of a "profound canyon" in the Rio Colorado that blocked the way north, and he turned his expedition west across the Mojave Desert to the Mission San Gabriel in California. His map of the Mojave Trail is the earliest record of the Route 66 corridor to California, with its dotted line along the Arroyo de los Mártires (the Mojave River) marking the old Indian path to the fresh springs in the Providence Mountains, and thence over the San Gabriel Mountains by the Cajon Pass into the Los Angeles Basin (Fig. 1.3).[22] Their knowledge of the deep incision of the Colorado River in the Grand Canyon taught the Spanish that a direct trail between Santa Fe and Los Angeles would not be easily realized. Consequently the Spanish circulated north *around* the canyon lands, unlike the route that would be followed by Route 66, looping up through southern Utah to Las Vegas in Nevada, and so down across the Mojave Desert to the Cajon Pass and Los Angeles (see Fig. 1.2). Because of this loop, the Pueblo lands of the upper Colorado remained isolated from European settlement until the Mexican War (1846–48).

As the Spanish searched for gold in the desert canyons of Nuevo Mexico, so the French followed the lure of furs west from the Great Lakes to the waterways of the Mississippi Valley. With the capital of Nouvelle France established on the St. Lawrence River at Quebec in 1608, the French *voyageurs* reached Sault St. Marie at the head of Lake Superior in 1668, searching for a western passage to the Pacific. Their interest, however, was soon diverted south to the base of Lake Michigan at the portage of St. Joseph at South Bend

PLANO

Que conti. las Provincias de Sonora, Pimerias, Papagueria Apache
ria, Rios Gila, y Colorado, y tierras descubert. hasta el Puerto de
fran.ca en la california Septembrional y hasta el Pueblo de Oraybe
en la Provincia de el Moqui, con arreglo a los diarios de el coronel d.
Ant.o Crespo y de los PP. Misioner. y fr. fran Garces en los
viages desde el la nacion Jabajaba en el Rio Colorado hasta la Mision de s.
Gabriel, a las naciones que estan al Norte de esta Mision. Su Egreso a lo
llamajabas, y camino que hizo al Moqui estan señalados con lineas de pun
tos: con cdia Señal Se manifiesta tambien la linea de Presidios de es
ta frontera
Los Presidios se notan con esta Señal
Los Reales de minas y Placer. Pobla.d

1.3. Fr. Garcés map, 1776. Detail showing the original Mojave River trail (shaded), from the Colorado River to Los Angeles along the Route 66 corridor through Cajon Pass. Collection of the Library of Congress.

and the headwaters of the Illinois River. Here in 1673 Father Jacques Marquette and Louis Joliet canoed south to the Mississippi and the Indian villages on the Arkansas. Returning via the Chicago portage, they opened the link between the Great Lakes and the Mississippi River across Illinois that Route 66 would follow from Chicago to St. Louis. A second voyage in 1682 by Robert de La Salle followed the Illinois to the mouth of the Mississippi at the Gulf of Mexico, and established French claims to Louisiana, setting the imprint of French culture in a great arc from Quebec to New Orleans (Fig. 1.2).[23]

The curiosity of the French about a waterway to the west from the Mississippi by way of the Missouri was tested in a series of expeditions that touched Spanish claims to the vast areas of the High Plains west and north of the Rio Grande. In 1714 French trader Etienne de Bourgmont reached the Omaha villages on the Platte River, and Du Tisné followed in 1719 to the Pawnee country in Kansas. By far the most adventurous voyage was by the brothers Pierre and Paul Mallet, Canadian traders living in the Illinois country. In 1739 they left New Orleans in hopes of reaching Santa Fe, traveling as far out of their way as the Dakotas along the upper Missouri and crossing south over the flooded channels of the Salmon and Arkansas rivers, where they found stones with Spanish inscriptions, likely from the Oñate exploration of 1601.[24] From here they followed an Indian guide south along the base of the Rockies to Santa Fe. The following year the Mallet brothers returned to New Orleans by way of the Canadian River, which they named after themselves, tracking its course east across the dry plains of Texas and Oklahoma to the Arkansas River (see Fig. 1.2).[25] Although native traders had taken the Canadian River for centuries as a way from the Rio Grande to the Ozarks, the Mallet brothers were the first Europeans to realize the strategic value of the river as a passageway across the buffalo country from New Mexico to New France, the vital connection that would become the basis for Route 66 from Albuquerque to Tulsa.

SANTA FE TRAIL

Within twenty-five years of the Mallets's voyage the entire Mississippi was lost to France in the Battle of Quebec of 1763, becoming British east of the river in Illinois and Spanish west of St. Louis (also founded in 1763). With the formation of the United States in 1783, the Illinois country became part of Indian Territory, while the western region acquired by Spain was returned to France in 1800, only to be sold to the United States in 1803 as the Louisiana Purchase. As new American settlements expanded across the Appalachian frontier into the Illinois and Missouri regions, the area, with its cultural center at St. Louis, and the crucial Great Lakes portage at Chicago, remained French in spirit. Nuevo Mexico, with Santa Fe isolated as the capital of the fertile Rio Grande, and Los Angeles being founded in California in 1781, remained Spanish.[26] These were the colonial capitals, separated from each other by culture, dry lands and Indians, that would later be connected by Route 66.

With the purchase of Louisiana, the Spanish frontier was opened to American interests, especially the lure of Santa Fe with its trade and potential wealth. In 1806, an army expedition was mounted from St. Louis by Lieutenant Zebulon Pike to explore the upper Arkansas prairie lands to the foot of the Rocky Mountains. There he named Pikes Peak after himself. Pike then turned south into New Mexico and reached Santa Fe in 1807, only to be captured and sent to

Mexico City.[27] Released by American protests, Pike published his accounts in 1810, which established the feasibility of the Arkansas River as a passage to Santa Fe.[28] A second American expedition to Spanish New Mexico was made in 1819 by Major Stephen Long. The expedition followed the upper Missouri west to the South Platte, and then south along the Rocky Mountain front to the edge of the Spanish claims, returning to Fort Smith in Arkansas Territory along the course of the Canadian River.[29] Mapping his route over the sun-bleached plains, Long labeled the area the "Great American Desert," and warned future travelers against crossing the prairie without water or firewood.[30] This stigma helped produce the popular conception of the Canadian River trail from Missouri to Santa Fe as a fearful void, a reluctance prefigured by the Anasazi and Mississippi peoples of Chaco Canyon and Cahokia.

In 1821, a year after the Long expedition, the Mexican revolution opened the Spanish border with New Mexico to eager Americans. The attraction of Santa Fe was soon tested by William Becknell, a Missouri trader, who, in the summer of 1821, took a company of some thirty men west along the upper Arkansas to the Rockies, following Long's trail south over the treacherous Raton Pass to Santa Fe in eight weeks. Becknell's real innovation came in his return route, which avoided the Raton Pass to cross diagonally over the desert lands of the Cimarron River cutoff through the Staked Plains, the *llano estacado*, of the Oklahoma panhandle. Without water this was a dangerous passage but of great advantage as an easy wagon grade. The following year Becknell took three loaded wagons down to Santa Fe by way of the Cimarron Cutoff and returned profitable. By 1825, federal troops had surveyed Becknell's Road and posted forts to keep unruly wagoners and Indian raiders from conflict with travelers.[31] Thus, the Santa Fe Trail from St. Louis to New Mexico went directly over the Ozarks and along the diagonal through Kansas Territory, rather than along the Canadian River. The fact that the Santa Fe Trail through Kansas took such a substantial detour around Indian Territory would, in the auto era, constitute an important argument for routing 66 through what had by then become Oklahoma (see Fig. 1.2).

One impediment that increased the difficulty of the Canadian River route to Santa Fe was the creation of Indian Territory in 1830 west of Missouri and Arkansas (and Fort Smith).[32] These Indian lands were filled with the displaced Appalachian tribes of Cherokee, Choctaw, and Creeks who had been forced on the Trail of Tears across the Mississippi and over the Ozarks into the reservation.[33] Although allowed independent authority, the Indian Nations were carefully controlled by the U.S. Army, who set the Canadian River lands aside as colonial territory. Yet the direct route to Santa Fe from Fort Smith continued to offer rewards. In 1839 Josiah Gregg pioneered the Canadian River trail and published maps in his book, *Commerce of the Prairie* (1844), that showed the way to New Mexico, a valuable guide soon sought by California Gold Rush emigrants of 1849.[34] Nevertheless, the popular belief that the Indian Nations of Oklahoma constituted a threat to safe passage remained, and the longer Becknell's road was considered safer. As a consequence, the Santa Fe Trail became ever more popular, and Indian Territory ever more isolated and feared.

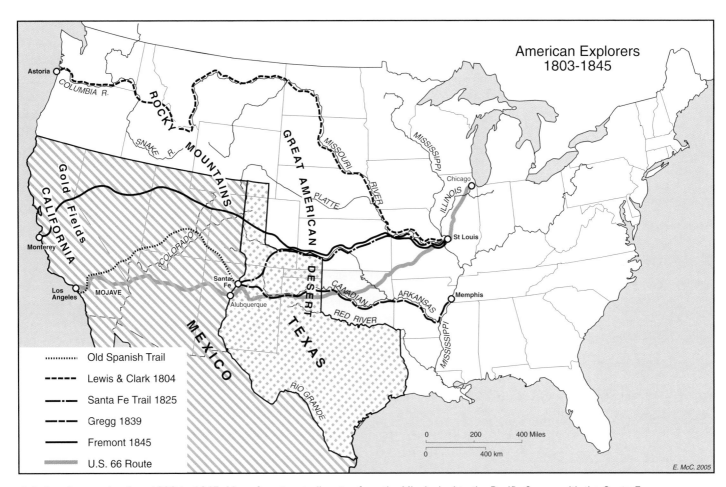

2.1. American exploration, 1803 to 1845. Map of western trail routes from the Mississippi to the Pacific Ocean, with the Santa Fe Trail from St. Louis to Santa Fe (1825) and the Gregg Trail along the Canadian River from Memphis (1839), following the pre-Route 66 corridor through the Great American Desert (Oklahoma). By the author.

Chapter Two
Thirty-Fifth Parallel Route

WHILE THERE IS LITTLE DOUBT that the prehistoric activities of the Anasazi and Mississippi peoples, and their extension at the hands of the Spanish, French, and Americans of the colonial and early national periods, prefigured the essential lineaments that Route 66 would eventually make between Chicago and Los Angeles, the inscription of the route as such was enormously advanced by the Pacific Railroad surveys of 1853. The most direct of these was the thirty-fifth parallel route from Fort Smith through Albuquerque to Los Angeles, which essentially preset the location of the future Route 66 from Oklahoma to California across New Mexico and Arizona before the Civil War abruptly curtailed further efforts. It would take another eighty years of nearly continuous development before this prefiguration could manifest itself in highway form.

BENTON AND FRÉMONT

In the sixteenth century, the conception of the way to the

Pacific took the form of a Northwest Passage, imagined as a continuous water route from the Atlantic to the Pacific. The Northwest Passage had achieved iconic status centuries before it was finally navigated, in 1903 to 1906, through the Arctic Archipelago.[1] The first specifically American effort to achieve this dream took shape in Lewis and Clark's expedition to Oregon from St. Louis in 1804, up the Missouri, over the Rocky Mountains, and down the Snake to the Columbia River (Fig. 2.1), effectively ending the dream of a national water route between the oceans. Subsequently the Oregon Trail, via the Platte River and South Pass, became the wagon trail west, especially after the national attention given it by Francis Parkman's *Oregon Trail* of 1849.[2] The idea of a wagon road spanning the continent was given new currency by the development of the steam railroad. By 1840 the Atlantic ports of Boston, Baltimore, Philadelphia, and New York had built railroads west to the Appalachians, and had projected routes across the Missouri.[3] The building of an iron road over the Rockies seemed only a matter of determined enterprise. As Missouri Senator Thomas Hart Benton put it in 1844: "The magic boat and flying car are not yet seen upon the plain, but they will be seen there; and St. Louis is yet to find herself as near to Canton as she is now to London."[4]

Out of his vision Senator Benton promoted a host of Pacific railroad projects from St. Louis in the years before the Mexican War. His agent was Lt. John Frémont, the handsome western explorer who had married Benton's beautiful daughter Jessie. During 1843 and again in 1845, Frémont crossed the Rockies over the Wind River Range in present-day Wyoming, and passed down into Mexican California. He returned along the Old Spanish Trail through the Mojave Desert and back over the mountains by fur trapper trails to the Arkansas River and St. Louis (see Fig. 2.1).[5] For Benton and Frémont, these backways over the Rockies seemed the logical way to reach the Pacific shore, and they established the federal government's backing for a railroad survey that would prefigure the initial line that Route 66 would follow to California.

CALIFORNIA GOLD

Today California with its wealth of cities seems so secure in its prosperity that its absence from the American realm is beyond comprehension. Yet in 1844, when the first Pacific Railroad projects were proposed, California was a distant Mexican province of scattered ranches and discarded missions, abandoned since the Revolution of 1821. A tentative American presence had been established in the port of Monterey and in the Sacramento Valley as Oregon-bound emigrants branched from the trail at South Pass to cross the Great Salt Lake and the Sierra Nevada Mountains into California.[6] The possibility of the American acquisition of California encouraged President Polk to send Frémont to Monterey in 1846 with a company of sixty men and sealed orders to foster an uprising of the American settlers in the Sacramento Valley. On June 14 Frémont inspired the Bear Flag Revolt in Sonoma and led his men to Yerba Buena in San Francisco to claim California as a Republic. Within two weeks a U.S. Navy warship was in Monterey and by August the American flag was raised in Los Angeles, capturing California for the United States.[7]

The same year a similar action led to war with Mexico over the issue of Texas statehood. During the summer of 1846, a military column under General Stephen Kearny departed Fort Leavenworth in Kansas, captured Santa Fe in August, followed the Gila River trail in Arizona, and reached San Diego in December. A year of bloody battles was to pass before the signing of the Treaty of Guadalupe Hidalgo in February 1848, which ceded California and New Mexico to the U.S.[8] Between Santa Fe and Los Angeles lay an expansive territory without any marked roads of which little was known (see Fig. 2.1). The New Mexico territory stretched from the Rio Grande to the Colorado River, a true *terra incognita* of hostile Indian lands, long ignored by the Spanish, forgotten by the Mexicans, and unknown to the Americans. It was the exoticism of this territory, still essentially intact, that was to prove such a lure to tourists traveling Route 66 in the period of prosperity that followed World War II.

In January 1848, just before the U.S. signed the Hidalgo treaty, gold nuggets had been discovered in the Sacramento

River. This was to trigger a rush to the Sierra slopes that would make California the new American horizon. News of the gold had reached New York by August and by December President Polk had reported its authenticity to congress with nuggets carried overland to Washington, D.C.[9] Within two months steamships in Boston and New York were packed with young men eager to seek their fortunes in California, setting in motion a great national Gold Rush, and the formation of San Francisco as the great new metropolis in the Pacific West.[10]

SIMPSON AND SITGREAVES

With California and New Mexico incorporated as American territory, an effort was undertaken to survey routes to San Francisco and the gold fields. Most relevant to the future Route 66 were the Army exploration parties sent from Albuquerque to Los Angeles across New Mexico and the Mojave Desert. The initial effort was made in April 1849, under Capt. Randolph B. Marcy and Lt. James H. Simpson of the Topographical Engineers. They led a large party of California emigrants from Fort Smith west along the Canadian River trail established by Josiah Gregg through Indian Territory to Santa Fe (see Fig. 2.1).[11] In 1851 Marcy supported the construction of a Pacific Railroad along the Canadian River, outlining the very corridor Route 66 would later take across Oklahoma and Texas: "I am, therefore, of the opinion that but a few localities could be found upon the continent which (for a great distance) would present as few obstacles to the construction of a railway upon this route."[12]

When Marcy reached Santa Fe in June 1849, he helped organize a series of Army expeditions which determined the future Santa Fe railroad route across New Mexico into the Grand Canyon lands of present-day Arizona. These surveys were mounted to explore the unknown Indian lands in the mountains west of Santa Fe and they revealed a difficult, though passable route around the deeply incised Colorado River canyons. The first of these expeditions, in August 1849, was made by Simpson to track Navajo raiders from the Rio Grande (Fig. 2.2). This expedition followed the Old Spanish trail northwest. As the first westerners to see the great stone ruins in Chaco Canyon and Canyon de Chelly, they were stunned by their encounter with these ancient cities. Simpson's party returned in September through the Zuñi Pueblo, following the traditional trail east past El Moro Rock.[13]

The Simpson expedition opened a new route into the Colorado Plateau region that would later mark the line of Route 66 across Arizona. In August 1851, a second survey into the Colorado country was made by Captain Lorenzo Sitgreaves with Antoine Leroux, a Taos trader who had discovered a shortcut around the canyon lands to the Colorado River at the edge of the Mojave.[14] From the Zuñi Pueblo, Sitgreaves followed Leroux's trail west along the Little Colorado canyon to the San Francisco Peaks near present Flagstaff, then west across the mesa lands and over the Black Mountains to the Colorado River by a pass he named after himself, later absorbed into Route 66 as the switchback Oatman Road from Kingman to Topock.[15] Although Sitgreaves avoided the Mojave Desert, turning south along the Colorado to Fort Yuma and so to San Diego, his detailed maps by surveyor Richard Kern, who had also assisted Frémont in 1848, provided the most accurate reconnaissance

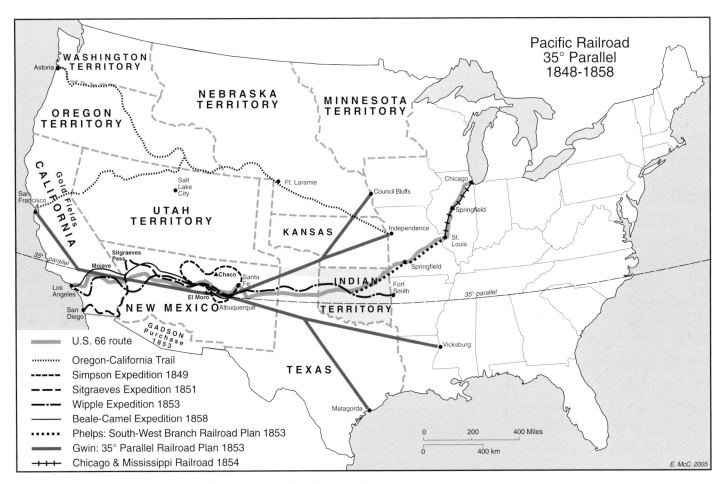

Pacific Railroad
35° Parallel
1848-1858

Legend:
- U.S. 66 route
- Oregon-California Trail
- Simpson Expedition 1849
- Sitgraeves Expedition 1851
- Wipple Expedition 1853
- Beale-Camel Expedition 1858
- Phelps: South-West Branch Railroad Plan 1853
- Gwin: 35° Parallel Railroad Plan 1853
- Chicago & Mississippi Railroad 1854

E. McC. 2005

2.2. Pacific Railroad, 35° parallel route, 1848 to 1858. Map showing U.S. Army exploration routes from Santa Fe to Los Angeles; the South-West Branch Railroad route from St. Louis to Springfield, Missouri; and the Chicago & St. Louis Railroad establishing the Route 66 alignment across Illinois. By the author.

28

if under the umbrella of the greater supervening concept), with each idea, each Sitgreaves Pass, helping to construct the possibility of its ultimate achievement.

GWIN AND KERN

Efforts to connect California with the continental U.S. were given national sanction when it was granted statehood in March 1850. The senate vote was part of the second Missouri Compromise by which New Mexico and Mormon Utah were to be organized as territories without reference to the issue of slavery, divided by the parallel of 36°30' first drawn for the original Missouri Compromise of 1820.[17] It was with such inked lines that the Pacific Railroad was projected over the Rocky Mountains to California along parallels of political compromise. In September 1850, California sent two new senators to Washington: John Frémont, the hero of the Bear Flag Revolt who had moved to his Mariposa estate, and William Gwin, a transplanted Mississippi congressman who had emigrated to San Francisco in the Gold Rush of 1849 with a network of Washington contacts for his new Pacific state (Fig. 2.4).[18]

Of the two senators, it was Gwin who immediately seized the initiative for a Pacific Railroad to California. Instead of adopting the route proposed by Senator Benton that Frémont had pioneered along the 38° parallel, Gwin suggested the route pioneered by Sitgreaves along the 35° parallel that went south around the Rocky Mountains and crossed the Colorado Plateau and the Mojave Desert. Reelected to Congress in 1852, Gwin offered "a railroad to unite the Atlantic and Pacific frontiers of the Republic" along the 35° parallel, the alignment which would later be followed by Route 66.[19]

2.3. Richard Kern, daguerreotype, ca. 1850. Kern was the surveyor of the 35° parallel route from Los Angeles to Albuquerque in 1852, following the line of pre-Route 66 across New Mexico Territory. Permission of Huntington Library Collection, San Merino, CA.

yet of the Colorado River canyon lands that were later to be traced by Route 66 (Fig. 2.3).[16] The ideal of connecting east and west, what we might call the great dream of the Northwest Passage, was actually achieved only bit by tiny bit (even

2.4. Senator William Gwin, California, line cut, ca. 1860. Gwin was the promoter of the Pacific Railroad Route along the 35° parallel from California to New Mexico in 1853. Courtesy of California State Library.

mountain trapper, Joseph Walker, who had trekked from California to Santa Fe in 1851.[20] Writing to Gwin in early January 1853, Kern recommended the 35° parallel as a Pacific Railroad route: "Its freedom from obstruction by snow, its easy passage through the Rocky Mountains, Zuñi Mountains and Sierra Nevada, and its location through a country already settled in more or less degree as far as the 110° meridian west from Greenwich, and the necessary material and labor can be obtained, and only needed an outlet to develop its various resources."[21]

With the Kern report in hand, and knowing Congress would fund but a single Pacific Railroad route, Gwin proposed an innovative trunk line with several branches to key cities.[22] These included spurs to the Mississippi and Missouri River ports of Vicksburg, Mississippi, and Council Bluffs, Iowa, and to Austin and Matagorda, Texas (see Fig. 2.2). The Gwin bill was presented to Congress in late January 1853 where opposition by Northern senators to a Southern railway project delayed approval until a compromise was offered by Senator William Broadhead of Pennsylvania.[23] The final bill for a Pacific Railroad approved five different government surveys along key western parallels: (1) 47°-48° parallels to Washington Territory; (2) 41°-42° parallels through the South Pass on the Oregon Trail; (3) 38°-39° parallels through the southern Rockies along the Frémont trail; (4) a 35° parallel across Indian and New Mexico Territory; and (5) a 32° parallel along the Gila River in the Mexican border regions. Within a week, the five Pacific Railroad surveys were authorized by Jefferson Davis, then Secretary of War, and approved by the newly elected president, Franklin Pierce, in March 1853.[24]

Gwin based his faith in the 35° parallel route on the survey experience of Sitgreaves's surveyor Kern. Much of Kern's knowledge in turn was based on reports of the famed

Of the five Pacific Railroad surveys, it was the original Gwin-Kern plan along the 35° parallel that laid the essential foundation for the future path of Route 66. While the Kern report had outlined the general topography of the New Mexico route over the Colorado Plateau, the Sitgreaves expedition of 1851 had characterized much of the area as difficult for steam locomotives due to the steep grades. Because of this, the 35° parallel survey was charged with a detailed reconnaissance of mountain passes, water supply, and deep canyons between Fort Smith and Los Angeles.

The 35° parallel survey was assigned to Lt. Amiel Whipple in June 1853. Whipple was a Yale-trained civil engineer who had marked the Mexican boundary in 1849. The Whipple party left Fort Smith in July, following the Canadian River trail through Indian Territory and the Texas panhandle to the Pecos River in New Mexico. The party ignored the trail north to Santa Fe and took a direct route though the Sandia Mountains into Albuquerque, the straight line cutoff that was later paved for Route 66 in 1937.[25] In Albuquerque they met with François Aubry, a Santa Fe trader who had just returned from Los Angeles along the Walker Trail through the Mojave and Colorado canyons. Aubry assured Whipple that an easy railroad grade could be located through northern New Mexico.[26] Whipple then hired Sitgreaves's scout Leroux as his guide, and the augmented expedition left Albuquerque for the Zuñi Pueblo in early November.[27]

From Zuñi the expedition followed the Little Colorado River, reaching the San Francisco Peaks near present-day Flagstaff on Christmas Eve. The survey then wound down the Bill Williams River and around the base of the Black Mountains to the Colorado, where they crossed into California in February 1854, at the landmark rocks they called the Needles. The final leg followed the old Mojave Indian Trail over the Providence Mountains, up the Mojave to the Cajon Pass, and down into the Los Angeles Basin, arriving there in late March.[28] The Whipple survey proved that a steam railroad could be constructed along the 35° parallel from Fort Smith to Los Angeles, though it expressed concerns about the lack of water, the fear of Indian attacks on the Staked Plains of Texas, and the steep canyons over the Colorado Plateau.[29]

The other Pacific Railroad surveys revealed similar problems with grades and Indians along their routes. The 48° parallel survey to Washington Territory found snow-bound passes during late summer, while the 42° parallel survey through the South Pass, led by Frémont, was never completed. The 38° parallel survey was beset by tragedy when expedition cartographer Kern and survey leader Lt. John Gunnison were murdered by Ute Indians in October 1853. The 32° parallel survey along the Gila River required the expense of the Gadsden Purchase from Mexico in 1853, and was favored only by Southern supporters.[30]

BEALE WAGON ROAD

Although the Pacific Railroad surveys had been simple paper projects, the publication of the Whipple report in 1855 opened the wilderness of New Mexico to emigrant demands for a posted government wagon road to California. With political pressure for a snow-free route around the southern Rockies, an Army survey was approved in 1856, headed by Lt. Edward Beale, the friend of both Benton and

Frémont who had carried the California gold nuggets to President Polk in 1848. Beale began his expedition in August 1857, importing an exotic caravan of Egyptian camels through Indianola, Texas, with camel driver Hadji Ali. The caravan gathered at Fort Defiance in Navajo country before heading south to the Zuñi pueblo. It followed Whipple's trail west along the Little Colorado, losing most of its wagons in the steep descent of the Sitgreaves Pass in October. The camels proved their value in crossing the Mojave Desert and the party reached Los Angeles by Christmas. To insure the practicality of the wagon route, Beale repeated the survey the following year. When Beale presented his report to Congress in December 1859, its publication was delayed by the sectional politics that would disintegrate into the Civil War.[31] The Beale Wagon Road provided a workable government route over the Colorado canyon lands and became the first federally funded highway to California, prescribing the line Route 66 would follow across New Mexico and northern Arizona (see Fig. 2.2).[32]

The outbreak of the Civil War in April 1861 forestalled any further interest in the southern surveys for a Pacific Railroad. Instead Union attention turned strategically toward the established transcontinental route already in use by the Pacific Telegraph and the Pony Express.[33] The Pacific Railroad, authorized by President Lincoln in 1862, was completed seven years later with the historic meeting of the Union Pacific and the Central Pacific at Promontory Point, Utah, in May 1869.[34] Thereafter efforts to construct a Pacific Railroad along the 35° parallel were delayed by the lingering factional effects of the Civil War. Two decades were to pass before a transcontinental line was built from Albuquerque to Los Angeles along the Route 66 axis.

SOUTH-WEST BRANCH

Of relevance to the future Route 66 was a secondary set of projects inspired by the 35° parallel route that issued from St. Louis to form a long diagonal across the Ozark Highlands to the Indian Territory of Oklahoma. These projects, too, suffered the effects of the Civil War, which postponed their construction to the key center at Springfield, Missouri.

The idea of connecting isolated Springfield with the 35° parallel route was promoted by John A. Phelps, a transplanted Connecticut Yankee. Phelps had been elected congressman from Springfield and sought to bind his home district to the westward migration route to the California gold fields.[35] The impetus for Phelps was the passage of the Missouri Grant Act of 1852 for Pacific Railroad projects that would connect to St. Louis.[36] Upon reading the Gwin-Kern report, Phelps proposed a South-West Branch Railroad to be built down to Springfield and then extended to Indian Territory to connect with the 35° parallel route along the Canadian River.[37] After many years of delayed construction, this diagonal finally established the idea for alignment of Route 66 from St. Louis through Tulsa to Oklahoma City.

Phelps found he had to defend the South-West Branch Railroad against Senator Benton, who favored the 38° parallel route west from St. Louis. Phelps's persistent promotion succeeded when the first spike was driven at Pacific, Missouri, in July 1853, twenty-five miles west of St. Louis.[38] The projected line was set over the crest of the Ozark Highlands along the Springfield Road, a highway that traced the pathway of an ancient Indian trail from the Mississippi to the

Arkansas River, as would later Route 66 (see Fig. 2.2). Construction proceeded slowly, however, and by 1857 track crews had reached only to Cuba, a mere fifty-five miles from St. Louis. Three years later the railhead was halted at Rolla by the outbreak of the Civil War.[39]

The Civil War turned the Ozarks into a battlefield of neighbors as the contending armies fought over the highland plateau. In 1862 Springfield was held by Confederate, and then by Union, forces.[40] The Rolla railhead became the headquarters for Union supplies with a telegraph line extended down to Springfield along the "Wire Road," a name later adopted for the Ozark section of Route 66. After the war Missouri took control of the South-West Branch, selling the line in 1868 to John Frémont as the Southwest Pacific Railroad. Frémont intended to extend the rails into Indian Territory and then on to Santa Fe as Phelps had originally proposed. Frémont was able to finance the railroad west from Rolla to Lebanon (in 1868) and Springfield (in 1870), but construction stalled when Frémont reorganized the survey to Indian Territory.[41] From this point the account of the Southwest Pacific becomes enmeshed with schemes for the transcontinental Atlantic and Pacific Railroad and the future path of Route 66, as detailed in succeeding chapters.

CHICAGO PULLMANS

The great diagonal line of the Southwest Railroad across Missouri was mirrored by a similar line across Illinois that extended a railroad line northeast from St. Louis to Chicago prior to the Civil War. It was this line, a straight shot from the Great Lakes to Missouri, that Route 66 would come to follow, and that itself followed routes pioneered by Marquette and Joliet, and earlier Native Americans at least as far back as those Mississippi peoples trading Lake Superior copper down the Illinois. Only the short portage from Chicago to the Des Plains River at Joliet interrupted the water passage, improved in 1836 with the construction of the Illinois and Michigan Canal.[42] As Chicago extended its canal westward, the settlement of the interior prairie progressed gradually from southern Illinois northwards to reach the central prairie counties after the Black Hawk War of 1832.[43]

To accommodate the expanding central settlement, the capital of Illinois at Vandalia was moved north to Springfield in 1837 with the help of a young Sangamon County lawyer, Abraham Lincoln.[44] With Springfield as the new state capital a network of railroads was projected across Illinois, but development was abruptly halted with the economic Panic of 1837.[45] When the financial markets finally recovered in 1844, Chicago had emerged as the new center of Illinois commerce, challenging St. Louis for future expansion of the Mississippi Valley trade.[46]

Initially the railroad projections between Chicago and St. Louis were based on the old Illinois River system to the port of Alton on the Mississippi above St. Louis. The first line was chartered in 1847 as the Alton and Sangamon, completed to Springfield in 1851. From Springfield a new railroad was granted as the Chicago & Mississippi Railroad, soon extended north to the town of Lincoln, named for the rising Springfield lawyer. It reached Bloomington in 1853 and Joliet the following summer. Yet it took two more years before trains were run directly by the Chicago & St. Louis Railroad to complete the long diagonal that would become that of the Route 66 across Illinois (see Fig. 2.2).[47]

This railroad was but one of a web of lines that helped establish Chicago, at St. Louis's expense, as the leading metropolis of the Midwest. As early as 1850, the *Chicago Daily Democrat* had foretold a vision of the new city:[48] "Chicago is the most favorably placed as the center of a great net-work of railway communication which will yet be constructed; but which requires the constant care of our citizens to provide that it shall inure to our benefit as well as the general prosperity of our country."[49]

The great innovation in travel to St. Louis was made in the fall of 1858: overnight sleeper trains running between the two Midwest metropoli. In Chicago, George Pullman, a newly arrived upstate New York carpenter, had realized the potential of nighttime travel, and converted two passenger cars into plush coaches with sleeping beds, the first such overnight sleeper service in the U.S.[50] It was this "Pullman service" across Illinois just prior to the Civil War that made the Chicago & St. Louis Railroad the most advanced for western travel. The service marked the triumph of Chicago over its rival St. Louis, and assured that the future western highway to California would be anchored at Lake Michigan rather than on the banks of the Mississippi.

It was in this way that the railroads, as the great innovation in nineteenth-century travel, etched ever more deeply into the land those lines previously drawn by wagon trains, trappers, colonial explorers, and Native American traders. Although few had the vision to encompass the spanning of the continent, each of these early actors appreciated the value of connecting disparate realms. Gradually the routes they projected, and often enough came to walk, paddle, or ride, coalesced into an image which precipitated, and doubtless more than once, the idea of a continent-spanning route. Through this process the dream of a Northwest Passage was gradually being transformed into the reality of a Southwest highway, one which would carry forward through the twentieth century all the promise of the original vision.

Chapter Three
Constructing the Route as a Railroad

I<small>T WAS ONE THING</small> to project railroads across the landscape as lines drawn on maps. Fragmented though they might have been, these were the purest expressions of the desire to connect East and West, unembodied prefigurations of the routes which would take their most iconic form in U.S. Route 66. But it was another thing altogether to lay steel ribbons along the ground, to construct the *facts* required to transform desires into icons. Yet it is in precisely these details, in the decisions to follow one alternative or another, in the precarious balancing act between pragmatics and politics, that the most valuable insights are to be gained into the character of the route that will propel 66, once commissioned, into the ethereal realm of national icon.

For example, the first segment of the 35° parallel route to be realized, the extended loop across the Mojave Desert between Needles and Barstow, took initial form in a north-south route between San Francisco and San Diego in the 1865 formation of the Southern Pacific Railroad.[1] An 1866 survey selected a route down the Central Valley and over Walker's Tehachapi Pass to join the 35° parallel route that had been chartered by the Atlantic and Pacific Railroad.[2] In January 1867, a charter map of the Southern Pacific route was published with the railroad projected across the Mojave to a junction with the Atlantic and Pacific at the Colorado River (Fig. 3.1).[3] While almost two decades were to elapse before the Southern Pacific was completed, the railroad surveys that were to establish the long crossing of the Mojave would also prescribe the future Route 66 from Needles to Barstow.

PALMER AND GREENWOOD

Independent of the Southern Pacific and Atlantic and Pacific projects, the Union Pacific Railroad had also proposed its own survey of potential routes to California. In early 1867, the Kansas Pacific Railway hired Gen. William J. Palmer, a Pennsylvania-trained railroad officer, to undertake detailed surveys of the 32° and 35° parallel routes to San Francisco and San Diego.[4] For the 35° parallel route Col. William H. Greenwood was selected as the topographic engineer. Greenwood was a New England-trained surveyor who had worked on Illinois railroads before the Civil War, and in Texas for the Union Army.[5] In July 1867, the Greenwood party left Fort Wallace in Kansas for Albuquerque, where the expedition was to follow the Whipple route into California.

The survey solved several difficult grade location problems in the mountains of western New Mexico that later highway engineers would use for Route 66. The first was a direct line from the Rio Grande up the Rio San Jose through Campbell's Pass, named for Richard Campbell, an early trapper, to Fort Wingate on the continental divide.[6] This route avoided the steep descent on the Old Spanish Trail to the Zuñi Pueblo while connecting with the Little Colorado along the Puerco River through the Zuñi Mountains. This would later constitute Route 66 between Grants and Gallup. The survey solved a second grade problem in 1868. Following the Whipple route across the Colorado Plateau, Greenwood's party descended to the Colorado River along the south flank of the Black Mountains rather than over the Sitgreaves Pass on the Beale Wagon Road (see Fig. 3.1).[7]

But the great innovation of the Greenwood survey was the route determined across the Mojave Desert. While the traditional trail had run over the Providence Mountains for the fresh water springs, the Greenwood survey located a level grade to the south, over the volcanic lava fields of the Perry (Amboy) Crater to the Mojave River at the foot of the San Gabriel Mountains. As Greenwood wrote in his report:

The worst features on the line run by Whipple, to wit, the detour from the head of Bill Williams River to the Colorado crossing, and the transit of the Aztec and Aquaris Ranges in Western Arizona have been entirely avoided, while west of the Colorado River a summit of 2,500 feet has been substituted for one of nearly 5,000, encountered by Whipple in crossing the Providence Mountains.[8]

While the Palmer-Greenwood survey was underway, the Southern Pacific was acquired by the "Big Four": the San Francisco financiers Collis Huntington, Mark Hopkins, Leland Stanford, and Charles Crocker, who in 1870 projected their new route across the Mojave to the Colorado.[9] The following year they revealed their larger strategy with a proposed line down the Central Valley and over the Tehachapi Pass to the Colorado River along the charter grants of the Atlantic and Pacific Railroad.[10] Construction was soon undertaken and by 1872 track had been laid as far south as Visalia. Local boosters in Los Angeles saw potential in this Southern Pacific line for connecting their isolated center with the new transcontinental railroad. Despite the financial Panic of 1873, Los Angeles merchants convinced Southern Pacific directors to build over the Tehachapi Pass in a spectacular wonder of engineering. In September 1876, flag-decked trains arrived from San Francisco, thereby linking Los Angeles with the Eastern seaboard and the potential for future growth that would dictate Los Angeles as the future terminus of Route 66.[11]

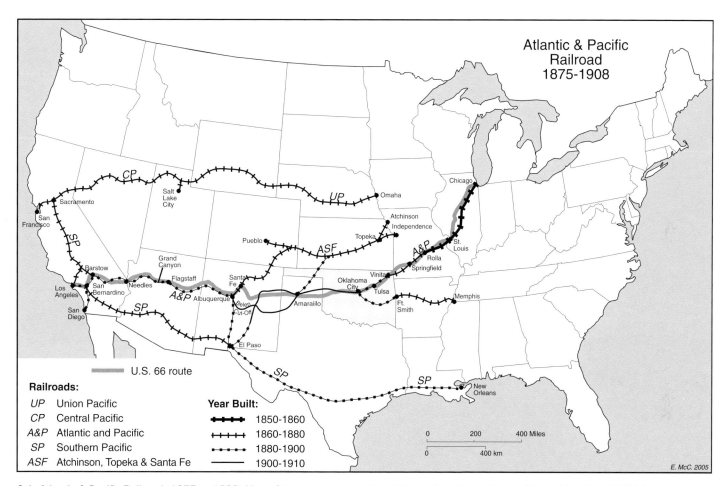

Atlantic & Pacific
Railroad
1875-1908

U.S. 66 route

Railroads:

UP	Union Pacific
CP	Central Pacific
A&P	Atlantic and Pacific
SP	Southern Pacific
ASF	Atchinson, Topeka & Santa Fe

Year Built:

━━━━	1850-1860
┼┼┼┼	1860-1880
▪▪▪▪	1880-1900
────	1900-1910

E. McC. 2005

3.1. Atlantic & Pacific Railroad, 1875 to 1908. Map of transcontinental railroad lines along the pre-Route 66 corridor, through Oklahoma (shaded), including the final link to the Grand Canyon (1901) and Belen, New Mexico (1908). By the author.

SANTA FE RAILROAD

While the Southern Pacific was laying track toward Los Angeles, a small Kansas-based railroad was extending its line west into New Mexico and across the Rio Grande towards California. Originally charted in 1859 as the Atchison & Topeka to connect the Missouri River port of Atchison with the Kansas state capital, the company was reorganized in 1863 as the Atchison, Topeka & Santa Fe Railroad, to extend its line along the Santa Fe Trail into New Mexico.[12] In 1877, when the railroad had reached Pueblo, Colorado, at the foot of the Rockies, it was purchased by William Barstow Strong, a New England Yankee with Chicago railroad experience. In January 1878, Strong sent his engineer, Lewis Kingman, to survey a route across the Raton Pass to Santa Fe. In a midnight raid against rival railroad crews, Kingman staked out the route into New Mexico and won the rights to Raton Pass for the Santa Fe. Within a year the railroad had been graded through the mountains, bypassing Santa Fe for a depot at Albuquerque on the Rio Grande, and so anchoring the commercial growth that would make Albuquerque an important stop on Route 66.[13]

With a railhead in Albuquerque, the Atchison, Topeka & Santa Fe turned its attention to California. A preliminary survey had been made in 1878 to determine whether the 32° or the 35° parallel was the best route to the Colorado River.[14] Although Santa Fe chief engineer, A. A. Robinson, favored the Gila River route through southern Arizona, Strong supported the northern route of the Whipple and Palmer surveys, concluding in November 1879 that, "The results show the line by the 35th parallel has so many things in its favor that with its great advantage in distance and accessibility from all parts of the United States, its claim on capital and enterprise far exceed those of any route or combination on the 32nd."[15]

The realization of the 35° parallel route as a railroad had a complex construction history in the post-Civil War period. The original Gwin-Kern proposal across New Mexico and Arizona to California was quickly completed in 1883 as the Atlantic and Pacific Railroad, with, before the turn of the century, its lines leased by both the Atchison, Topeka & Santa Fe and Southern Pacific. However, the South-West Branch Railroad from Missouri to Indian Territory, which Phelps had proposed, dissolved into a host of deferred projects that remained incomplete until Oklahoma statehood in 1907. The result was a disconnected web of railroad lines west from Oklahoma City to Albuquerque that encouraged local automobile use and so helped open the way for transcontinental highway links in the early twentieth century.

With his survey of the western routes assured, Strong began negotiations for government railroad grants along the 35° parallel owned by the Atlantic and Pacific, now controlled by the St. Louis and San Francisco Railroad. In January 1880, the Santa Fe signed a Tripartite Agreement with the St. Louis company that gave each railroad a fifty-percent interest in the original Atlantic and Pacific grants along the 35° parallel.[16] The agreement allowed the Santa Fe to build the Pacific Railroad originally proposed in 1853 by Gwin.

LEWIS KINGMAN

Construction of the Atlantic and Pacific lines across New Mexico and Arizona began immediately after the Tripartite Agreement was signed. As chief engineers, the Santa Fe appointed Lewis Kingman, and the Atlantic and Pacific, H. R. Holbrook, both memorialized in town names along the northern Arizona route.[17] Kingman, together with other railroad personnel who had towns named for them, would later become true household names in the iconic Route 66 song, "(Get Your Kicks on) Route 66!" Here we are watching specific elements of what will become an important component of the highway icon being laid down as landscape facts with the construction of the railroad that prefigured the highway.

Kingman was under immense pressure to complete track to the Colorado River. By February 1881, the railroad was extended from Albuquerque up the Rio San Jose to Fort Wingate. Along the way the towns of Grants and Gallup were named for the Atlantic and Pacific contractor and auditor respectively, with Gallup, like Kingman, being immortalized in "Route 66!" At the continental divide the grading continued down the Little Colorado to the town they named Holbrook in September. At Winslow the depot was named for Edward G. Winslow, the St. Louis and San Francisco president. Construction was stalled at Canyon Diablo until a high timber trestle could be completed, which it was in May 1882. By this time the track crews had reached Flagstaff, a third "Route 66!" place name, in the San Francisco Mountains, settled five years earlier by Mormon ranchers and New England emigrants. By October, Kingman had followed the Palmer and Whipple surveys west around the base of Bill Williams Mountain and down the Ash Fork grade to Seligman, named for the Santa Fe's New York bankers. In early 1883 the project reached the foot of the Black Mountains, where they named the depot Kingman.[18]

The final push to the Colorado River was underway in May. Tracks were laid around the south flank of the Black Mountains as recommended by Palmer, rather than up the steep grade of the Beale Wagon Road through the Sitgreaves Pass, which Route 66 would take. The Colorado River was first bridged in June but washed out in spring floods and rebuilt in July. On August 9, 1883, formal ceremonies were held at the new Atlantic and Pacific depot in Needles to celebrate the opening of the "Thirty-Fifth Parallel Transcontinental Line" to California (Fig. 3.2).[19]

WILLIAM HOOD

As Lewis Kingman rushed Santa Fe track crews west from New Mexico to the Colorado River, a similar effort was underway at the hands of William Hood, the chief survey engineer for the Southern Pacific. In January 1882, Hood was directed to build the Southern Pacific line across the Mojave to the Colorado in order to block the Santa Fe from acquiring the original Atlantic and Pacific Railroad grants to Los Angeles. Hood organized his survey in two phases, the first east from the Tehachapi Pass, the second west from Needles, to meet midway in the lava fields near the Perry Crater, a level route around the south flank of the Providence Mountains.[20]

Construction of the Mojave lines proceeded at a hurried pace, beginning in February under the direction of the Pacific Improvement Company with crews of Chinese laborers working in the searing desert heat. By October the railroad had reached Waterman's Station (Barstow) and, in December, Ludlow and the Calico silver mines. By February 1883 trains were running to the Perry Crater. From this point eastward Hood suggested a series of alphabet depot names beginning with Amboy and Bristol, and including Cadiz, Danby, Edson, Fenner, Goffs, Homer, Ibis, and Java. Depots from Tehachapi were given equally fanciful names: Bagdad, Daggett, and Siberia.[21] The result was a geography of exotic names that identified the Mojave crossing and

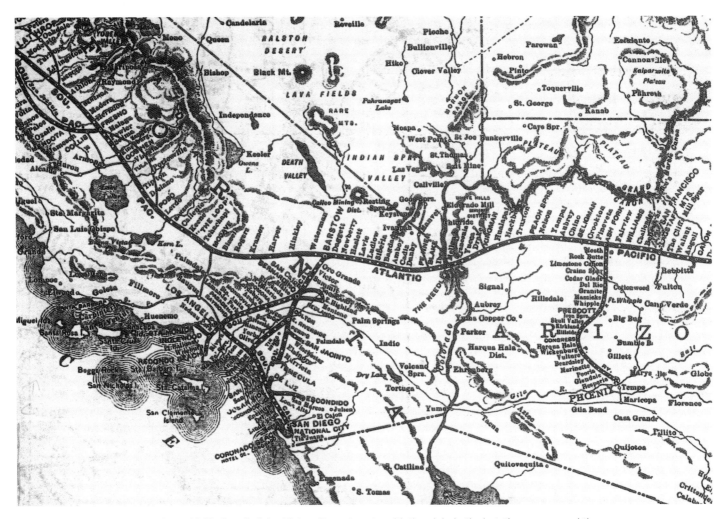

3.2. Atlantic & Pacific Railroad, ca. 1885. Detail of the Mojave Desert route, with the alphabetical station names and the Arizona-California depots. By permission of Harvard University Map Collection.

would later entertain desert travelers on Route 66 with their curious order (see Fig. 3.2).

Although the Mojave Desert route was less demanding than the one over the Providence Mountains, the ascent around the south flank required tight curves and trestles to reach the summit at Goffs.[22] Through trains to Needles were running on April 19, 1883, when the Santa Fe crews reached the Colorado from the east. When the rails were finally joined in August, the Southern Pacific had effectively prevented the Santa Fe from its transcontinental entry into California, at the same time that it had inscribed across the desert the line that Route 66 would follow from Needles to Barstow.

GRAND CANYON

Despite the rivalry of the Southern Pacific and the Santa Fe, through connections from Chicago were allowed for Santa Fe passengers at the Needles depot, to provide a direct transcontinental route to California by October 1883. Nevertheless, the transcontinental service was of secondary interest to both railroads, as both the Southern Pacific and the Santa Fe regarded the Colorado River routes as branch lines from Tehachapi and Albuquerque respectively. The importance of the Colorado crossing became evident only with the completion of the California Southern over the Cajon Pass from Waterman's Station (Barstow) to San Bernardino in 1885.[23] As an affiliate of the Santa Fe, the California Southern was projected as a railroad south to San Diego. With Waterman's Station renamed Barstow in 1885, after the Southern Pacific president, yet another "Route 66!" place name, the Santa Fe was allowed to run trains over the Southern Pacific tracks into Los Angeles. Two years later

the Santa Fe opened its own line along the foothills of the San Gabriels through Cucamonga, Pomona, and Pasadena, platting towns that would constitute an entryway for Route 66 into Los Angeles.[24]

With the transcontinental Atlantic and Pacific route opened directly to Los Angeles, a fare war was declared between the Southern Pacific and the Santa Fe. Originally Union Pacific tickets from Chicago to San Francisco were $130 but were cut to $100 on the Southern Pacific by 1886. Within a year coach fare from Chicago to Los Angeles was slashed to $8, then $6. By March 1887, $1 would buy a passenger ticket for anyone west of the Missouri River to California.[25] These rates finally realized the Gold Rush vision of Gwin for the $35°$ parallel route and triggered a rapid real estate boom in Los Angeles. With increased passenger traffic, the Santa Fe Railroad now recognized the tourist potential of its Colorado River short line from Albuquerque to Los Angeles; in 1896 it rebuilt the single track for heavy passenger traffic and, in September 1901, opened a scenic branch line to the South Rim of the Grand Canyon from Williams, Arizona.[26] In January 1902, just as the railroad reached the Canyon, an enterprising Los Angeles motorist, Winfield Hogaboom, had driven his steam-powered Toledo car to the Grand Canyon from Flagstaff (Fig. 3.3).[27] Within the decade the success of this motoring venture promoted automobile tourist roads in the Southwest, generating demand for a national auto highway across northern Arizona. Thus, no sooner had the railroad been completed than it was providing a foundation for an auto route whose far more rapid development would effectively replace the railroad line across Arizona.

3.3. Toledo steam car at the Grand Canyon, January 1902. Photo showing the first automobile at a scenic sight along the pre-Route 66 corridor, within six months of the completion of the Grand Canyon Railroad (1901). Collection of the Library of Congress.

INDIAN TERRITORY

As the automobile met the railroad at the Grand Canyon, so the motor car succeeded the passenger train in finally completing the 35° parallel route across the Indian Territory of Oklahoma in New Mexico after 1900 (see Fig 3.1). The original impetus for a transcontinental line across the Indian Nations can be traced to Phelps and his South-West Branch Railroad. As detailed in the last chapter, after the Civil War this railroad had been reorganized by Frémont as the Atlantic and Pacific but, as noted, he had only completed seventy-five miles of track within the Cherokee Nation to Vinita.[28] The railroad had been opposed by the Cherokees as an ill omen, a view reported by the government agent to Washington: "Desirous as they are of maintaining their nationality and of holding their lands, the great majority of these people regard these [rail]roads as the introducers of calamities rather than blessings."[29]

As the Cherokee Nation halted extension of the railroad, the Panic of 1873 completely disrupted the financial security of the Atlantic and Pacific, reorganized as the St. Louis and San Francisco Railway in 1876. Recovering its initiative, the "Frisco" continued to press the Indian Nations in legal maneuvers and by 1882 had successfully extended the line southwest to Tulsa on the border of the Creek Territory. With further agreements the railroad crossed the Arkansas River another ten miles to Sapulpa in 1886. Three years later the Great Run of 1889 opened the Indian lands of Oklahoma Territory to white settlement, and in 1898 the Frisco finally reached the Canadian River at Oklahoma City. It thus created the line of railroad towns of Bristow, Daven-

port, and Chandler, which would become familiar to later-day Route 66 travelers.[30]

ROCK ISLAND LINE

While the Atlantic and Pacific extended its line southwest to the Indian lands, the construction of the 35° parallel route east from Arkansas along the Canadian River was likewise delayed by the Indian nations and financial problems. An Arkansas railroad had reached Fort Smith from Little Rock and Memphis in 1879, based on the Pacific Railroad Bill of 1853, but no line had yet been chartered to Indian Territory for the Canadian River route to Texas and New Mexico.[31] After the Great Run of 1889 a railroad along the 35° parallel was completed from Fort Smith to Oklahoma City in 1895 as the Choctaw, Oklahoma & Gulf Railway, then extended further west to El Reno and the Canadian River at Bridgeport in 1898.[32] In 1902, the line had reached Clinton and Elk City when it was purchased by the Chicago, Rock Island and Pacific.[33] The new company continued work westward across the Texas panhandle to Amarillo in 1903 and Tucumcari, New Mexico, the following year.[34] Yet even as the track realized the 35° parallel route west, a motor bus route was established in 1907 as the Lubbock and Amarillo City Auto Line to serve the cattle towns not yet reached by rails (Fig. 3.4). This created a new system of auto highways in the Texas panhandle that would form the basis of Route 66 after the First World War.[35]

Even with the extension of the Rock Island Railroad into eastern New Mexico, the 35° parallel route was never fully completed before the advent of automobile travel. The last section from Tucumcari to Albuquerque was projected by the Santa Fe Railroad as a bypass around Raton Pass through Clovis, New Mexico, in 1899. An elaborate scheme known as the Belen Cutoff was under construction in 1903 just as the financial markets collapsed. After construction resumed in 1904 it was halted again by the Panic of 1907, and only opened in 1908 (see Fig. 3.1).[36] The Santa Fe hardly realized the savings of the new line, as it still maintained the familiar route through the Raton Pass to Albuquerque. Thus, the Canadian River corridor remained a jumble of three separate railroads' disconnected routes: the Frisco, the Rock Island, and the Santa Fe. At the same time the Santa Fe maintained its California trains from Chicago through Kansas City, effectively bypassing Oklahoma as a route to California. With statehood in 1907, Oklahoma boosters organized to create a transcontinental auto highway on the 35° parallel railroad route from Tulsa to Albuquerque, a road network that would form the basis for Route 66.

At this point, the route that U.S. 66 will roll over between Chicago and Los Angeles had been all but completely worked out. Over much of it, in fact, a through railroad service had existed for more than twenty years. The neces-

3.4. Lubbock and Amarillo City Auto Line advertisement, 1907. For an early auto stage line in the Texas Panhandle before railroad links had been completed along the pre-Route 66 corridor. Courtesy of Amarillo Public Library.

sary technology required for the development of an auto highway had been invented. Thus, with the idea of transcontinental travel very much in mind, and a completely viable route between Chicago and Los Angeles articulated, the stage was set for Route 66 to be born. It was time for the fact of Route 66 to emerge from the chrysalis of its railroad prefiguration.

Part II

From Idea to Fact:
Putting Route 66
on the Ground

Chapter Four
National Auto Trails

As the steam railroad prefigured Route 66's path in the decades following the Civil War, so early automobile use prefigured many of its actual highway locations in the decade before World War I. An early form of the idea of a transcontinental highway had been to construct an auto trail between New York and San Francisco. Experience and the efforts of local activists gradually transformed this into the idea of a national tourist highway from Chicago through the scenic landscapes of the Southwest to Los Angeles. These early motor routes were initially developed as privately sponsored auto trails. Among these were the National Old Trails Road from Kansas City to Los Angeles, and the Ozark Trails Highway from St. Louis to Oklahoma City, Amarillo, and Santa Fe. Each had its regional promoters and advocates for local attractions.

In the organization of these early motor routes, what is inescapable is the importance of the role played by the predecessor routes worked out by the railroads in the nineteenth century. An apt metaphor for the whole process might be that of developing a photographic negative. First to appear are the Native American trails, then those of the colonists and European settlers; next the railroads emerge, then the early auto trails. In the next chapter, Route 66 itself will finally materialize. At that point we would have a picture of the highway itself, the fact constructed on top of these layers of history. The last third of the book is concerned with the transformation of this fact into a great national icon.

AUTOMOBILING

In this story, the role of the early automobile is pivotal. The first practical motor cars were being perfected as the last links of the $35°$ parallel railroad were being constructed across Oklahoma to Texas and New Mexico. While primitive steam-powered wagons had been driven on the streets of Philadelphia in 1804, the true innovation of the American automobile combined the flexible rubber tires of the bicycle with the internal combustion power of the gasoline engine. This was first devised in Springfield, Massachusetts, by bicycle makers Charles and Frank Duryea with their clutch-geared motor carriage in 1893.[1] Such gasoline horseless carriages had already been perfected in Europe. The most notable was the Motorwagon of Karl Benz in Germany, driven sixty miles from Heidelberg to Pforzheim by his wife Bertha in August 1888. In France, Peugeot and Panhard drove their motor cars from Paris to Brest in 1891, and then to Nice in 1892, establishing the basic technology for long-distance road travel.[2]

Within two years of Duryea, the first scheduled race of motor carriages was held along the Chicago lake shore to suburban Evanston on Thanksgiving Day in 1895. Six vehicles were entered, including two electric-powered wagons, and two German Benz cars, with the race won by Duryea at the speed of five miles an hour.[3] Within the year, horseless carriage races were being held at the Rhode Island State Fair, and, in May 1897, inventor Thomas Edison predicted that "the automobile is bound to be in general use before long," using the new French word for self-propelled motor vehicles. Later that summer, Alexander Winton drove his car from Cleveland to New York in ten days, completing the first long distance auto trip in the United States.[5]

By the turn of the century, the American automobile had been established as viable mechanical transportation, albeit limited to upper-class amusement and determined inventors in the industrial cities of the Northeast. In November 1900, the first National Automobile show was held in New York with U.S. motor registration already at almost 8,000 vehicles, a figure that doubled within two years.[6] The forma-tion of the American Automobile Association (AAA) with the Good Roads Organization of bicyclists in 1902, resulted in a proposal for a transcontinental auto highway between New York and San Francisco, and a proposal for "An American Appian Way" from the Atlantic to the Pacific by 1906 (Fig. 4.1).[7]

NEW YORK TO PARIS

In 1900, the idea of cross-country auto travel was beyond reasonable belief. Paved roads hardly existed outside city limits. Even graded roads were limited to settled sections between New York and Chicago. Nevertheless, in May 1901, Alexander Winton attempted the impossible, a transcontinental motor trip to San Francisco. He reached the Nevada desert before he abandoned the effort. Within two years, however, practical success was achieved by a Vermont doctor, H. Nelson Jackson, who wagered fifty dollars he could drive an automobile from San Francisco to New York in three months. Jackson won his own prize by driving a Winton motor car along the Union Pacific Railroad through Wyoming and Nebraska to Omaha, and on to Chicago, reaching New York in July 1903, to complete the longest overland journey yet made by an automobile.[8]

Another transcontinental auto trip was made in 1908 as part of the New York to Paris road race. Beginning in Times Square, a half dozen motor cars started for Los Angeles. They followed the familiar route to Chicago, then proceeded west along the Union Pacific tracks to Great Salt Lake. From Great Salt Lake the projected path cut diagonally through Nevada. Death Valley was reached in March. The lead car, a German Zust driven by Antonio Scarfoglio

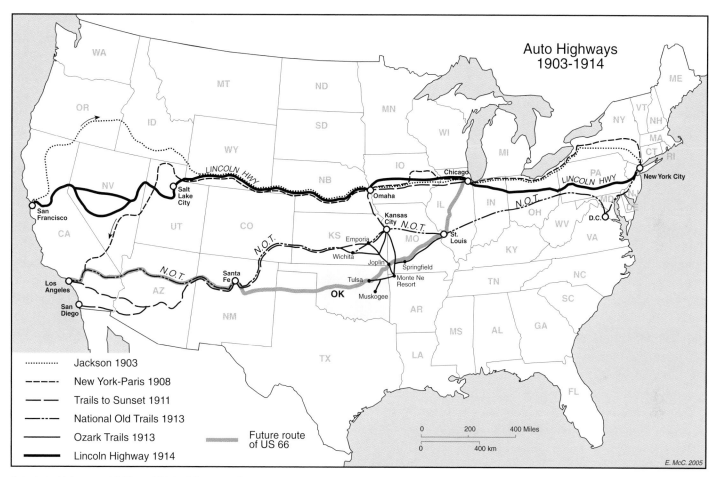

Auto Highways
1903-1914

Jackson 1903
New York-Paris 1908
Trails to Sunset 1911
National Old Trails 1913
Ozark Trails 1913
Lincoln Highway 1914

Future route
of US 66

E. McC. 2005

4.1. Auto highways, 1903 to 1914. This map of early auto routes, from the Mississippi River to the Pacific Coast along the pre-Route 66 corridor, included the National Old Trail (N.O.T.), from Los Angeles to Santa Fe, and the Ozark Trails, from St. Louis to Tulsa. By the author.

and Herr Haaga, struggled through the sand dunes where the drivers used tent canvas to pave their way across the salt flats to reach the Mojave River at Daggett.[9] The Zust drivers followed the eventual path of Route 66 from the Mojave Desert, winding their way up the Cajon Pass and so down into the Los Angeles Basin. Scarfoglio described the transforming experience that John Steinbeck would retell in the Dust Bowl period:

49

Behold the Land of Promise! It came to meet us this morning across the mountains with arms full of flowers, opening out to view the sweetest, greenest, most fertile landscape that ever delighted the human eye. The desert came to an end, cut off clean by a wave of trees and leaves which advanced from Los Angeles towards San Bernardino, into which the road plunged like a thirsty man into a spring of fresh water.[10]

The Zust team arrived in Los Angeles on April 1, the first transcontinental motorists to have come over the San Gabriel Mountains on a pre-modern section of Route 66. The remaining auto tour vehicles crossed the Pacific Ocean by steamship from San Francisco to Japan, then journeyed to Vladivostock, Russia, and followed the Trans-Siberian Railroad to Moscow, reaching Paris in August 1908.[11]

SIXTY-SECOND MILE

In the decade after the first American auto race, speed records were achieved that showed the automobile a worthy competitor to the railroad, especially on hard flat surfaces. The sixty-second mile was broken on Ocean Beach Parkway in Brooklyn in November 1901; and, in January 1904, Henry Ford drove his hand-built speedster, No. 999, at almost ninety-two m.p.h. on the ice of Lake St. Clair near Detroit. Although gasoline engines had proven themselves highly efficient, the thirty-second mile was made by a Stanley Steamer Rocket at Daytona Beach, Florida, in January 1905, with Fred Marriott at the wheel; and again in 1907 at 150 m.p.h. before the rocket car flew apart and Marriott barely escaped with his life.[12]

As racing cars challenged speed, associations of more conservative automobile owners were formed in major American cities to promote paved roads and offer touring services. New York organized the first Automobile Club in 1899. The Automobile Club of Southern California was chartered in Los Angeles in 1900, and the Chicago Motor Club in 1906.[13] As national auto ownership soared to well over 100,000 vehicles, engineering advances allowed Henry Ford to put his Model T into production, and Col. Vanderbilt opened his Motor Parkway on Long Island, the first limited access toll road.[14]

SUNSET TRAIL

Among the early auto pioneers who determined the future routes for U.S. 66 was A. L. Westgard, who promoted many of the first motor highways in New Mexico, Arizona, and California. Born in Norway, Westgard emigrated to the United States in 1883. He found work as a topographic engineer for the Santa Fe Railroad when it opened the Atlantic and Pacific line across northern Arizona. In 1903 Westgard purchased his first automobile, motoring to the Grand Canyon with his wife Helen, among the first auto tourists to the area.[15] With his surveying experience, in 1907 Westgard became Touring Chief for the Auto Club of America and, in October 1910, mapped the first motor road from New York to Los Angeles, billing it the "Trail to Sunset."[16]

The Trail to Sunset headed west from Chicago across Iowa to Omaha, then south to Kansas City, and so along the Santa Fe Railroad to Albuquerque. From Albuquerque, Westgard marked a circuitous route southwest through

Laguna and over rugged mountains to Fort Apache, Globe, and Phoenix.[17] From that point the trail paralleled the Southern Pacific Railroad to San Bernardino and Los Angeles. Writing about the trip in *Collier's*, Westgard described the true nature of the auto trail for this premodern section of what would become Route 66 west of Albuquerque.[18]

> After leaving our pilot some ten miles out, we certainly did encounter plenty of deep sand and a bunch of coyotes, on which we assiduously practiced sharpshooting, but we crossed the Puerco River without knowing it was a river. There was no water whatsoever, merely a sandy wash and no quicksand, but we ran into a lot of confusing trail.[19]

In his work on the Trail to Sunset, Westgard directed the first transcontinental crossing of heavy motor trucks for the Touring Club of America in March 1911. The three-ton Sauer Motor trucks started from Denver, again following the Trail to Sunset to Albuquerque and so across the Arizona mountains to Phoenix, and to Los Angeles along the railroad.[20] Thanks to his survey experience, Westgard was able to produce the first useful road maps for the American Automobile Association, *Strip Maps of the "Trail to Sunset"*, in September 1911. These are the earliest detailed diagrams of a prototype Route 66 in New Mexico and California.[21] Here the black lines show the tenuous conditions of the primitive roads of the early auto era, crossing small streams and railroad tracks in rutted ways (Fig. 4.2).

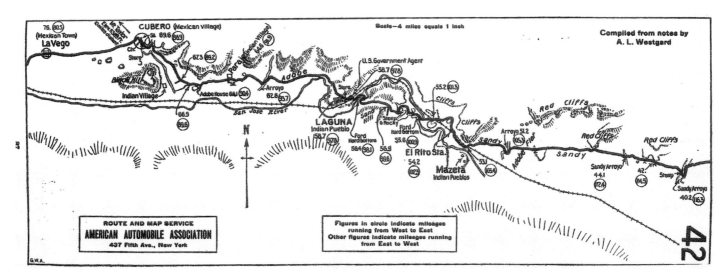

4.2. *Trail to the Sunset*, 1911. Strip map of the early auto trail along the pre-Route 66 corridor in New Mexico west of Albuquerque that was surveyed by A. L. Westgard for the American Automobile Association. Courtesy of Federal Highway Administration (FHA) Archives.

With Westgard's Trail to Sunset as an example, an auto highway was organized in Missouri that also took the Santa Fe Trail as a motor route to California. Initially, two independent groups were formed to the same end, both in the latter months of 1911: the Women's National Trail Association and the Old Trails Association (OTA). A convention of OTA delegates met in Jefferson City, Missouri, during July under Governor Herbert Hadley to mark out an "Ocean-to-Ocean Highway" that would also connect St. Louis and Kansas City. In October a final vote was made for an "Old Trails Road" west to Kansas City, then south along the Santa Fe Trail to New Mexico.[22]

As the men had convened in Jefferson City, the Women's National Trail Association met in Kansas City in December 1911, under the direction of Elizabeth Butler Gentry of the Daughters of the American Revolution (DAR).[23] She proposed a national motor route to the upcoming 1915 Panama Exposition in San Francisco which would follow the National Road to the Santa Fe Trail, and cross northern Arizona to Flagstaff along the Santa Fe Railroad as a way to the Grand Canyon (as Route 66 would in later years).[24] From Flagstaff, the Gentry route connected south to Phoenix and on to Los Angeles on the trail To Sunset. At the same time, an Ocean-to-Ocean Highway Association was formed in Phoenix by Col. D. M. Potter to adopt the Westgard route across southern Arizona to Los Angeles.[25] Despite this attention to the southern route, a northern route to the Grand Canyon remained an active interest among highway proponents.

With momentum for a transcontinental motor road building in Missouri, in April 1912, a National Old Trails (NOT) convention was held in Kansas City for the selection of the route to California. The new NOT president, Judge J. M. Lowe of Kansas City, who had worked with Gentry and the DAR, maintained that the Westgard route through Phoenix was the best option.[26] In Washington, Gentry lobbied Congressman William Borland of Missouri for a national highway bill, writing:

> A countrywoman said to me: "My men folks have left me stuck in the mud all my life. I am mighty thankful the D.A.R. are trying to pull me out." While individually we are concerned with this phase of good roads, as an organization we are dedicated to the historic and patriotic side, and are here to urge that a great national ocean-to-ocean highway be built as a memorial to the pioneer patriots of the Nation.[27]

To survey the practicality of the national route, Lowe and Potter drove the National Old Trails Road from Los Angeles to New York in May 1912, evidently following the Trail to Sunset through Phoenix.[28] However, by February 1913, Potter had formed his own Southern National Highway for a route from Phoenix to San Diego, and, with the second National Old Trails meeting in April 1913, the Ocean-to-Ocean Highway was disbanded.[29] In its place Lowe adopted the Grand Canyon Route across northern Arizona suggested by a Santa Fe Railroad engineer, O. T. Parker. With this decision, the National Old Trails established the location that

Route 66 would use to connect Albuquerque to Flagstaff, Kingman, and Barstow along the original 35° parallel route of the Santa Fe Railroad (see Fig. 4.1).[30]

By the summer of 1913, complete road maps of the National Old Trails Road were published for transcontinental tourists. The final route went from New York to St. Louis and along Boon's Lick Road to Kansas City. There it connected with the Santa Fe Trail and the Grand Canyon Route to Los Angeles. Detailed photo maps were likewise offered by various state auto organizations, the most elaborate by the Arizona Good Roads Association, in the *Illustrated Tour Book* it issued in 1913 to celebrate the statehood of the former territory. Most instructive for the later route of U.S. 66 is the strip map of the National Old Trails Road over the Sitgreaves Pass. Instead of following the Santa Fe around the Black Mountains the highway wound up to the gold mining town of Oatman in steep grades of twisting turns that would become notorious for later Route 66 drivers (see Fig. 4.3).[31]

With Lowe as president and Parker as engineer, construction of the National Old Trails Road was organized to improve the difficult Grand Canyon Route where inadequate roads had forced detours from the official maps. During the summer of 1914, the Auto Club of Southern California had marked the entire section from Los Angeles to Kansas City with blue and white "N.O.T." enameled signs.[32] The following year Parker supervised the grading of the mountain pass from Williams to Ash Fork in Arizona,

4.3. *Arizona Illustrated Tour Book*, 1913. Strip map showing the National Old Trails auto route from Kingman to Needles over the Oatman Gold Road, anticipating the Route 66 alignment. Courtesy of Arizona Highway Department.

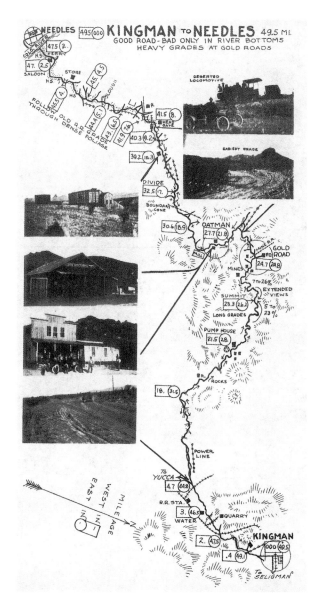

and also realigned the treacherous Mojave Desert section from Needles to Barstow.[33] In 1915, a modern concrete bridge was built over Canyon Padre east of Flagstaff, and Westgard declared that the National Old Trails had opened the "first transcontinental" motor route to the Panama-Pacific Exposition in San Francisco.[34] The only gap was the Colorado River ferry at Needles, soon closed with the construction of a 600-foot steel arch bridge in 1916.[35] The bridge completed the Grand Canyon Route to Los Angeles and created a landmark that would symbolically mark the entry into California for Dust Bowl emigrants.[36]

OZARK TRAILS ASSOCIATION

In 1912, a National Highway Association was founded under the direction of Charles Henry Davis with Lowe and Westgard as officers, its creation prompted by the emergence of all the regional auto organizations.[37] By the First World War, a network of primary auto trails defined the basic corridors of travel between Chicago and California, the Lincoln Highway following the Union Pacific Railroad to Utah and so on to San Francisco, and the National Old Trails Road following the Santa Fe Railroad to Los Angeles. Both had bypassed the former Indian Territory of Oklahoma, and they thus encouraged the local promotion of a motor trail that would tap tourist traffic to the Ozark Highlands. This movement would lead directly to the creation of an auto trails association that would mark the future Route 66 through Missouri and Oklahoma and west across the Texas panhandle to New Mexico and the National Old Trails Road.

The origins of an auto highway association in the Ozarks and Oklahoma are found in the early efforts of William "Coin" Harvey, a free silver advocate and advisor to presidential candidate William Jennings Bryan in 1896.[38] In 1900, Harvey retired from Chicago to his Ozark estate at Monte Ne in northwest Arkansas. There he constructed a "character-building" conference center with its own railroad spur direct to the resort.[39] When the rail line was abandoned in 1910, Harvey sought alternative transportation to his mountain center and, in the following June of 1911, offered an auto route as a "Great White Way" from Muskogee, Oklahoma, eastward to Monte Ne.[40] With the establishment of the National Highway Association, Harvey expanded his proposed auto road into a regional network. In May 1913, he published a regional map of an Ozark Trails system radiating from Monte Ne to St. Louis, Kansas City, Wichita, and, most importantly, Oklahoma City via Tulsa, thereby presaging the path of Route 66 in Oklahoma.[41]

Formal organization of the Ozark Trails Association (OTA) was made by Harvey in July 1913, at Monte Ne.[42] More than 300 delegates attended from neighboring states to hear Harvey promote the Ozark Trails as a Good Roads movement and morally uplifting civic experience. The following year the OTA convention was held in Tulsa. Most significantly, this was sponsored by Cyrus S. Avery, the Tulsa County Commissioner and Good Roads advocate for Oklahoma highways, who would become the pivotal figure in the creation of Route 66 after the First World War.[43] Avery had emigrated from Pennsylvania to Oklahoma with his family when it was still Indian Territory, and he moved to Tulsa in 1907 as a civic booster of Sooner statehood to bring Oklahoma into the national highway network (Fig. 4.4).[44]

4.4. Cyrus S. Avery, Tulsa County Commissioner, 1916. The Oklahoma promoter of Ozark Trails Highway to Tulsa and Oklahoma City anticipated the Route 66 alignment. Reprinted from *History of Oklahoma* (Chicago: American Historical Society, 1916). By permission of Harvard College Library.

With Harvey as president and Avery as regional coordinator, membership in the OTA expanded dramatically. Some

7,000 delegates attended the November 1916 meeting in Oklahoma City, complete with marching bands and motor car parades.[45] Avery proposed to expand the Ozark Trails across Oklahoma and Texas to reach the National Old Trails Road at Santa Fe, providing the link for the future Route 66 that would connect the isolated Sooner state with the tourist traffic to California.[46] In January 1917, Harvey voiced this westward vision of the OTA in *Better Roads*: "The Ozark Trail will not only be constructed, but it will be the 'mother' of other great roads feeding or intersecting this road that will span the state in continued mileage in every direction."[47]

It was in promotional phrases such as these that Harvey ballyhooed the central function of the Ozark Trails as a trunk highway of transcontinental traffic, literally a "mother" road, an image reinvented by John Steinbeck for Highway 66 in *The Grapes of Wrath* two decades later.

With the western network proposed, the OTA marked a system of alternative routes across Oklahoma and the panhandle of Texas into eastern New Mexico with green and white "O.T.A." signs. The Association also sponsored the construction of tall obelisks in key town centers, modeled after Harvey's own monumental pyramid at Monte Ne. In June 1917, the annual meeting was held in Amarillo, Texas, where the Ozark Trails were projected south to El Paso to serve as a military highway against the Mexican border raids of Pancho Villa.[48] By 1918, the main OTA route had been located from St. Louis through Rolla and Springfield to Joplin, Missouri, southwest into Oklahoma at Miami, and so on through Tulsa to Oklahoma City, a diagonal axis that followed the original line of the South-West Branch Railroad that Phelps had proposed in 1853. From Oklahoma City a series of alternate routes reached south and west, with the main auto trail through Amarillo, Tucumcari, and Santa Rosa into New Mexico to hook up with the National Old Trails Road at Santa Fe, a pathway later directly taken by Route 66 (Fig. 4.5).[49]

After the First World War, the momentum of the OTA stalled and much of the proposed highway remained no more than a paper trail throughout western Oklahoma and

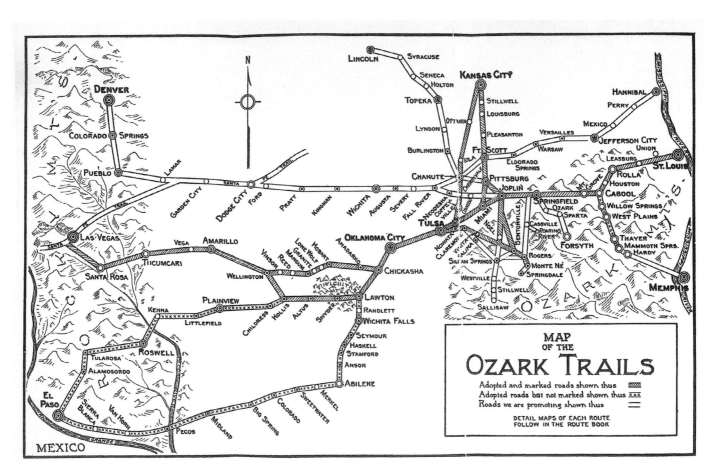

4.5. *Map of the Ozark Trails*, 1917. Ozark Trails Association routes from St. Louis to Santa Fe, anticipating the Route 66 alignment through Missouri, Oklahoma, and Texas. Courtesy of Springfield-Greene County (Missouri) Library.

the Texas panhandle. Later the OTA devolved into sectional debates over local routings, with the last recorded meeting in Duncan, Oklahoma, in September 1924.[50] At the Duncan convention, the new president, S. E. Hodgdon of St. Louis, spoke before a gathering that included the Oklahoma governor, Martin Trapp, and Avery, now the Oklahoma Highway Commissioner. In an effort to revitalize the booster spirit, Hodgdon proposed that the Ozark Trails construct a paved highway from "the Great Lakes to the Pacific coast."[51] It was this goal of a single signed auto road connecting Oklahoma with Chicago and Los Angeles that inspired Avery to provide direction for a new network of federally numbered routes through Oklahoma in 1925, a network that would include U.S. Highway 66 along the lines of the former Ozark Trails between St. Louis and Santa Fe.

STANDARD ROUTE MARKER
ADOPTED BY THE JOINT
BOARD ON INTERSTATE HIGH-
WAYS FOR USE ON ALL UNITED
STATES HIGHWAY ROUTES

The color scheme will be black and white

5.1. U.S. 56 federal highway shield, 1925. Sample route sign designed for the American Association of State Highway Officials (AASHO) meeting in Kansas City, May 1925. Courtesy of Federal Highway Administration (FHA) Archives.

Chapter Five
Route Number 66

THE FEDERAL NUMBERING OF ROUTE 66 is among the most complex and convoluted aspects of the early iconography of the highway proper. The transformation of private auto trails into a national network of designated routes involved politicized campaigns to maintain regional identity in the switch from named trails to numbered roads. Such was the case with the Ozark Trails and Route 66.

While the use of numbers seemed a simple solution to state and federal highway officials, the new numbers were unavoidably inflected with the complicated legacy of the named auto tourist trails, especially in the West where the new numbered routes promised commercial prosperity in the economic boom that followed World War I. The highway numbers became points of contention between regional interests, each trying to secure some special signet of identity. The choice of 66 for the federal highway between Chicago and Los Angeles, insuring a unified route through St. Louis and Tulsa to California, provoked a drama that involved Missouri and Oklahoma highway officials, the Bureau of Public Roads, and the Governor of Kentucky. It also concluded, by stringing together under a single designation, the development of a connection which had initially been no more than a happenstance chain of hundreds, perhaps thousands, of Native American trails; then dozens of explorer's routes and wagon trails; next a handful of railroad routes; and finally a couple of named auto trails. With the federal designation Chicago and Los Angeles were for the first time linked as termini of a *single* path, one with an incredibly rich legacy, and as will be seen, a thoroughly prepotent name.

FEDERAL-AID ROADS

Federal support of interstate routes can be traced to authorization of the National Road under President Thomas Jefferson in 1808, a highway that crossed the Allegheny Mountains between Cumberland, Maryland, and the Ohio

River at Wheeling.[1] Built to the highest standards of the time with a European-style Macadam crushed-stone surface, the National Road was opened in 1818. When completed in 1850, it extended from Baltimore to Vandalia, Illinois.[2] While soon replaced by canals and railroads, and converted to state toll roads, the National Road remained an example of federal highway construction for regional improvement.[3] Other early examples can be found in the government support of the western wagon roads that evolved from the surveys for the Pacific Railroad, most notably the 1857 Beale Wagon Road across New Mexico Territory that would presage the route of U.S. 66 across northern Arizona.[4]

Except for the military highways on the western frontier, no further federal support of national highways was made until the great bicycle craze of the last decade of the nineteenth century. In 1892, New Jersey passed the first state-aid road bill, which permitted one-third support for highway improvement projects; and, in 1893, the U.S. Department of Agriculture created the Office of Road Inquiry for the support of farm-to-market roads in rural areas. In 1905, the new agency was expanded into the Office of Public Roads, again for farm-to-market highway projects, under Logan W. Page. Within the decade a more expansive Federal-Aid Road Act was passed (July 1916) that permitted government support of regional highways in rural areas in conjunction with the newly formed American Association of State Highway Officials (AASHO).[5] With the sudden death of Page in 1918, Thomas H. MacDonald became the Director of Public Roads, a post he would hold for the next thirty-three years as the principle administrator of national highway development in the U.S. It was MacDonald who conceived

of the partnership between the Bureau of Public Roads (BPR) and AASHO state engineers for regional federal projects, which was enacted into law with the Federal Highway Act of 1921.[6] This encouraged both rural market roads and long distance interstate routes, but posed a potential problem of competition with private auto trails and regional railroads.

FEDERAL ROUTE NUMBERS

By the end of World War I, the multitude of private auto trails had created a confusion of regional highways across the U.S. Such a complex web of routes prompted the idea for a national highway signage system, enacted into law in the Federal Highway Act of 1921. This became the basis for a comprehensive mapping of a national road network under MacDonald beginning in November 1923. The following year, MacDonald organized the first set of regional AASHO meetings to consider how to give order to the overlap of the 250 private auto trails and state road projects.[7] In the Midwest, the Wisconsin Highway Department had devised a numbered system for trunk routes in 1918, which had been adopted by Illinois and Michigan two years later and followed by highway departments in New York and New England.[8] Using these Midwestern sign systems as models, MacDonald proposed that a national marking standard be designed for all the major regional trunk routes in the United States. At AASHO's Tenth Anniversary meeting in San Francisco in November 1924, E. W. James, Chief of Design for the BPR, proposed that a "comprehensive and uniform scheme" for the designation of primary national highways be developed through the joint efforts of the BPR and AASHO in a series of regional meetings with state officials. Under direction from MacDonald, a Joint Board on Interstate Highways was approved in March 1925, which held a preliminary session in Washington, D.C., in early April. Among those attending were several Midwest state highway engineers, including Frank T. Sheets of Illinois, B. H. Piepmeier of Missouri, and Cyrus Avery, the Chairman of the Oklahoma Highway Commission. All of these men were to play crucial roles in the designation of Route 66.[9]

SHIELD SIGNS

The Washington meeting had developed a working plan. This proposed that long-distance interstate highways should be marked with a systematic scheme of route signs. The question of whether to maintain the existing auto trails or devise a new network of numbered highways was still in debate among the state engineers. For Midwest members, a regional conference of the Mississippi Valley AASHO group was held in Kansas City on May 27, 1925, organized by BPR Chief James with Avery and Piepmeier in attendance. At the meeting James showed a sample federal route shield he had developed from a sketch with Frank T. Rogers of Michigan that read "MAINE/US 56" (Fig. 5.1).[10]

Among the board members, it was Avery who was most insistent about routing a national highway number through his home state of Oklahoma.[11] At the Kansas City meeting, he offered his own State Highway No. 7 as the best graded road from St. Louis to Santa Fe, noting the historic problem suffered by Oklahoma:

The fact that trans-continental railways have for the most part missed the state, because it was so long

Indian Territory, has also helped turned travel to other states. But with the shortest route, the best improved route, and a route marked from coast to coast, Oklahoma will experience a wonderful increase in tourist traffic.[12]

In order to demonstrate that a nationally numbered highway route across Oklahoma could be realized, Avery showed the Board members his own sample metal shield he had made at the McAlester State Penitentiary. According to the *Tulsa Tribune*, the sample shield showed "U.S. 66" in black letters on a yellow background. It is the first recorded use of the double six for the future Route 66, presented a full year before the federal designation of the highway in 1926.[13]

Avery likely conceived of his sample U.S. 66 shield from the example of the BPR U.S. 56 shield exhibited by James earlier in May.[14] Possibly Avery had used the BPR "U.S. 56" signet as a national base number, with a ten-step for his own national highway, "U.S. 66," across Oklahoma. Avery wrote to James in June, sending him the sample Oklahoma marker signs in a new pressing in black-and-white to match the sample shield developed by the Bureau.[15] The only recorded image of the Oklahoma shield appears in a photo from *Studebaker Wheel* of February 1926, showing MacDonald with a table of state signs, including the 1925 sample markers for Oklahoma and Missouri, the numbers hidden by MacDonald's hand (Fig. 5.2).[16] The fact that Avery had selected "66" by May 1925 demonstrates that the double sixes had already been attached to the concept of a transcontinental route across Oklahoma, even though the

The Tourist "Moses"

5.2. U.S. highway shields, 1925. Sample route signs shown by Bureau of Public Roads Chief T. H. MacDonald, with the U.S. 66 Oklahoma shield "KLA" designed by Cyrus Avery above MacDonald's hand. From *Studebaker World* (February 1926). Courtesy of Federal Highway Administration (FHA) Archives.

Avery "U.S. 66" shield was a simple demonstration project for the Joint Board meeting in Kansas City.

FINAL NUMBERING

A second meeting of the Joint Board on Interstate Highways was held in Washington, August 3-4, 1925, with BPR's James as chairman. The decision to number the national highway routes now seemed certain, although the problem of how to appease the political power of the private auto trail associations was still to be considered. Working from a large wall map of the United States, James devised a practical system of route numbers in which even numbers were assigned to the east-west transcontinental highways and odd numbers to

the north-south trunk roads.[17] More importantly, the primary transcontinentals took steps of ten, starting with the "zero" roads: U.S. 20 between Atlantic City, New Jersey, and Astoria, Oregon, and U.S. 40 between Wilmington, Delaware, and San Francisco.[18] Similarly, the primary north-south highways were signed with "one": U.S. 1 between Fort Kent, Maine, and Miami, Florida, on the East Coast, and U.S. 101 between Port Angeles, Washington, and San Diego on the West. Intermediate routes were given intermediate numbers: U.S. 25 between Toledo, Ohio, and Augusta, Georgia, and U.S. 42 between Cleveland and Cincinnati.[19] To select the national routes, a Numbering Committee was formed, with Avery and Piepmeier as members, which submitted its final report on August 4, 1925. The report recommended eight primary east-west and ten primary north-south routes, along with fourteen intermediate routes, for a total of thirty-two nationally numbered highways.[20]

With Avery of Oklahoma, Piepmeier of Missouri, and Sheets of Illinois on the select Numbering Committee, the choice of highway numbers in the Mississippi Valley region was within their obvious discretion. Although no written minutes of the committee have been discovered, it appears that Piepmeier and Avery, with Sheets, designated a "zero" number, U.S. 60, for a *diagonal* national trunk route through their home states of Illinois, Missouri, and Oklahoma. The selected route followed the Ozark Trails from St. Louis to Tulsa and Oklahoma City, and then proceeded to Amarillo and Santa Fe, where it connected with the National Old Trails Highway into Los Angeles (Fig. 5.3). While not a true transcontinental highway, the route of U.S. 60 was apparently justified by the volume of traffic between

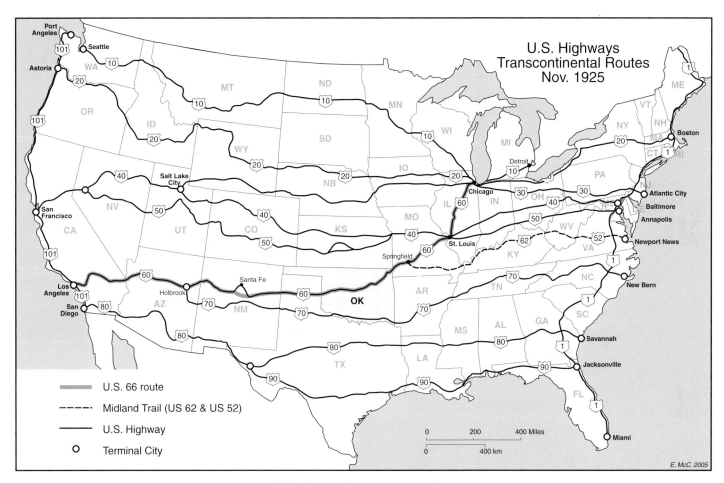

5.3. U.S. highway transcontinental routes, November 1925. Transcontinental "zero" numbered routes designated by AASHO, showing U.S. 60 from Chicago to Los Angeles as the pre-Route 66 number, and U.S. 52/62 as the Midland Trail through Kentucky to Springfield, Missouri. By the author.

Chicago and Los Angeles; and the fact that some primary highways, including U.S. 30 from Atlantic City to Salt Lake City, did not extend fully from coast to coast.[21] Thus, U.S. 60 marked a primary trunk route from the Midwest to California, and it established federal numbering for the continental highway that the next year would become Route 66.

The federal route system was made final in October, and the Report of the Joint Board published on November 18, 1925. In all, 145 numbered highways were designated, with national attention given to the transcontinental "zero" numbered routes such as U.S. 20 between Boston and Portland, Oregon, and U.S. 80 between Savannah, Georgia, and San Diego.[22] The scheme immediately provoked reaction from the auto trail associations and state highway departments. Among the most vocal was Governor William J. Fields of Kentucky, who openly protested the lack of a national "zero" route through his state. The primary highway west from Washington, D.C., the former Midland Trail, had been numbered U.S. 62 (see Fig. 5.3).[23] Fields found this secondary route a disservice to Kentucky and was outspoken at the Lexington Automobile Club in December: "I particularly object to the obliteration of my idol, my dream, the Midland Trail, running from Ashland to Lexington to Louisville. I have worked hard for this great road."[24]

Fields had let his priority be known to the Kentucky Highway Commission at the time of his election as "Honest Bill from Olive Hill" in 1924.[25] With his political contacts in Washington, Fields wrote to MacDonald and James at the BPR to lobby for a change in the numbering of U.S. 62 to U.S. 60.[26] Although U.S. 60 was already assigned to the Chicago and Los Angeles route, James quietly agreed to meet with Fields in Chicago in February 1926. Learning of the potential move of U.S. 60 from Missouri to Kentucky, Piepmeier immediately telegraphed AASHO Director W. C. Markham in Washington:

WE BITTERLY PROTEST THE CHANGE IN ROUTE NUMBERS SIXTY AND SIXTY TWO STOP CHICAGO TO LOS ANGELES IS THE IMPORTANT ROUTE AND SHOULD CARRY THE ZERO NUMBER STOP WE HAVE PUBLISHED SIX HUNDRED THOUSAND MAPS SHOWING NUMBERS AS ORIGINALLY ASSIGNED STOP B. H. PIEPMEIER[27]

The renumbering of U.S. 60 now threatened to disrupt the entire national route scheme. A second BPR Executive Committee meeting was held in Washington on February 16, 1926, to work out a compromise between Piepmeier and Fields. The solution was to renumber U.S. 62 as U.S. 60 from Norfolk, Virginia, to Springfield, Missouri, and then create an alternate *spur*, U.S. 60 North, for the section from Springfield through St. Louis to Chicago.[28] The numbering debate continued through March, when Avery wrote to AASHO President Frank Page:

I want to say to you Mr. Page, as president of this association, that I was not advised of any tentative agreement with Kentucky after the agreement in Chicago and only learned of it indirectly. We are proceeding to put up our No. 60 markers and have State Highway maps showing U.S. 60 on it, and will not consent to any change. We feel we have not been treated squarely in this matter.[29]

NUMBER 66

As the matter of resolving the U.S. 60 controversy extended into the spring, the political situation in Oklahoma began to unravel for Avery's future as Chairman of the Highway Commission. When appointed by Governor Martin E. Trapp in February 1924, Avery had expanded the Highway Commission into an effective department for the Trapp administration.[30] The upcoming state primary in August 1926, however, posed a problem for Democrat Trapp. He had been Lt. Governor under Governor John C. Walton, who had been impeached in November 1923. As Acting Governor of Oklahoma since December 1923, the state constitution prohibited Trapp from serving a second successive term.[31] Moreover, Trapp had initiated an active campaign against the Ku Klux Klan in Oklahoma which, by early 1926, had aroused bitter opposition to Avery and the Highway Commission.[32] One state newspaper reported: "There are many other counties than Oklahoma and Tulsa, too, where the klan will find itself in alliance with the county commissioners who are seeking to hog-tie or destroy the highway commission."[33]

The growing opposition to Governor Trapp resulted in the Klan offering its own gubernatorial candidate, Henry S. Johnston, who announced his campaign in late March 1926.[34] A legal case was immediately filed challenging Trapp's eligibility with the Oklahoma County Election Board to prevent his second term succession.[35] By early April, Trapp, and so Avery, faced a problematic political future due to the legal and electoral problems posed by Johnston and the Klan.

In April, with growing political uncertainty in Oklahoma, Avery sensed that trying to hold on to the U.S. 60 numbering would jeopardize the greater objective of a single-numbered through-route between Chicago and Los Angeles. On April 6, Avery wrote to MacDonald proposing that a compromise *number* might be arranged, and that he would make a "personal trip to see Mr. Piepmeier" in Missouri in order to help resolve the issue with Kentucky (Fig. 5.4).[36] The compromise solution was to maintain the single U.S. 60

5.4. B. H. Piepmeier, Missouri Highway Commissioner, ca. 1925. Piepmeier was the promoter of the original U.S. 60 route from Chicago to Los Angeles. Courtesy of Missouri Department of Transportation (MODOT).

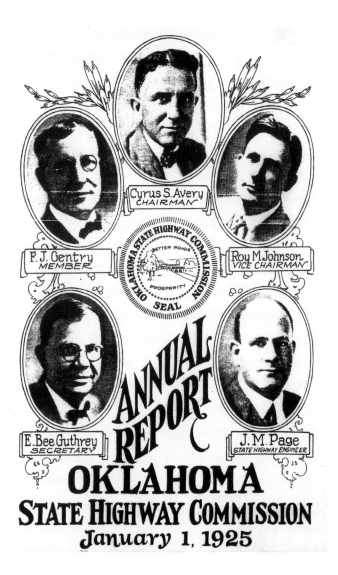

Cyrus S. Avery
CHAIRMAN

F. J. Gentry
MEMBER

Roy M. Johnson
VICE CHAIRMAN

E. Bee Guthrey
SECRETARY

J. M. Page
STATE HIGHWAY ENGINEER

ANNUAL REPORT

OKLAHOMA
STATE HIGHWAY COMMISSION
January 1, 1925

5.5. *Annual Report, Oklahoma State Highway Commission*, January 1925. The title page showing Cyrus Avery as chairman (top) and John M. Page as chief engineer (bottom right). Courtesy of Oklahoma Department of Transportation.

marker signs between Chicago and Los Angeles and renumber the former U.S. 62 as a spur, U.S. 60 South/East, from Springfield, Missouri, through Kentucky to Virginia Beach, Virginia.[37] Kentucky immediately rejected any additional signage on Route 60 through the state.[38] However, as Avery had promised a compromise meeting with Piepmeier, he was now pressed to convince his Missouri colleague to change the Chicago-Los Angeles route number before the upcoming Oklahoma primary in August.

On April 14, Avery received support from James at the BPR for meeting with Piepmeier to "clear up" the troubled situation.[39] Avery arranged to meet Piepmeier in Springfield, Missouri, midway between the two state capitals on Friday afternoon, April 30.[40] Local Springfield newspapers reported the meeting:

> Mr. Piepmeier was in the city today to confer with representatives of the Oklahoma highway department in regard to connecting Missouri highways which have been designated United Sates roads with extensions of the same national highways through Oklahoma.[41]

The meeting was likely held in the local offices of the Missouri Highway Commission in the Green County Courthouse in downtown Springfield.[42] Avery arrived with his Chief Engineer, John M. Page, originally from the Texas

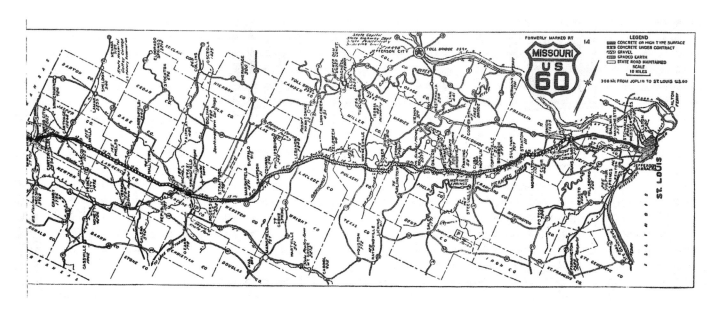

5.6. U.S. 60, Missouri, 1925. Strip map showing the original U.S. 60 route number from St. Louis to Webb City before the change to U.S. 66 in 1926. Courtesy of Missouri Department of Transportation (MODOT).

Bureau of Public Roads, whom Avery had hired in 1924 (Fig. 5.5).[43] Evidently Avery persuaded Piepmeier to relinquish U.S. 60 in Missouri for an alternate number for the Chicago to Los Angeles highway (Fig. 5.6). The choices appear to have been narrowed to even numbers between U.S. 60 and U.S. 70. With a national map as reference, the group pondered available numbers, including U.S. 62 formerly through Kentucky, as well as route numbers 66 and 68. They discounted U.S. 64 as already assigned to the route between Conway, Arkansas, and Des Moines, New Mexico, following the former Albert Pike Auto Trail through Tulsa.[44]

While no available record of the 1926 Springfield meeting survives, a later account by Avery summarized the final numbering choice: "At this meeting Mr. John Marshall Page, Chief Engineer of the State Highway Department of Oklahoma, in checking over the U.S. map used by the committee, discovered that the Number 66 had not been assigned."[45]

Page's "discovery" of "Number 66" opens the question of whether it was truly a revelation that came from looking at the map at the meeting, or was, in fact, a recollection of the sample "U.S. 66" shield sign presented to the earlier

AASHO Kansas City meeting by Avery in 1925. Reconstructing the logic of the Springfield meeting, the choices were likely limited to 66 or 68, as U.S. 62 was probably dismissed because of its association with Kentucky and the Midland Trail. Perhaps the "discovery" of "Number 66" did reflect the old AASHO "U.S. 66" signs from Kansas City, but it also showed a preference for a double number. There were only three of these double numbers assigned by the Joint Board in 1925: U.S. 22, U.S. 77, and U.S. 99.[46] Did the rarity of paired numbers enter into the discussion? These and other questions were doubtless debated at the Springfield meeting, where the primary objective had to be the maintenance of a *single* distinctive number for the Chicago-Los Angeles highway. Indeed, the double sixes with their appealing alliteration could have convinced the group that "Number 66" was perhaps an even better choice than "U.S. 60."

That afternoon, Avery and Piepmeier sent a telegram to MacDonald announcing their willingness to accept "SIXTY SIX" instead of "SIXTY." The Springfield telegram, now in the AASHO archives in Suitland, Maryland, is the first printed reference to Route 66. It can be considered the "birth certificate" of the highway, with the route numbers spelled out in telegraphic style (Fig. 5.7):[47]

REGARDING CHICAGO LOSANGELES ROAD IF CALIFORNIA ARIZONA NEWMEXICO AND ILLINOIS WILL ACCEPT SIXTY SIX INSTEAD OF SIXTY WE ARE INCLINED TO AGREE TO THIS CHANGE WE PREFER SIXTY SIX TO SIXTY TWO AVERY PIEPMEIER 4PM[48]

On May 17, Avery wrote to Markham at AASHO to inquire about Kentucky's position on the new proposal.[49] Unaware of the Springfield compromise, Kentucky officials were continuing to object to any change in the U.S. 60 designation. In the meantime, Piepmeier and Avery continued posting U.S. 60 signs in their states until MacDonald suggested, on June 11, that Avery should "postpone erection of signs on the route in your state" until the numbering matter with Kentucky was resolved.[50]

At the same time the political situation in Oklahoma was unraveling for Trapp. Avery wrote in his reply to MacDonald: "We think it would do us a lot of good politically, to get out U.S. markers up throughout the State before the primary, and unfortunately, the road that has now become a sort of question-mark with many citizens along the route, is U.S. 60."[51]

The Trapp case reached a climax when, on June 28, the Oklahoma Supreme Court overturned a lower Oklahoma County Court decision of May 1, that had recognized Trapp's eligibility for a second term.[52] Justice Thomas D. Lyons ruled that Trapp was "ineligible to immediately succeed himself," since he was already acting governor of the state.[53] With Trapp unable to run in a second term, Avery sensed that his future as chairman of Oklahoma Highway Commission was very much in question. In the meantime, he was eager to resolve the numbering of the Chicago-Los Angeles highway. On June 23, MacDonald wrote Avery that the "controversy which has been running for sometime" had finally been settled and that Kentucky would be satisfied with Number 60 if Oklahoma and Missouri would accept Number 66 for the route from Chicago to Los Angeles.[54]

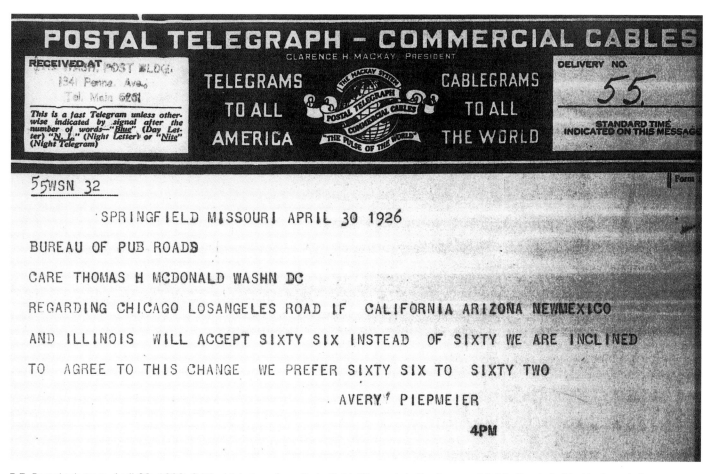

5.7. Postal telegram, April 30, 1926. Original telegram from Springfield, Missouri, to the Bureau of Public Roads in Washington, stating the agreement by Avery and Piepmeier to accept "SIXTY-SIX" for "CHICAGO LOS ANGELES ROAD," the first printed statement of the U.S. 66 numbering. Courtesy of American Association of State Highway Officials (AASHO) Archives.

Avery wrote James: "I wish to especially thank you for your interest in this matter, and assure you that the only object we, of Oklahoma, have had, was to have a continuous number from Chicago to Los Angeles without any branches. We assure you that it will be a road through Oklahoma that the U.S. Government will be proud of."[55]

Despite the agreement, a sense of hesitation still affected state highway departments. On July 30, Sheets, the Illinois Chief Engineer, wrote to James that he had "refrained from erecting any markers" on the U.S. 60 route until a decision was settled.[56] A letter to AASHO Board members supported the change, with the ballots counted in favor of the new numbering on August 6. The following day James wrote to Avery that he regretted the delay, but that the "situation is now ironed out."[57] Finally, on August 11, the change was officially announced to AASHO members:

> Please be informed that the Executive Committee has settled a controversy of long standing in reference to the use of Number 60 by assigning Number 60 to the route from Virginia Beach, Virginia . . . [to] Springfield, Missouri, and Number 66 to the route from Chicago . . . to Los Angeles.[58]

Another three months were to pass before the full AASHO membership voted its approval of the Interstate Highway route numbers on November 11, at its annual meeting in Pinehurst, North Carolina.[59] Among the continuous numbered routes, "United States Highway No. 66" was listed from Chicago to Los Angeles at 2,448 miles, while "Highway No. 60" extended from Virginia Beach to Springfield, Missouri. At 1,382 miles, it was hardly the transcontinental route Kentucky had wished, but, in fact, only three of the primary "zero" routes reached from coast to coast: U.S. 20, U.S. 40, and U.S. 80. The remaining "zero" routes, such as U.S. 10 between Detroit and Seattle, extended east-west between major cities, but without reaching the coasts. U.S. Highway 66 was among the ten longest routes, a through route with a single number, as Avery and Piepmeier had intended.[60]

With official AASHO approval, local state highway departments began to post the new U.S. 66 shield signs along highways and on highway maps. Among the first was Arizona, which published its revised state road map in October, with the double six shields stamped as large signs along the road from Navajo to Winslow, Seligman, and Kingman, even though much of the route was still gravel beyond Flagstaff (Fig. 5.8).[61] In neighboring New Mexico, the new signs were first posted on the section between Santa Fe and

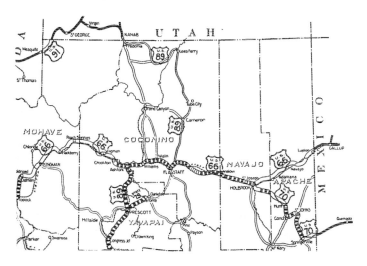

5.8. "GET ACQUAINTED WITH ARIZONA" map, *Arizona Highways*, October 1926. Road map detail showing the first uses of U.S. 66 shield signs on a state highway map. Courtesy of Federal Highway Administration (FHA) Archives.

5.9. *New Mexico Highway Journal*, January 1927. Photo showing the first posted U.S. 66 shield sign on the Santa Fe-Albuquerque highway, together with U.S. 85. Courtesy of New Mexico Highway Department.

Albuquerque where U.S. 85 overlapped with U.S. 66 (Fig. 5.9).[62] In Oklahoma, Avery reported in January 1927 that, "We have marked all the state roads and are now engaged erecting the U.S. Markers on Federal Routes," suggesting that U.S. 66 shields were replacing the U.S. 60 signs.[63]

RESIGNATION

Even as the new U.S. 66 marker signs were being erected, Avery's political situation was deteriorating. The Democratic primary of August 3, 1926, had given the nod to Johnston, the Ku Klux Klan candidate, and, in November, Johnston had won with a substantial majority over Republican O. K. Benedict.[64] When Johnston took office on January 10, 1927, the Highway Commission was among the first targets of change.[65] Within two weeks of the inauguration, Avery was forced to resign as chairman, leaving Oklahoma City for his home in Tulsa. Speaking to supporters on January 27, Avery said, "But it seems they have me licked."[66]

Avery's resignation sent shock waves into Missouri where, in Springfield, front-page headlines declared, "POLITICAL BLASTS IN OKLAHOMA HIT HIGHWAY 66 PLAN."[67] Though Johnston had forced Avery to retire, Page remained as chief engineer through May when pressure for his removal became a personal burden: "I couldn't afford to quit under fire, and until recently, I thought it was decided for me to stay for a time anyway. Then the trouble came and I have my reputation to consider and it became a question then of them firing me if they wanted me out."[68]

In Missouri, a series of similar events had affected Piepmeier and the Highway Commission in Jefferson City. In November 1926, Commission Chief Theodore Gary had announced plans to retire to private business and had offered Piepmeier a position as engineering director of the Gary Group in Kansas City.[69] Piepmeier announced his resignation that December 14, exiting in February 1927.[70] Thus, by early 1927, both Avery and Piepmeier had left office with their hard-won U.S. 66 signs only recently posted in Oklahoma and Missouri.

NUMBERED LEGACY

The fate of the political personalities that had forced the compromise of 1926 proved as fickle as that affecting Avery and Piepmeier. In Kentucky, Fields lost his bid for reelection in the Democratic primary of March 1927, and left office in November.[71] In Oklahoma, Johnston was threatened with impeachment for calling out the state militia against legislators on Christmas Day 1927, and was removed from office in March 1929 for financial improprieties.[72] All the state politicians embroiled in the controversy over the numbering of U.S. 60 had now been removed from office.[73]

As Avery had predicted in April 1926, establishing a single number for the Chicago to Los Angeles route through Oklahoma had proven to require a spirit of compromise, even before the politicians got involved in the process. As it was, Piepmeier's insistence on the Number 60, the intransigence of Kentucky highway officials for their Number 60, and the threat of Klan elections all played into the need for selecting an alternative at the Springfield meeting of late April 1926. Even after agreeing on 66, holding the numbering in place required Avery's continuous attention until the AASHO Board's approval was secured in August, at the very moment Avery's mentor, Trapp, was effectively removed from office in the Oklahoma primaries.

In light of these political events, the numbering of U.S. Route 66 can be seen as the seizing of a brief window of opportunity for maintaining the promise of a single signed highway across Oklahoma. For Avery, the unified route was but an extension of his work with the Ozark Trails to mark a continental highway through Tulsa. Though removed from office, Avery soon found opportunity to promote the new U.S. Highway 66 as a tourist route through Oklahoma in the years before the Great Depression destroyed the prosperity the new national route to California had promised.

But there was also more encapsulated in this number than the political drama of that tumultuous year. Caught in it as well was the longer history to which Trapp, Avery, Piepmeier, Fields, and all the rest were heirs. After all, the decision to create a federal system arose out of the system of privately named auto trails, these following the railroad lines whose paths had largely been worked out by wagon masters, taking their lead from the trappers and explorers who had benefited so lavishly from the knowledge of Native Americans. U.S. Highway 66 wasn't conceived in a conference room on a Friday afternoon in Springfield, Missouri, in 1926, but in the thousands of years of human effort to forge a connection across the Southern High Plains between the Great Lakes and the Pacific Ocean. It was the pregnancy of this connection that was given a name that interesting afternoon, a connection through which Avery foresaw the tourist and commerce of the nation flowing, and from which his state of Oklahoma could benefit. What Avery saw was the potential power of the road, an open road of unlimited promise, and it was this promise that those paired sixes would come in time to represent.

Chapter Six
Main Street Highway

THE FEDERAL NUMBERING OF U.S. 66 gave highway boosters a distinctively signed route for tourist travel from the Midwest to California, especially in Oklahoma where the double sixes became advertisements for local businessmen. In the brief period between the final AASHO numbering in 1926 and the Los Angeles Olympic Games in 1932, U.S. 66 became established in the heartland of the Midwest as a distinctive signet on highway maps, adopted by auto road associations, oil companies, and marathon road runners as the new tourist route to the West. The unique number gave U.S. Highway 66 an appealing identity as a road of scenic wonders through New Mexico and Arizona before the Great Depression and the Dust Bowl migration reset the sixes as signs of exodus to California.

HIGHWAY 66 ASSOCIATION

Before Avery lost his job with the Oklahoma Highway Commission, he had organized a group of Tulsa businessmen to promote the new highway as a tourist route to Los Angeles. Johnston's Klan-supported election as governor had convinced Avery that, in Oklahoma, Highway 66 could be compromised by the new administration. In February 1927, John T. Woodruff of Springfield, Missouri, was elected president at the inaugural meeting in Tulsa of the National Highway 66 Association.[1] Avery had known Woodruff through the Ozark Trails Association. Rephrasing the original objectives of the Ozark Trails, Woodruff named Highway 66 "AMERICA'S MAIN STREET," promising to pave the entire route from the "Great Lakes to the Pacific Coast."[2] A second Springfield meeting in early May was attended by more than 500 delegates. There, Avery traced the origins of the Highway 66 Association back to the Ozark Trails, prior to World War I:

> Mr. Avery, former chairman of the Oklahoma state highway commission, is one of the founders of the

movement to create a great transcontinental highway along the route of U.S. 66 and he gave the history of the movement, which really dates back to June 1917, when a meeting was held here to develop what was then known as the "Ozark Trail," now "the Main Street of America."[3]

The Highway 66 Association revived the former booster spirit of the Ozark Trails in Missouri and Oklahoma, with its promise to extend its promotional campaign westward to California. In June 1927, a third meeting was held in Amarillo, Texas, to form a western division in New Mexico and Arizona, giving "Main Street" the commercial identity of the highway.[4] While the Highway 66 Association found the new numbers appealing, many in the nation did not. These sentiments were captured by the *Lexington* [Kentucky] *Herald*, as reprinted in a *New York Times* editorial:

> The traveler may shed tears as he drives down the shady vista of the Lincoln Highway or dream dreams as he speeds over a sunlit path on the Jefferson Highway, or see noble visions as he speeds across the unfolding ribbon that bears the name Woodrow Wilson. But how in the world can a man get a kick out of 46 or 55 or 33 or 21?[5]

BUNION DERBY

In order to advertise Highway 66 to a national audience, the Main Street Association devised a promotional campaign for a long-distance marathon foot race along U.S. 66 that attracted attention far beyond the dreams of its local boost-ers. In late 1927, at a banquet in Oklahoma City, the question of national publicity was raised. Audience member Alex Singletry jovially shouted out, "Put on a foot race!"[6] At first, the suggestion was taken in jest, but the appeal of Singletry's idea soon encouraged Avery and local member Lon Scott of Springfield to contact C. C. Pyle, a Midwest sports promoter, who found the highway marathon an attractive challenge. With a $60,000 pledge from the Highway 66 Association and "Main Street of America" maps, Pyle scouted the route along U.S. 66 from Los Angeles east to Chicago, and on to New York, to promote the "First International Transcontinental Footrace" (Fig. 6.1).[7]

By early February 1928, Pyle had assembled an impressive organization in Los Angeles with several prominent European runners and the registration of some 300 entrants.[8] Pyle offered a substantial $25,000 prize to the best time for the 3,400-mile race. On February 12, a test meet was held at the Ascot Speedway for local newsmen who dubbed the spectacle "The Bunion Derby." When the starting gun fired on March 4, a crowd of 50,000 lined Highway 66 in Los Angeles to watch 275 runners on their way east to the first overnight station at Puente in the San Bernardino Valley. With its special Transcontinental Clipper motor coach and an oversized Maxwell House Coffee truck, the marathon paced slowly up Cajon Pass, down to Barstow and across the Mojave Desert, to reach Needles by March 11, with the Englishman, Arthur Newton, and the Hopi Indian, Nicholas Quomahwahu, in the lead. Having crossed the Colorado River by ferry, the runners climbed the Black Mountains to Oatman, Arizona, and cruised downhill to Kingman, to reach Flagstaff on March 17. The field had been reduced to 110, with Newton

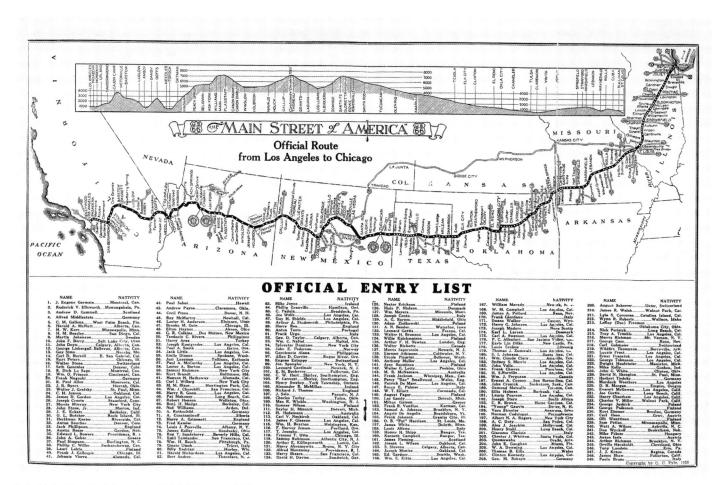

6.1. *Main Street of America, Official Route*, 1928. Map showing the Bunion Derby marathon route along U.S. 66 from Los Angeles to Chicago, with the runners listed below. By permission of Jim Ross Collection.

in the lead. Quomahwahu had dropped out due to leg cramps. It was at this point that a Cherokee Indian runner, Andy Payne from Foyil, Oklahoma, emerged for the first time as a strong contender among the daily leaders.[9]

The Transcontinental Foot Race pushed eastward along U.S. 66 during March and April, much of the roadway still loose gravel from the National Old Trails Highway, especially in the desert stretches in Arizona and New Mexico (see Fig. 6.1). By the time the runners reached the Texas border at Glenrio on April 1, Andy Payne and the Italian-born Englishman, Peter Gavuzzi, were in the lead.[10] Crossing the Oklahoma line at Texola on April 7, Andy Payne, No. 43, was greeted as a favorite son. In Oklahoma City, Payne was given a hero's welcome by Governor Johnston on April 13, and three days later another by Avery's Highway 66 Association in Tulsa.[11] Most rewarding was the home-town welcome in Claremore by famed Oklahoma cowboy humorist, Will Rogers, who gave Payne a check for $250 as a gesture of good will. The *New York Times* reported: "Throngs lined the highway route to see Payne dog-trotting steadily along. It was estimated that 1,000 automobiles followed him, blocking the highway."[12]

The excitement of the Bunion Derby is seen in a series of snapshot photos taken by Pyle in April in western Oklahoma, with Payne surrounded by auto flivvers and admiring crowds on the dirt road of U.S. 66 (Fig. 6.2).[13] These pictures capture the popular spirit of Highway 66 boosters and convey the significance of the Great Transcontinental Road Race as an event that brought Oklahoma from its territorial isolation into national attention.

When on April 19th the Bunion Derby reached Baxter Springs, Kansas, the field had been reduced to eighty runners, with Payne and Gavuzzi still in the lead.[14] When the front runners crossed the Mississippi to East St. Louis on April 26, only seventy-three contestants remained. The concrete highway in Illinois had pruned the field to seventy by the time the racers reached Chicago on the weekend of May 5, 1928. From Chicago east, the race took U.S. 20 across Indiana to Cleveland, thereafter following the Lake Erie shoreline to Jamestown, New York. Crossing through Pennsylvania in Bradford, the runners returned to New York State on Highway 17, reaching Bath on May 19. By this time, Gavuzzi had dropped out with a torn hamstring and Andy Payne had clearly become the front runner, though often holding back to conserve his energy.[15] When the fifty-five runners approached the New Jersey line at Suffrin, newsfilm cameras began recording the final lap into Manhattan. The runners crossed the Hudson River on the Weehawken Ferry before taking their victory lap around Madison Square Garden, May 26, after eighty-four days on the run. As reported by the *New York Times*, the finish was anticlimactic:

Andrew took it as a trot. He was saving himself for his future, and was not interested in winning applause by showing the crowd a burst of speed here. The crowd consisted of only a few hundred people at the ferry and there was no crowd along Tenth Avenue, where the runners took their way into the Garden. A crowd started to gather. As shouts and tooting of horns and whistles of motorcycle policemen called attention to the wind-up of history's longest footrace, thousands began to see what it was all about.[16]

Congratulatory telegrams were sent to Payne care of Madison Square Garden, from family and friends in Oklahoma, together with Pyle's check for $25,000. Payne returned to Oklahoma a genuine local hero. The Highway 66 Association had achieved its goal to promote the Main Street road as a national route to and from California. In fact, the only casualty was Avery, who was suddenly dismissed

6.2. Bunion Derby, Oklahoma, April 1928. Photo by C. C. Pyle showing Andy Payne (43) as the lead runner and U.S. 66 as a graded road in western Oklahoma. By permission of James H. Thomas Collection.

from the Highway 66 Association the weekend of Payne's victory, "double-crossed" for undisclosed reasons.[17]

The Bunion Derby had inscribed Highway 66 in the regional culture with poems written in its honor. L. R. Davee of Tulsa, likely a Main Street Association member, penned a twenty-four verse epic that read in part:

Thinking of the mud and ruts traversed in the good old balmy days,
As I sadly wonder where will end this jazzy speed bug craze,
I shake my head and heave a sigh; my eyes to heaven raise.
But down this Highway 66 "America's Best Highway,"

I look for joys unknown before, on Spring or Summer day.
From Chicago to Los Angeles, she winds her ribbon way,
Inviting jitney, limousine, Old Dobbin and the Shay.[18]

PHILLIPS 66

As the Bunion Derby was being run, another innovation of Oklahoma boosterism was promoting U.S. 66 by using the new federal route numbers as an advertising gimmick. In the fall of 1927, a local Oklahoma oil company, Phillips Petroleum of Bartlesville, near Tulsa, had perfected a cold-weather, high-gravity, naphtha-based auto gasoline. Its new wells in the Texas Panhandle at Borger near Amarillo along

6.3. Phillips Petroleum "66" logo, 1927-30. Evolution of the Phillips "66" logo. Courtesy of Phillips Petroleum Company.

U.S. 66 had created an instant city, with the discovery of new wells. The Borger oil rush was captured by Missouri artist Thomas Hart Benton in *Boomtown*, painted during his visit to the city in February 1927, with oil wells sprouting black geysers behind a bustle of Model T Fords on Main Street. Oil company founder Frank Phillips had just opened a chain of new Phillips service stations throughout the Midwest, and in this sudden prosperity he sponsored the Dole Air Race to Hawaii in August 1927.[19] It was at this moment that Texas oil and Highway 66 numbering converged to create a name that became part of Midwestern folklore.

According to company history, sometime in September or early October, Phillips Company executive John F. Kane and his driver, Salty Sawtell, were returning from Oklahoma City on U.S. 66 for a meeting in Bartlesville to name the new high-gravity auto gasoline.[20] Approaching Tulsa, Kane said:

"This car goes like 60 with our new gas," he remarked to the driver, who glancing at the speedometer, said excitedly, "Sixty, nothing! We're doing 66!" At the con-

ference the next day someone asked where the incident occurred. The reply was, "Near Tulsa, on Highway 66."[21]

The "66" campaign was approved in Bartlesville in October before Frank Phillips left for an international petroleum conference in Paris. When he returned on November 18, 1927, "Phil-Up and Fly with Phillips 66" banners were hung over the new Wichita station on East Central Avenue.[22] The following year, 66 was incorporated into the design of the Phillips Company disk, and in 1930 the federal route shield was adopted as the "Phillips 66" logo, eventually modernized in stylized form (Fig. 6.3).[23] By the onset of the Great Depression, regional marketing for Phillips 66 had spread the double-six shields throughout the Midwest, well beyond its original Oklahoma core and into the national culture. Whether because of the appealing graphics of the paired sixes or their liquid, alliterative sound, Phillips and 66 became entwined, a new part of the roadside landscape, transforming 66 from a federal highway number into travel-

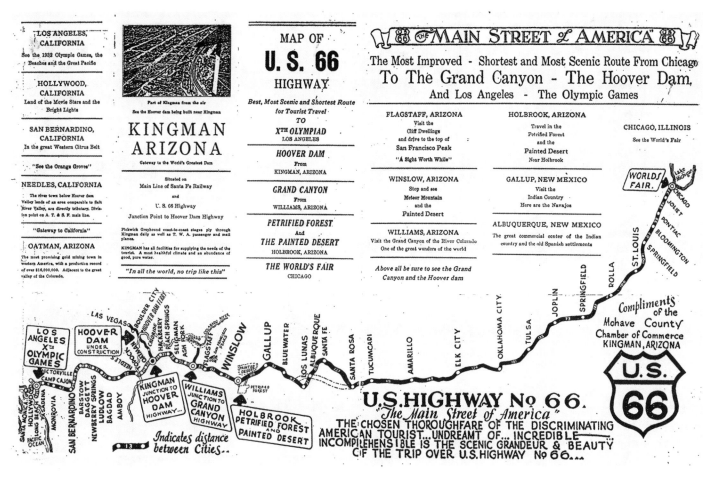

6.4. *Main Street of America, U.S. No. 66 Highway*, 1932. Map of U.S. 66 for the tenth Olympics in Los Angeles, showing the Grand Canyon and Hoover Dam (under construction). Courtesy of Arizona Route 66 Association.

ers' beacons from Illinois to California. Scarcely in use for a year, the new route number was already beginning the process of symbolization that would preserve it as a potent icon long after the highway itself had been decommissioned.

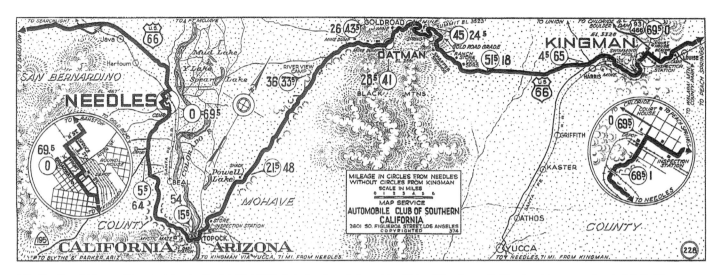

6.5. *Sectional Maps of Los Angeles to Flagstaff,* 1937. Details of an Automobile Club of Southern California strip map, showing U.S. 66 over the Oatman Gold Road between Needles and Kingman. By permission of Automobile Club of Southern California.

LOS ANGELES OLYMPICS

The momentum of American prosperity was suddenly broken by the stock market crash in October 1929, an economic downturn that quickly became a national financial crisis. Despite the dire conditions, the promotion of Highway 66 continued through the early years of the Depression, with national attention turned towards the tenth Olympic Games to be held in Los Angeles in 1932.[24] Like the Panama-Pacific Exposition of 1915 in San Francisco, the Los Angeles Olympics encouraged transcontinental road travel to the West, especially along the newly marked U.S. 66, the most direct route to Southern California.

A wealth of cartographic talent was employed to map the Olympic highway from Chicago to Los Angeles. At first, simple outline maps were printed in local papers. In December 1929, the Sunday *St. Louis Post-Dispatch* illustrated the route as a bold black line, crested with a "66" shield near the Grand Canyon.[25] In Kingman, Arizona, the local Highway 66 Association produced an illustrated map in 1932 for the new Hoover Dam, urging travel for the "Scenic Grandeur & Beauty of the Trip over U.S. Highway No. 66" (Fig. 6.4).[26] The most elaborate tourist maps were produced by the Automobile Club of Southern California in Los Angeles, compiled by professional surveyors in the form of carefully detailed strip maps based on earlier editions of the National Old Trails Highway.[27] A sample of the Needles to Kingman section from 1937 reveals the tight turns and switchbacks of the Oatman Gold Road through the Black Mountains, with the U.S. 66 shield printed securely by the road (Fig. 6.5). Finally, with the Olympic Games at hand, the Highway 66 Association took out an advertisement in the *Saturday Evening Post* that described the appealing logic of the route:

> One of America's few great diagonal highways, U.S. 66 is the shortest, best and most scenic route from Chicago through St. Louis to Los Angeles. From the bustling middle west it is a high speed carry-all into the historic and romantic west, the land of limitless panorama and the home of ageless antiquity.[28]

When the Los Angeles Olympics finally opened in August 1932, the impact of the Depression was entirely evident. The optimism that had created the Highway 66 Association and Phillips 66 gasoline had turned the Main Street of America into a route of exodus from the drought and economic collapse of the Midwest and Southern Great Plains. Now, the U.S. 66 shield became a guidepost on the overland trek to California, the land of last resort from the dust storms of Oklahoma. Route 66 was fulfilling its promise as a road to opportunity, albeit in times harder than any of the highway's creators could ever have imagined.

7.1. *The Plow that Broke the Plains*, 1935. A Texas Panhandle scene showing a migrant car on Dust Bowl drought land, from the Farm Security Administration film directed by Pare Lorentz. Photographic still by Paul Strand. By permission of University of Nevada Press.

Chapter Seven
Dust Bowl Highway

THE DECADE OF DESPAIR that followed the stock market crash in 1929 transformed U.S. 66 into a road of flight. In western Oklahoma and the Texas panhandle, a drought of biblical magnitude forced an exodus of farm families onto Highway 66 toward the hopeful horizon of work in the fruited fields of California. The compassion of those concerned about the travail of the destitute migrants found voice in the work of a group of gifted San Francisco Bay artists and writers who portrayed the drought refugees as heroic figures in the documentary style of the New Deal period. Beginning in 1935, these artists created masterworks of lasting impact: Pare Lorentz in his film, *The Plow That Broke the Plains* (1936), John Steinbeck in his novel, *The Grapes of Wrath* (1939), and Dorothea Lange in her photo-essay, *An American Exodus* (1940). These works focused national attention on the plight of the drought-driven families and immortalized Highway 66 as an icon of the Dust Bowl exodus to California.

BLACK SUNDAY

The first sign of a massive drought in the High Plains was evident in April 1930, when a deadly heat wave was reported across a wide area of the Southwest. By August, national magazines were calling it the "Great Drought" as it burned out the cotton crop in Oklahoma, Arkansas, and Kansas.[1] In 1931 a second season of hardship seemed underway. The cowboy humorist Will Rogers raised nearly $90,000 in his home state of Oklahoma, and a similar amount in Texas, before spring rains brought welcome relief.[2] Still, a sense of dread spread across the High Plains, and discouraged families began trekking the western highways in search of opportunity. Speaking in October to a radio audience in Los Angeles on behalf of President Hoover's Unemployment Relief, Rogers offered his ironic insight on the auto mobility of the Depression period: "We'll hold the distinction of being the only nation in the history of the world that ever went to the poor house in an automobile."[3]

With the election of Franklin D. Roosevelt in 1932, Washington offered the nation hope with its New Deal recovery program. In the Heartland, however, the searing drought worsened, with topsoil blown about in great dust storms across Kansas and Nebraska and the first blackout occuring in November 1933. The following spring, still more destructive dust clouds smothered the fragile economy of the High Plains, forcing ever more families from their homesteads. Although climatologists explained the persistent drought as the result of the Bermuda high pressure cell moving west from the Atlantic Ocean to sit over the Gulf of Mexico, thus blocking tropical moisture from moving into the Mississippi Valley, a decade of overgrazing and overplanting following World War I compounded the crisis on the High Plains.[4]

In the spring of 1935, a dust storm of immense magnitude overwhelmed the region on Black Sunday, April 14, blanketing the whole panhandle of Texas and Oklahoma and on into Kansas, blotting out the sun, and choking those who tried to seal their doors and windows against the swirling soil.[5] On Monday, April 15, Robert Geiger, an Associated Press reporter from Denver, wired the *Washington Evening Post* from the Oklahoma panhandle town of Guymon the phrase that tagged the region with the lasting label, "DUST BOWL OF U.S." Geiger began his dispatch: "These little words, achingly familiar on a Western farmer's tongue, rule life in the dust bowl of the continent, 'If it rains.'"[6]

In Washington, "Dust Bowl" was immediately adopted to describe the wide region of agricultural crisis extending from the high grasslands of Wyoming south to New Mexico, with its heart in the panhandle region. In response to the national disaster, the Department of Agriculture established the Resettlement Administration (RA) on April 30, 1935, an agency that was to foster a number of creative projects that would document the Dust Bowl migration on Highway 66.[7]

Yet another tragedy struck the Dust Bowl on August 15, 1935, with news that Will Rogers had died in an Alaska air crash with his friend Wiley Post.[8] To honor the man whose humor had lifted the spirits of the nation in hard times, the Texas Centennial Commission in January 1936 designated the entire length of U.S. 66 from Chicago to California as the "Will Rogers Highway."[9] At the same time, New Deal relief projects improved much of the basic alignment of the road. The Los Angeles portion of U.S. 66 was extended from downtown west along Sunset and Santa Monica boulevards to the Pacific Ocean at the Santa Monica Pier in June 1935, finally linking the Great Lakes and the Pacific. In New Mexico, a significant shortcut was opened in 1937, directly to Albuquerque from Santa Rosa through Clines Corners, bypassing the route north to Santa Fe that had been established by the National Old Trails Highway in 1914.[10] Such Depression-era projects upgraded U.S. 66 to a fully paved route through the Southwest, just as Avery and the Highway 66 Association had envisioned.

PARE LORENTZ

By the fall of 1935, national attention had been focused on the dust storm disaster in the High Plains by movie theater newsreels. During September, Pathé News showed "Dust Bowl Victims" in auto caravans moving slowly west on the highways out of Oklahoma and Texas.[11] The historic significance of the Dust Bowl migration equally inspired New Deal agencies to document the farm crisis through movie film. In fact, Rexford Tugwell, at the Resettlement Administration of the Department of Agriculture, had authorized a feature film on the Great Plains drought in June 1935.[12] Tugwell hired Pare Lorentz to direct the government film project. Lorentz had published a photo-essay called *The Roosevelt Year 1933* and had written several lead articles on the farm crisis for *News-Week*.[13] From his wife's family farm in Iowa, Lorentz had seen firsthand the Midwest drought, and he envisioned a movie-essay documenting the erosion of American agriculture.[14] He hired avant-garde filmmakers Paul Strand, Leo Hurwitz, and Ralph Steiner, who had formed the NyKino group in New York, a group inspired by the documentary style of the Soviet Kino Pravda (Film Truth).[15]

With approval of government funding in September, Lorentz took his film crew out to the High Plains and began shooting scenes in eastern Montana, then moved his crew southward, to reach the heart of the Dust Bowl in the Texas panhandle, at Dalhart, in October 1935.[16] One Dalhart sequence captured the migrant exodus in a black sedan headed west through the stubble of corn fields outlined by its own shadow on the stark horizon (Fig. 7.1). Such imagery of auto mobility symbolized the populist spirit of the Dust Bowl migration as families moved on their own free will out onto the western highways.

In Dalhart, a disagreement between Paul Strand and Pare Lorentz erupted over the film script, and the NyKino crew quit the project and went back to New York. Lorentz continued to work on the film, traveling to Hollywood to finish the editing with the famed director King Vidor and Dorothea Lange, a young Resettlement Administration photographer, who set up shots of migrant caravans arriving in the camps of California's Central Valley.[17]

With the editing completed, Lorentz entitled the movie *The Plow That Broke the Plains*. Its script was read by opera baritone Thomas Chalmers; the musical score was by Nebraska-born Virgil Thompson. When the movie opened in New York in May 1936, the combination of stark drought scenes, deep-voiced narration, and swelling musical score created a powerful effect.[18] The movie follows an auto caravan moving west from Texas to California, introduced with Chalmers narrating the lines:

Once again they headed into the setting sun,
Once again they headed West,
Out of the Great Plains,
And hit the highways for the Pacific Coast,
The last border.[19]

The Plow That Broke the Plains proved that a government-sponsored film portraying a powerful drama on the dust storm crisis could succeed in commercial theaters. *Time* magazine called it the "first motion-picture document" in the United States, and critics lauded Lorentz for his evocation of traditional American themes and the depiction of authentic people in daily circumstances.[20] More importantly, the film focused popular attention directly on the migrant exodus, and it became a landmark for other artists seeking to record Dust Bowl families on the western highways to California.

DOROTHEA LANGE

Lorentz's contact with photographer Lange was to prove of significance for the documentary record of Highway 66 in the Dust Bowl period. Lange, based in San Francisco, had come west as a young portrait photographer from New York inspired by Clarence White at Columbia University. With the onset of the Depression, Lange had turned her lens outside the studio window to photograph the bread lines and labor strikes of San Francisco. Her carefully crafted photographs of homeless men were applauded by the avant garde photographers of Group f/64 in Berkeley, where University of California economics professor Paul Taylor saw her images in gallery shows. A photographer for his own research on Mexican migration, Taylor found Lange's portraits of working men particularly moving. Early in 1935, Taylor used his influence to arrange a position for Lange with the California State Emergency Relief Administration to document the migrant camps in the Central Valley.[21]

Working together, Taylor and Lange produced an illustrated article for the influential social arts magazine, *Survey Graphic*, in July 1935, entitled "Again the Covered Wagon."[22] Using her black-and-white photos to portray the tattered migrant cars arriving in California, Lange quoted migrants directly in their own Dust Bowl dialect, "God only knows why we left Texas 'cept my man is in a movin' mood."[23] The text by Taylor gave the highway migration a biblical dimension:

> Dust, drought, and protracted depression have exposed also the human resources of the plains to the bleak winds of adversity. After the drifting dust clouds drift the people; over the concrete ribbons of highway which lead out in every direction come the refugees. We are witnessing the process of social erosion and a consequent shifting of human sands in a movement which is increasing and may become great.[24]

It was through articles such as these that Lange and Taylor became known to Resettlement Administration officials in Washington. Lange's portrait work attracted the attention of Roy Stryker, who headed the new Information Division for documenting the people and places affected by the Depression and Dust Bowl crises. In September 1935, Stryker hired Lange as a documentary photographer and assigned her field work in the migrant camps of California from Los Angeles to Marysville. In March 1936, Lange was returning north on coastal highway U.S. 101 when she stopped to photograph a pea pickers' camp at Nipomo. Here she shot a pensive portrait of a migrant mother with her children, published in the *San Francisco News* and again in *Survey Graphic* in September 1936. The Nipomo mother quickly became an iconic madonna of the Great Depression and brought Lange national recognition as a portrait photographer for the Resettlement Administration, recognition which permitted her a certain artistic freedom with Stryker in Washington.[25]

SALLISAW

In late 1935, Lange and Taylor were married. For their 1936 summer field work, they were given a Southern tour. After a visit to the Resettlement Administration offices in Washington, they returned home through the Dust Bowl states to California, taking U.S. 64 from Arkansas into Oklahoma through Sequoyah County.[26] On August 4, 1936, they stopped in the small town of Sallisaw on the Arkansas border, where Lange photographed local farmers squatting in the shade of Main Street stores. In her notebook, she quoted the sidewalk conversation: "These fellers are goin' to stay right here till they dry up and die too."[27] A few days after Lange and Taylor stopped in Sallisaw, Oklahoma state officials declared a drought emergency for the eastern counties and asked the Resettlement Administration for additional aid from the heat wave.[28] That Dust Bowl conditions extended as far east as Sallisaw was an indication of the depths of the agricultural crisis in Oklahoma that summer, of which Lange's photographs are a poignant record.

Lange's Sallisaw photos found an immediate reception with the Resettlement Administration, now renamed the Farm Security Administration (FSA). Among those who saw her Oklahoma prints was the poet Archibald MacLeish, who selected several Lange images with those of other FSA photographers for a photo-essay book on the Great Depression. Inspired by Lorentz's film, MacLeish published the *Land of the Free* in April 1938, using Lange's Sallisaw Main Street to frame his "Sound Track" of the Dust Bowl drought (Fig. 7.2).[29]

ON U.S. 66

In March 1938, Paul Taylor testified before the Senate in Washington on the plight of the migrant workers in California. As revised for an April speech to the Commonwealth Club in San Francisco, Taylor described the dire situation of the migrants:

> We call them "Dust Bowlers." Ever since the droughts of 1934 and 1936 they have been streaming westward from the Great Plains. A count at the California border records the entry to our state by automobile alone of 221,000 refugees between the middle of 1935 and

the end of 1937. More than four-fifths of them came from the drought states. In vivid phrases they tell us the tragedy of nature: "Burned out, blowed out, eat out." What are we to do with them?[30]

7.2. Sallisaw, Oklahoma, August 1936. Farmers discussing drought in front of the Sallisaw State Bank, site of Pretty Boy Floyd's notorious 1934 robbery. Farm Security Administration photo by Dorothea Lange. Collection of the Library of Congress.

7.3. "On Highway 66 near Weatherford, Oklahoma," August 1938. A Missouri family hitchhiking to a lumber job in Arizona, one of the few period photos of Dust Bowl migrants taken directly on Route 66. Photograph by Dorothea Lange. By permission of Oakland Museum, Oakland, CA.

highways and families wandering along the side of the road.[31] Increasingly stark highway shots became a theme in her photography, seemingly symbolizing the hope lost on the high-speed roads to California.

After meeting with Roy Stryker at the Farm Security Administration in Washington, Lange and Taylor drove south into Georgia; then, having passed through Arkansas and the Missouri Ozarks, headed along U.S. 62 for Muskogee, Oklahoma.[32] With classes at Berkeley looming early in September, they drove quickly to Oklahoma City, where they picked up U.S. 66, following it west past El Reno over the Canadian River bridge near Weatherford on Friday, August 12.[33] Climbing the concrete grade, they spotted a migrant family hitchhiking west on the grassy shoulder. Turning their car aside, Lange stopped for a photograph. The wife was wearing sunglasses and a bold striped dress of chevron patterns, as if to catch the eye of passing traffic, as Claudette Colbert had done hitchhiking for Clark Gable in the 1934 movie film, *It Happened One Night*.[34] The wife was holding a baby boy in her arms, her husband held a suitcase and a box of their possessions, and their little girl in her Sunday dress walked between. They told Lange they were "hitch-hiking from Joplin, Missouri to a sawmill job in Arizona" (Fig. 7.3).[35]

Seeing an opportunity for a full photographic record, Lange apparently asked if she could take more pictures with her Rolleiflex. Moving closer, Lange set her lens looking back up U.S. 66 to the west, posing the family as if thumbing a ride, with cars and trucks on the horizon of the concrete highway. Although Lange did not number the negatives, the seven photos (now in the Oakland Museum)

For their summer tour of 1938, Lange and Taylor retraced much of their previous work through the rural South and Dust Bowl states. Beginning in June, they drove east into Arizona, New Mexico, and Texas, turning north into central Oklahoma, where Lange photographed vacant can be sequenced by the restless movements of the little girl. At first, she is sitting on the suitcase near her father; then she moves left to her mother, holding her hand toward the oncoming traffic. Reconstructed, the photos are a virtual stop-action film of westbound migrants hitchhiking in the summer of 1938.[36] These photos are apparently unique as the only dated documentary photos discovered of Highway 66 taken by a Farm Security Administration photographer during the Dust Bowl period (Fig. 7.4).[37]

The rare record raises questions, especially about the fate of the family. Field notes reveal that Lange and Taylor were interviewing farmers in the Oklahoma panhandle town of Boise City two days later, suggesting that they traveled north after the Weatherford stop, possibly discouraging them from offering a ride to the hitchhiking family.[38] Curiously, the Oklahoma U.S. 66 photo negatives were never filed with the FSA in Washington.[39] Perhaps Lange saw the Ozark "Family on the Road" as a private moment and kept the negatives as her own record for the Dust Bowl photo essay-book planned for the fall.[40]

In 1939, Lange and Taylor again went to Washington to meet with Stryker and seek publishers in New York for their projected Dust Bowl book. They sought advice from fellow Californian John Steinbeck, whose 1939 migrant novel, *The Grapes of Wrath*, had already received national attention. Without success, they returned west through Oklahoma in July, driving north to Oregon and Washington for fieldwork in August. Finally, in the fall of 1939, Paul Kellogg, the editor of *Survey Graphic*, found a New York publisher for Lange and Taylor. In January 1940, their photo-essay book, *An American Exodus, A Record of Human Erosion*, was released, just as the new motion picture *The Grapes of Wrath* debuted in New York and the European War began to distract Americans from the Dust Bowl and Depression.[41]

The U.S. 66 hitchhiking series played an important role in *An American Exodus*. Of the eight negatives, Lange chose her first instinctive shot taken east towards the Canadian River. It shows the Missouri family standing silent on the vacant highway, as lonely figures in the large landscape. The starkness captures the iconic reality of U.S. 66 as the main route of exodus from the Dust Bowl, with Lange's caption underscoring the highway's significance as a ribbon of reference in a lost region:

THROUGH OKLAHOMA STREAM EMIGRANTS FROM KANSAS, MISSOURI, ARKANSAS, WESTBOUND. "They're goin' every direction and they don't know where they're goin'."—FARMER On U.S. 66 near Weatherford, western Oklahoma.[42]

To emphasize the magnitude of the Dust Bowl exodus, Taylor included a bold outline map showing the "Origins of Migrants to California" from FSA data for 1935-37 (Fig. 7.5).[43] Three distinct streams are shown flowing into California: the first from the Pacific Northwest, a second from the Upper Midwest, and a third, the broadest line, from the Southwest following the axis of migration from Oklahoma, through the Texas panhandle, across New Mexico and Arizona to California. Taylor uses a highway metaphor to describe the Dust Bowl migration this way: "The winds

7.4. "On Highway 66, Oklahoma," August 1938. Alternate shots by Dorothea Lange of a Missouri family hitchhiking on U.S. 66, on concrete pavement looking west from the Canadian River bridge. By permission of Oakland Museum, Oakland, CA.

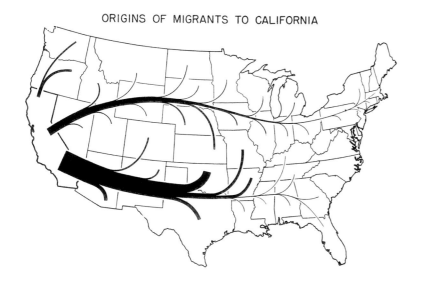

ORIGINS OF MIGRANTS TO CALIFORNIA

7.5. "Origins of Migrants to California," 1939. Paul Taylor's map showing the origin of migrants to California, 1935-37, for his and Lange's 1939 book, *An American Exodus*. The U.S. 66 stream is clearly dominant. Courtesy of California State Library.

churned the soil, leaving vast stretches of farms blown and hummocked like deserts or the margins of beaches. They loosened the hold of the settlers on the land, and like particles of dust drove them rolling down ribbons of highway."[44]

POSTSCRIPT

On September 1, 1939, German forces invaded Poland, thereby igniting war in Europe. With war in Asia also threatening, the plight of Dust Bowl migrants was overshadowed and the national economy turned to full-scale military production. Popular interest in *An American Exodus* seemed to fade with the war effort. Respected critics found fault with the photo-essay format. Pare Lorentz said it was "not well presented," and Paul Strand noted a "lack of a basic photographic structure."[45] By the fall of 1940, Paul Taylor found the book remaindered in Berkeley's second-hand stores. Nevertheless, the national press gave Dorothea Lange praise for her moving photos of the migrant experience.[46] Her images of Dust Bowl immigrants, whether actually on Route 66 or not, helped to cement in the popular imagination the idea of the road as the migrant highway to California. In this way, the route of the Bunion Derby, America's Main Street, was grafted with a profound sense of human pathos, even tragedy, essential ingredients of the book which was to apotheosize Route 66 as the "Mother Road," John Steinbeck's *The Grapes of Wrath*.

Part III
From Fact to Symbol:
The Route 66 of Our
Imagination

Chapter Eight
Mother Road

Jоhn Steinbeck immortalized Highway 66 as the "mother road" of the western frontier in his documentary novel, *The Grapes of Wrath*. Out of his experience in the Central Valley migrant camps, Steinbeck created a fictional family, the Joads of Sallisaw, Oklahoma, and traced their journey during the summer of 1938 west to California along Highway 66. The translation of Steinbeck's novel into German, Japanese, and Russian before the outbreak of World War II internationalized U.S. 66 as *the* iconic American highway, a process furthered by John Ford's filming of the novel in 1939. The work of Steinbeck and Ford made the numbers "66" a powerful symbol for people around the world who gathered together disparate threads of American life focused on the image of the open road.

SALINAS

The genesis of *The Grapes of Wrath* can be traced to the labor strikes in the farm fields of Central California during 1933.

These transformed John Steinbeck from a writer of historical novels into an eyewitness to the Dust Bowl migration just outside his door. Steinbeck had grown up in the small farm town of Salinas south of San Francisco. As an English major at Stanford University, Steinbeck first sought a job in New York as a cub reporter, but returned to California for family reasons and completed his first novel, *A Cup of Gold*, in 1929. This was a fictional account of the pirate, Henry Morgan. The following year Steinbeck married Carol Henning of San Jose and published a number of short stories, before moving to Los Angeles where he struggled on a writer's income during the early years of the Depression. When his mother became ill in 1933, Steinbeck returned to Salinas. This brought him into closer contact with the increasingly grave migrant labor situation.[1] Through family friends, he began exploring the Mexican neighborhoods and writing short stories about the sugar mill workers. Steinbeck was introduced to Lincoln Steffens, the famed populist muckraker who had retired in nearby Carmel, and, during the spring of 1933, he met radical labor organizers from the Central Valley.[2] Among these was a young migrant from central Oklahoma, Cecil McKiddy, who took Steinbeck out to the field camps to show him the brutal reality of labor in the fruit fields.[3] McKiddy proved to be a rich source of Oklahoma migrant culture that helped set the foundation for *The Grapes of Wrath*.

During 1934, Steinbeck turned his writing skills to labor conditions in Salinas. His first effort in the new social documentary style was *Tortilla Flat*. This satirical account of Mexican-American life in Monterey was published in 1935, along with several short stories. Among these was "The Breakfast," set in a roadside migrant camp, which used the frank naturalism that Steinbeck would later develop into his documentary style for *The Grapes of Wrath*.[4]

HARVEST GYPSIES

The field excursions with McKiddy inspired the writing of *In Dubious Battle*, a fictional account of Central Valley labor strikes. Published in 1936, the book brought Steinbeck national attention as a New Deal social writer.[5] During that summer, the progressive editor of the *San Francisco News*, George West, asked Steinbeck to write a daily series about the migrant labor situation in the Central Valley with Eric Thomsen of the Resettlement Administration.[6] In mid-August, Steinbeck bought an old bakery truck he called the "pie wagon" and drove south with Thomsen to the new RA camp at Arvin, near Bakersfield. Here they met the manager, Tom Collins, who had written detailed reports on the migrants that contained direct quotations of the Dust Bowl

dialects of Arkansas and Oklahoma. Collins had been born in Virginia and was a high school headmaster with the U.S. Navy in Guam before being assigned to the new Resettlement Administration camp in 1936.[7] Steinbeck and Collins found a common interest in documenting the lives of the Dust Bowl refugees, and they forged a friendship that would last through the writing of *The Grapes of Wrath*.

When Steinbeck returned from the Arvin camp, he wrote his first impression for *The Nation*, a magazine of liberal social views. His September 1936 article, "Dubious Battle in California," used a plain journalistic style to portray the hard reality of the Dust Bowl migrants:

> They bring wives and children, now and then a few chickens and their pitiful household goods, though in most cases these have been sold to buy gasoline for the trip. It is quite usual for a man, his wife, and from three to eight children to arrive in California with no possessions but the rattletrap car they travel in and the ragged clothes on their bodies.[8]

Steinbeck expanded his migrant field reports into a full series for the *San Francisco News* during October. The articles ran under the title "The Harvest Gypsies," with documentary photos from the Resettlement Administration files by Dorothea Lange:[9]

> The drought in the middle west has driven the agricultural populations of Oklahoma, Nebraska and parts of Kansas and Texas westward. Their lands are destroyed and they can never go back to them. Thousands of

them are crossing the borders in ancient rattling automobiles, destitute and hungry and homeless, ready to accept pay so that they may eat and feed their children.[10]

OKLAHOMA TRIP

During the fall of 1936, Steinbeck invited Collins to his new house in the Los Gatos hills near San Jose to discuss collaboration on a "big book" about the Dust Bowl refugees. It is likely that it was during this visit when Steinbeck began to understand that the migrant route from the Dust Bowl was U.S. 66. He and Collins took the pie wagon and explored the Central Valley's migrant camps, as Collins continued his reports to the San Francisco Resettlement office.[11] In November 1936, Dorothea Lange was sent down to Arvin to photograph Tom Collins, recording his fatherly pose in white shirt and knit tie.[12]

Steinbeck's collaboration with Collins on the migrant book continued through the spring of 1937, when he and Carol left Los Gatos for Europe. Arriving in New York by Panama Canal steamer in May, they departed for Ireland and then traveled east to Sweden and the Soviet Union. Returning to New York in August, the Steinbecks were invited to New Hope, Pennsylvania, the summer home of George Kaufman, playwright for the Broadway production of Steinbeck's book, *Of Mice and Men* (Fig. 8.1).[13] From there the Steinbecks went to Washington, D.C., returning to California along U.S. 66 through the Oklahoma Dust Bowl.

This trip has become a legend wrapped in its own myth, largely due to the absence of a road map or diary. Various accounts have been related, some with the Steinbecks

acquiring a showroom car in New York and driving west; others getting them to Detroit by train, then westward in a new car; a third taking them to Chicago to visit a cousin, then west on U.S. 66 to Oklahoma. Different varieties of cars are alleged, most notably "a red Chevrolet" bought with the royalties from *Of Mice and Men*. What seems certain is the route: U.S. 66 into Oklahoma during September 1937, through New Mexico and Arizona, and on to Los Gatos by October.[14] While the details remain hazy, there is a sense that Steinbeck travelled U.S. 66 into the heart of the

8.1. John and Carol Steinbeck with George S. Kaufman, in August or September 1937, New Hope, PA. Photo by Beatrice Kaufman, showing John Steinbeck (left) and Carol Steinbeck (center) with Kaufman (right) at the Kaufmans's farm, just before the Steinbecks' Highway 66 road trip to California. By permission of Center for Steinbeck Studies, San Jose State University.

migrant Oklahoma homeland, and that the actual trip was quickly made in a bright new car.

Upon his return, Steinbeck immediately contacted Collins for another field trip down the Central Valley to retrace the migrant route. Starting out in October, Steinbeck and Collins took the pie wagon from the Resettlement camp at Arvin down to Barstow, following U.S. 66 back to the Colorado River bridge at Needles, then south to the emigrant inspection station at Blyth, returning north through Brawley by November. In later years, this excursion was called the "Oklahoma" trip, although Steinbeck never left California and apparently confused it with his auto return trip from New York.[15]

THE OKLAHOMANS

It was at this time, after he had traveled U.S. 66, that Steinbeck began writing the Dust Bowl manuscript he called "The Oklahomans." Little is known of this work except the title, since Steinbeck destroyed the draft after a year's effort. An alternate version was also reported as "L'Affaire Lettuceberg," apparently using the same Oklahoma migrant theme, of which only the title and general subject were revealed to reporters. It was also during this period, in the fall of 1937 or early 1938, that Steinbeck helped Collins collect his Arvin camp reports into a narrative book on the migrant experience, again a project known only from brief references.[16] All of this activity points to an increasing interest by Steinbeck in Oklahoma and the Dust Bowl culture as the migrant crisis mounted in California.

During the winter of 1938, devastating floods swept through the migrant camps of the Central Valley. Because of Steinbeck's experience with the migrants, *Life* magazine asked him to write an account.[17] With *Life* photographer Horace Bristol, Steinbeck drove to Visalia in late February, where he was overwhelmed by the absolute misery of the migrants whose camps were swamped by mud and rain.[18] Recalling the floods in later years, Steinbeck said: "I saw people starve to death. That's not just a resounding phrase. They starved to death. They dropped dead."[19]

Horace Bristol photographed the flooded camps as Steinbeck interviewed the stranded families. Again, as with Collins and his narrative reports, there was some discussion with Bristol about using his photographs for an illustrated book on the situation; but, by the time they returned to San Francisco, Steinbeck had withdrawn his support and the project was postponed, along with the *Life* story and the Bristol photographs.[20] Nevertheless, the Visalia flood proved to be a turning point for Steinbeck, who now refocused his attention on the "big book" about the Dust Bowl migration.

SALLISAW

Steinbeck called film director Pare Lorentz and the two met to discuss a documentary style of writing, intercutting dialogue with scenic passages, as one would edit a movie. With this cinematic approach in mind, alternating background and character chapters, Steinbeck prepared to begin the "big book" by recording his plot progress in a journal diary that would document the saga of his Dust Bowl migrant family.[21]

On June 1, 1938, Steinbeck began writing the Dust Bowl novel in a large ledger book, with his wife Carol typing up the completed manuscript pages.[22] The novel was set in central Oklahoma near Shawnee, introducing a hitchhiker named Tom Joad returning home after his release from the state prison at McAlester. By mid-June, Steinbeck had developed detailed characters for his fictional family. The dynamic matriarch, Ma Joad, defended her son, Tom, to neighbors with the analogy of Oklahoma outlaw Pretty Boy Floyd: "I knowed Purty Boy Floyd. I knowed his ma. They was good folks."[23] Floyd had been killed by federal agents in October 1934, and his body brought back to his hometown of Sallisaw, in eastern Oklahoma, amid widespread publicity.[24] On June 20, Steinbeck wrote in his journal that he was changing the Joads' locale from "Shawnee to Sallisaw," likely because it was Floyd's hometown. With this change, Steinbeck set the Joads' homestead "Right near Sallisaw" in the Ozark Hills of eastern Oklahoma.[25] Steinbeck had doubtless seen MacLeish's *Land of the Free*, which included Lange's photo of Sallisaw's Main Street.[26] Perhaps Steinbeck changed Shawnee to Sallisaw for the familiar salt-sounding name of his home town of Salinas.[27] By whatever means Steinbeck selected Sallisaw, the Joad family exodus began from this small Oklahoma town on the Arkansas border.

HIGHWAY 66

By the end of June 1938, Steinbeck had completed eleven chapters of his Dust Bowl book. Exhausted by a month of writing, Steinbeck allowed himself the respite of the July 4th weekend before beginning the second section, which would narrate the journey from Sallisaw to California.[28] Writing in his diary on July 5th, Steinbeck outlined what he hoped to achieve in his prose: "Beginning the second book today and it must have the rolling sound of wheels and the clutter of cars and the panting across the country."[29]

To plot the progress of the Joad family, Steinbeck apparently worked from a road map to locate place names and route numbers, perhaps the very map he used the previous summer on his Oklahoma trip.[30] He began by presenting the migrant road as a persona with its own graphic identity: "Highway 66." At first Steinbeck started to write out the route name in full script, "S[ixty-six]," but quickly revised the form by striking the "S" and overwriting with the paired numbers, "66", which became powerful icons on the page.[31] The original manuscript, now at the University of Virginia, shows how this looked to Steinbeck (Fig. 8.2):

Highway 66 is the main migrant road. S/66, the long concrete path across the country, waving gently up and down on the map, from the Mississippi to Bakersfield— over the red lands and the gray lands, twisting up into the mountains, crossing the divide and down into the bright and terrible desert and across the desert to the mountains again and into the rich California valleys.[32]

With his second sentence, Steinbeck created the immortal identity of Highway 66 as the matriarchal pathway that draws the migrants westward out of the Dust Bowl region. With confidence he wrote the double sixes as bold numbers paired on the ledger page:

66 is the path of people in flight, refugees from dust and from shrinking ownership, from the desert's slow northward invasion, from the twisting winds that howl up out of Texas, from the floods that bring no richness to the land and steal what little richness there is. From

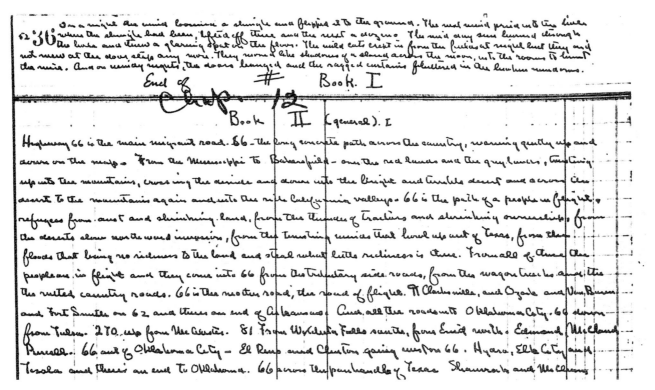

8.2. John Steinbeck's *The Grapes of Wrath* manuscript, July 1938. Ledger book manuscript of Book II (Chapter Twelve), with the original "S[sixty-six]" changed to "66," and the handwritten "66 is the mother road, the road of flight." By permission of John Steinbeck Collection, Clifton Waller Barrett Library, Special Collections, University of Virginia.

all of these the people are in flight, and they come into 66 from the tributary side roads, from the wagon tracks and the rutted roads. 66 is the mother road, the road of flight.[33]

To follow the Joads from Sallisaw, Steinbeck traced the highway routes from U.S. 64 at Fort Smith, Arkansas, to U.S.

66 at Oklahoma City, obviously guided by place names and numbers from a road map.[34] He continued to follow U.S. 66 across Texas and New Mexico, to Albuquerque and into the mountains at the Arizona border, then across the Colorado River into California. With a vivid sense of reality derived from his own field trips, Steinbeck describes the Mojave Desert crossing: "Up from Needles and over a

burned range, and there's the terrible desert. And 66 goes on over the terrible desert, where the distance shimmers and the black center mountains hang unbearably in the distance."[35]

Finally, Steinbeck brings the Joads across the desert to Barstow and then turns the family north to Bakersfield and the field camps of the Central Valley. Though in actuality the highway is signed U.S. 466 at Barstow, Steinbeck retains U.S. 66 in the narrative when Tom Joad discusses going alone with his road map in hand: "Ma said worriedly, 'How you gonna find us?' 'We'll be on the same road,' said Tom. '66 right on through. Come to a place name' Bakersfiel'. Seen it on the map I got.'"[36]

THE GRAPES OF WRATH

It would take another month of writing into August 1938 before Steinbeck had taken the Joad family along Highway 66 to the government resettlement camp at "Weedpatch," the Arvin Camp of Collins.[37] Here the family encounters the first signs of disdain for their Oklahoma origins, as Steinbeck adopts the crude California slang for the Dust Bowl migrants, "Okie," likely heard on his travels through the Central Valley.[38] By mid-summer, however, events beyond the cloistered writing in Los Gatos began to affect the pace of the book. The failure of his publisher, Covici-Friede in July, forced Steinbeck to seek a new firm: Viking Press in New York on August 9, 1938, transferring his Dust Bowl book to the East Coast and his new editor, Elizabeth Otis. At the same time, events in Europe brought a foreboding of unsettled times, as Steinbeck discussed world events and current film projects with Pare Lorentz and Charlie Chaplin in mid-

August. By early September, the sense of the approaching completion of the book and the ominous war clouds in Europe prompted Carol Steinbeck to name the book *The Grapes of Wrath*, a phrase taken from the Civil War song, "Battle Hymn of the Republic," a title Steinbeck immediately adopted for the novel.[39]

With the writing almost finished, Steinbeck maintained an intense pace through September and into October, finally closing his ledger book on October 26. An editorial debate over the final passage threatened to upset publication, while the rest of the manuscript was left intact as Steinbeck had written it, including the signet numbers "66" for the migrant road printed on the page as he had written them.[40] The black "66", a literal road marker, marched through the original text as the primary sign of the exodus, achieving an iconography of graphic power as Steinbeck intended (Fig. 8.3).

For a book cover, Viking proposed a realistic illustration by Elmer Hader, a California artist living in the New York area. Hader had composed the cover for Steinbeck's *The Long Valley*, published in September 1938, and he knew the regional setting of the Salinas area from his student training in San Francisco. During November and December, Hader corresponded with Milton Glick at Viking about the cover, suggesting a caravan of migrant trucks moving down a highway into a mountain valley. While Hader had neither seen Steinbeck's final manuscript nor knew specifically of the Joads or Highway 66, the final watercolor painting captures Steinbeck's sense of documentary Dust Bowl realism.[41] In the foreground, a migrant family looks out over a convoy of trucks and overloaded cars twisting down a long highway

8.3. John Steinbeck's *The Grapes of Wrath*, 1939. Page from the first edition, Chapter Twelve, showing the graphic power of the "66" numerals on the printed page, especially the opening line in paragraph two. By permission of Viking Press Penguin Group.

Chapter Twelve

HIGHWAY 66 is the main migrant road. 66—the long concrete path across the country, waving gently up and down on the map, from the Mississippi to Bakersfield—over the red lands and the gray lands, twisting up into the mountains, crossing the Divide and down into the bright and terrible desert, and across the desert to the mountains again, and into the rich California valleys.

66 is the path of a people in flight, refugees from dust and shrinking land, from the thunder of tractors and shrinking ownership, from the desert's slow northward invasion, from the twisting winds that howl up out of Texas, from the floods that bring no richness to the land and steal what little richness is there. From all of these the people are in flight, and they come into 66 from the tributary side roads, from the wagon tracks and the rutted country roads. 66 is the mother road, the road of flight.

Clarksville and Ozark and Van Buren and Fort Smith on 64, and there's an end of Arkansas. And all the roads into Oklahoma City, 66 down from Tulsa, 270 up from McAlester. 81 from Wichita Falls south, from Enid north. Edmond, McLoud, Purcell. 66 out of Oklahoma City; El Reno and Clinton, going west on 66. Hydro, Elk City, and Texola; and there's an end to Oklahoma. 66 across the Panhandle of Texas. Shamrock and McLean, Conway and Amarillo, the yellow. Wildorado and Vega and Boise, and there's an end of Texas. Tucumcari and Santa Rosa and into the New Mex-

16ᴄ

toward a mountain pass. One can imagine it is U.S. 66 along a stretch in New Mexico or Arizona, Hader's vision of the exodus road (Fig. 8.4).

DIE ROUTE 66

In the spring of 1939, Viking prepared to release *The Grapes of Wrath*. An advanced proof was sent to Los Gatos in March for approval, with release scheduled for April 14.[42] Viking had enough confidence to print nearly 200,000 copies, and it was immediately rewarded with brisk sales and lavish reviews.[43] The *New York Times* called the book "A Magnificent Novel of America" and gave particular attention to the role of "Route 66, the wanderer's trail" from Oklahoma to California.[44] This East Coast description of the highway was repeated by the *Saturday Review of Literature*, which brought U.S. 66 to Eastern readers unfamiliar with the Western road:

> It is the particular story of one family, the Joads from a farm near Sallisaw. You have seen them going west through Texas and New Mexico on Route 66, or you have seen them in Resettlement Administration photographs: three generations in a second-hand truck piled high with everything they own.[45]

The Grapes of Wrath achieved success well beyond the expectations of Steinbeck and Viking. Within two weeks of its release, a bid for the film rights was offered by Twentieth

8.4. Elmer Hader's jacket design for *The Grapes of Wrath*, 1939. The original watercolor showed an imaginary landscape of migrant trucks on a Dust Bowl highway in a Southwest setting. By permission of Viking Press Penguin Group. Author's collection.

Century-Fox.[46] The national publicity also brought Steinbeck threatening letters from those who read the novel as socialist propaganda or immoral literature. In California, the Kern County Farmers Association organized a protest, while school boards in Kansas City and Buffalo banned the book. An outright book burning was reported in East St. Louis in November 1939.[47] Despite such outrage, sales reached more than 450,000 copies by May 1940, when Steinbeck won the Pulitzer Prize in Literature for the book.[48]

Beyond the United States, interest in Steinbeck and the Dust Bowl was matched with foreign editions of *The Grapes of Wrath*, even as World War II engulfed Europe and Asia. These translations inscribed the exodus route of Highway 66 into the imagination of a wartime world that sought escape through the Joad family and its trek from the devastations of the Dust Bowl. The mobility of destitute Americans traveling national highways across a continent in their own cars fascinated Europeans and Asians confined within their borders and restricted by passports and political oppression.

English editions of Steinbeck were available in Canada and Great Britain by the end of 1939, with a printing in British Palestine by 1940.[49] Translations of *The Grapes of Wrath* found receptive audiences in Scandinavian- and German-speaking countries, a popularity derived from Steinbeck's own German heritage and from a fascination with America.[50] A Danish translation, *Vredens Druer* (*Angry Grapes*), was available in Copenhagen in 1939, with a Swedish edition of *Vredens Druvor* in Stockholm by 1940, and a second printing in occupied Norway the same year.[51]

8.5. *Fruchte des Zornes*, jacket cover, 1943. The Berlin edition, in wartime Germany, of *The Grapes of Wrath* showing a migrant truck. By permission of Harvard College Library.

German translations of *Die Fruchte Des Zornes* (*The Fruits of the Wrath*) were printed in Switzerland by Humanitas Verlag of Zurich in 1940, with a German edition in Stuttgart the same year.[52] Both translations were made by Klaus Lambrecht in a careful, literal style that conveyed Steinbeck's simple landscape descriptions, rooted in common Anglo-Saxon words, intact.[53] The power of Steinbeck's numerical iconography in the opening paragraph of Chapter Twelve is maintained as well: "Die Route 66 ist die Hauptwanderstrasse. Route 66, der lang Betonweg durch das Land . . . Sie ist die Mutterstrasse, die Strasse der Flucht" (The Route 66 is the Headtravelroad. Route 66, the long Concreteway through the land . . . She is the Motherroad, the Road of Flight).[54]

A second translation of remarkable skill was made in wartime Berlin during 1943 by Karen von Schab, again as *Fruchte des Zornes*.[55] The inked artwork on the cover shows an army truck overloaded with people on a lonely highway, evoking an exodus from a war-torn land (Fig. 8.5). Moreover, a full-color map of the Joad family's route from Oklahoma to California is shown on the endpapers (Fig. 8.6). Such cartographic artwork delivered Highway 66 to readers confined by war and disorientation. Similar realism is maintained in the text which retains the double sixes: "Uberlandstrasse 66 ist de gross Treckweg. Die 66, ein langer Pfad aus Beton in der Landschaft . . . Die 66 ist die Strasse inher gemeinsamen Flucht" (Overland 66 is the great Trekway. The 66, along Path of Concrete is the Landscape . . . The 66 is the Road of their common Flight).[56]

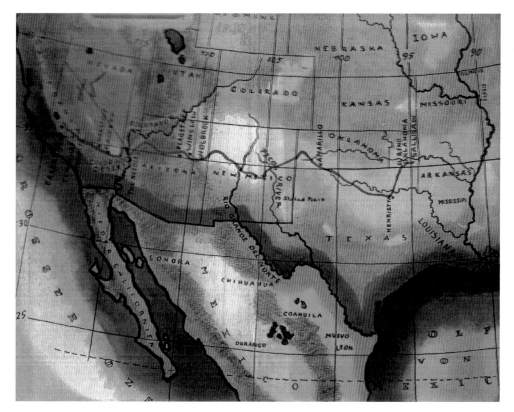

8.6. *Fruchte des Zornes*, endmap, 1943. The Berlin edition of *The Grapes of Wrath,* showing the route of the Joad family from Oklahoma to California on "Die 66." By permission of Rockefeller Library, Brown University.

IKARI NO BUDO

A similar transformation of the migrant highway took place in Asia, then on the brink of war. The earliest effort was made in Japan by Itaru Nii with his edition of *Ikari No Budo* (*Rage of Grapes*), published in Tokyo by Shigen Sha in 1939. While only the first seventeen chapters were translated, the citation of Highway 66 as "Rokujuu Roku-ban douro wa" (Sixty-six Number road) presented the highway as an extraordinary concept to insular Japanese, a free road that spanned half a continent from a distant place called Oklahoma to the familiar state of California where many Japanese had themselves settled to work in the fields of the Central Valley. The complete edition of *The Grapes of Wrath* was available in 1940 before the declaration of war severed relations between Japan and the United States. A Chinese translation was available in Shanghai by 1941, with a final edition published in Hong Kong within weeks of the invasion.[57]

8.7. *Grozdya Gnyeva*, 1940. The Russian edition of *The Grapes of Wrath* published by the Soviet State printer just before the German invasion, showing an imaginary Highway "66" illustrating the first page of Chapter Twelve. By permission of Stanford University Library, Special Collections.

In the Soviet Union, where Steinbeck had been appreciated for his visit in 1937, a Russian translation of *Grozdya Gnyeva* (*Bunches of Anger*) was published by the state printer in Moscow during 1940 before the German invasion cut cultural links to Europe (Fig. 8.7).[58] By December 1941, when the U.S. declared war on the Axis nations, the power of Steinbeck's words and the numerical icon of Highway 66 as the "mutterstrasse" had been dispersed throughout the world where it would act as a reservoir of interest that would be released during the American occupation of the post-war period. In the process, the route number had been transformed from a metal highway marker into a symbol of the open road, into an apotheosis of the open road, a transformation laid out before us on the opening page of Chapter Twelve in the Russian edition. Nine 66s march down the page, usually preceding or following a dash or a space between sentences, so that the numbers are set off, amplifying their impact on the page. Above the text is an evocative drawing of an open road dwindling toward a horizon closed by distant mountains. It is all but a graphic equation: *66 = open road*, where *open road = America*. With *The Grapes of Wrath*, the process that had begun with the use of the paired sixes by Phillips was ratcheted into high gear.

Chapter Nine
Filming Highway 66

STEINBECK'S SUCCESS was immediately repeated by Hollywood, whose film adaptation replayed the Joad family saga on neighborhood movie screens. *The Grapes of Wrath* proved as powerful on screen as on the written page, inspiring folk songs and ballads among the migrants who watched the movie as their own exodus to California. The black-and-white documentary style gave newsreel authenticity to the Steinbeck story. In fact, much of the background footage relating to the Joad family trek on U.S. 66 had been shot on U.S. 66 in Oklahoma, Texas, and Arizona, and in the migrant camps of California. The film captured the highway's roadside reality and provided a cinematic record of the road before World War II redirected American attention overseas.

DARRYL ZANUCK

Within a week of Viking's publication of *The Grapes of Wrath*, Hollywood movie producers expressed interest in filming it. The most persistent was Darryl Zanuck of Twentieth Cen-

tury-Fox who outbid two other studios and signed Steinbeck for the extraordinary sum of $75,000 on April 20, 1939. Steinbeck had been approached by film studios as early as 1936 for *Tortilla Flat* and *In Dubious Battle*. During the spring of 1938, Steinbeck had discussed the problem of rewriting his narratives into working scripts with Lorentz, and had visited Hollywood for the filming of his novella, *Of Mice and Men*. The Zanuck offer was given serious consideration by Steinbeck's agent, Annie Laurie Williams, although Steinbeck was anxious about his documentary vision of the Dust Bowl being debased by studio writers.[1]

Zanuck was confident of his ability to film *The Grapes of Wrath* as a profitable commercial venture, and he found echoes of his own Nebraska background in Steinbeck's story. Beginning in 1935, Zanuck had expanded Twentieth Century-Fox with Western historical dramas presented in a realist documentary style, assembling an experienced company of actors and directors.[2] During 1938 and 1939, Twentieth Century-Fox had several Western films under production, including two with the Nebraska-born actor Henry Fonda, directed by John Ford: *The Young Mr. Lincoln* and *Drums Along the Mohawk*. When Zanuck acquired the rights to *The Grapes of Wrath*, the theme of a western migration of a Dust Bowl family fit an established frontier formula, and Zanuck naturally selected Henry Fonda to play Tom Joad and John Ford to direct him.[3]

NUNNALLY JOHNSON

In May 1939, Zanuck assigned his best script writer, Nunnally Johnson, to condense the 600 pages of the Steinbeck novel to a two-hour film. Johnson had well-grounded experience with such literary projects, having worked with William Faulkner on the script for *Paths of Glory* and the Western melodrama *Jessie James* for director Henry King. Johnson started the Steinbeck script with some hesitation, contacting Lorentz for his insights into Steinbeck and to talk about the problem of what to do with the scenic background chapters such as those describing U.S. 66. Lorentz encouraged Johnson to talk directly with Steinbeck. The two met in Los Angeles during June, and, with Steinbeck's approval for the abridgments, the first draft for *The Grapes of Wrath* was submitted on July 19. Zanuck had objections, especially to the final scene in which Rose of Sharon gives her milk to a starving man, even as she was going to be played by Johnson's wife, Doris Bowden.[4]

More pressing than the script was the shooting schedule. During July, Ford was in Monument Valley, Arizona, editing *Stagecoach* for United Artists. Ford requested a personal break until Labor Day before starting *The Grapes of Wrath*.[5]

News of the German invasion of Poland, however, made immediate production of the Steinbeck script imperative, since Zanuck realized that the Dust Bowl drama would soon be overshadowed by war news from Europe. Johnson had a revised script by August 5 in which he proposed covering the scenic chapters in montages edited in Lorentz's documentary manner.[6] For the narrative sections of the Joad family trek, Johnson proposed U.S. 66 shields to mark the exodus road as Steinbeck had intended: "The scene dissolves to a MONTAGE: Almost filling the screen is the shield marker of the U.S. Highway 66. Superimposed on it is a montage of jalopies, steaming and rattling and piled with goods and people."[7]

For the Dust Bowl setting, Zanuck and Ford researched the public file of Farm Security Administration photographs by Dorothea Lange and *Life* magazine images by Horace Bristol. The success of the Steinbeck book had prompted *Life* to publish Bristol's Visalia flood photos in June 1939, with captions in the form of quotations from *The Grapes of Wrath*. Several Twentieth Century-Fox contract players were cast from the faces of the migrant photos by Bristol and Lange, including Jane Darwell as Ma Joad and John Carradine as Casy.[8] In addition, Steinbeck suggested to Johnson that Tom Collins be hired as a set consultant for the migrant camp scenes, a position Collins gladly accepted.[9] To complete his crew, Ford selected Greg Toland as his cameraman. Now known for his classic noir work with Orson Wells in *Citizen Kane* (1940), Toland had recently completed the stunning ambient photography for *Wuthering Heights* and was considered an asset for the dark drama of the Steinbeck film.[10]

Filming began in September and continued through the fall. Much of it was done by Ford and Toland on Fox sound stages, but Zanuck insisted on authentic location scenes for the migrant camps and the Joad family journey on U.S. 66. With controversy over the Steinbeck book still alive, Zanuck disguised location shooting under the working title, "Highway 66," and put his second unit director, Otto Brower, in charge of the project.[11] Michigan-born Brower had come to Hollywood in 1914 in the early silent era, becoming a specialist at Fox Studios in background footage on such Zanuck films as *Heidi* and *Safari*.[12] His location work for *Jesse James* in 1938 had made him familiar with the Ozarks, to which he now returned to scout for locations for the background scenes of the Joad family homestead in eastern Oklahoma.

The "Highway 66" unit retraced the narrative sequence of the novel beginning in Sallisaw, where it shot farm scenes using local extras.[13] For each background, a sequence of moving shots was made at various speeds on silent film, as were static shots of U.S. 66 shield markers and city limit signs, including those of Sallisaw and Oklahoma City. The Brower unit followed the Joad family from Sallisaw on U.S. 64 west to Oklahoma City and U.S. 66 at the Canadian River bridge, where Lange had taken her hitchhiking family photos. The work continued into Texas at Amarillo and Vega, and then into New Mexico at Glenrio and the railroad bridge at Santa Rosa. From Albuquerque the "Highway 66" crew continued west to Grants and the inspection station at the Arizona state line, with additional shots of the Painted Desert. A detour was made from Flagstaff to the Navajo Reservation near Monument Valley where *Stagecoach* had

been made the previous year. A special effort was taken to film the difficult Goldroad Grade through the Sitgreaves Pass between Kingman and Oatman, as well as on the Colorado River bridge and night footage of the Joshua trees in the Mojave Desert.[14] Altogether the Brower location unit filmed more than 2,000 feet of "Highway 66" footage, about three-and-a-half hour's worth.[15]

To replicate the Joad family experience, Brower first attempted to film the journey along U.S. 66 in documentary fashion, using real migrant trucks and cars. This proved an awkward experience, although a similar authentic filming of migrant camps was successfully made in the San Fernando Valley near Los Angeles under the advice of Tom Collins.[16] Instead, Brower went to used car lots and purchased twenty-four jalopies for his Okie caravan down Highway 66 with studio extras as Dust Bowl migrants.[17] The only time the lead actors came out to the highway was for the Colorado River bridge swimming scene when the Joads enter California. As Fonda recalled: "The second unit went out and shot all the footage between Oklahoma and California. The river outside Needles, California, where we take our bath was the farthest away we went. The rest of the picture was shot on real 'Okie' camps in the vicinity of Los Angeles."[18]

JOAD FAMILY TREK

By October, second unit work had been completed and edited as montages.[19] With Ford on vacation during December, Zanuck supervised much of the final cut using Robert Simpson as his editor. Simpson edited Brower's three hours of 66 footage down to three minutes. This included scenes in Sallisaw and Oklahoma City and U.S. 66 shield signs in

Oklahoma, Texas, New Mexico, Arizona, and over the Colorado River bridge into California (Fig. 9.1). Some of the staged shots at the Arizona border station and the Navajo Reservation were kept as brief scenes, but the crossing of the Canadian River bridge in Oklahoma and the switchback drive up the Goldroad Grade to Oatman were cut entirely from the release print.[20]

Despite its brevity, the montage of U.S. 66 shield signs lent authenticity to the "mother road" migration. Even though rented jalopies had been staged for Brower's cameras, his footage recorded authentic cars on the real highway, preserving motion pictures of the Dust Bowl migration as it took place.[21] When the final cut was shown to Steinbeck in mid-December 1939, he wrote his agent:

Zanuck has more than kept his word. He has a hard, straight picture in which the actors are submerged so completely, that it looks and feels like a documentary film and certainly has the truthful ring. No punches were pulled, in fact with the descriptive matter removed, it is a harsher thing than the book.[22]

The Grapes of Wrath opened at the Rivoli Theater in New York on January 24, 1940, to rave reviews, eventually winning two Academy Awards for John Ford as director and Jane Darwell as Ma Joad.[23] The film had achieved the power that Zanuck had felt in the original. The Joad family saga found a deep well of sympathy in the American public, which came to see the picture as a modern Western, one in which the wagon train had been turned into the auto caravan and the Oregon Trail into U.S. 66.[24] Lorentz, however,

confusing the brightly shot Brower location footage with the dark, atmospheric studio work of Toland, found fault with the film's scenic tone, arguing that, "But for all the beauty of his night effects and the difficult trick shots he made, Toland did not get the size of the Southwest, nor the feeling of the sky and the land in his camera, and John Ford didn't make him do it,"[25] but most of America got it without any trouble.

To promote the film, Twentieth Century-Fox distributed a press packet of lobby cards that featured a "Blow Up Map of the Joad Family Trek" showing their route from Sallisaw to California with movie stills mounted at appropriate locations (Fig. 9.2). These highlighted the pathway of Highway 66 as the road from the Dust Bowl and gave cartographic credence to the movie as a documentary film of the migration.[26] The lobby maps promoted *The Grapes of Wrath* as a scenic highway film across the Southwest, even though U.S. 66 itself had only brief seconds of screen time.

WOODY GUTHRIE

When the Steinbeck movie opened, its impact was most immediate on the radical political community which saw in *The Grapes of Wrath* a story of American socialism. Among these was Woody Guthrie, a song balladeer from Oklahoma, who had hitchhiked out to California from Pampa, Texas, in 1936.[27] His Los Angeles radio show on KFVD promoted Western cowboy songs and ballads that Guthrie had written about the Dust Bowl migration, including "So Long It's Been Good To Know You," about the Black Sunday dust storm of 1935, and "Do Re Me," about the California inspection stations on U.S. 66.[28] After seeing the Joad family saga on screen, Guthrie wrote a review for *People's World*

9.1. *The Grapes of Wrath*. U.S. 66 location shots by the second unit director, Otto Brower, for Twentieth Century-Fox's "Highway 66," taken in September 1939 and showing a highway sign and an Arizona inspection station. By permission of Twentieth Century-Fox Film Corporation.

which identified his own story with those of the characters in the film:[29]

> Seen the pitcher last night "Grapes of Wrath," best cussed pitcher I ever seen. "The Grapes of Wrath" you know is about us a pullin' out of Oklahoma and Arkansas, and down south and out, and driftin' around over the state of California, busted, disgusted, down and out, and lookin' for work.[30]

Seeing *The Grapes of Wrath* was a transforming experience for Guthrie that inspired a wealth of songwriting which defined his later career. When a Steinbeck Committee benefit concert for agricultural workers was held in New York on March 3, 1940, Guthrie was featured as "a real Dust Bowl refugee." His authentic performance caught the ear of RCA Victor record producers who asked him to their New Jersey studios to make *Dust Bowl Ballads* in May 1940. Among the many songs, Guthrie had composed a long ballad inspired by the Steinbeck movie about "Tom Joad" that became the album's signature.[31]

As RCA Victor had heard commercial profit in the Dust Bowl voice of Guthrie, folk song collector Alan Lomax invited the singer to the Library of Congress in Washington in March 1940, to record his repertoire of Western songs

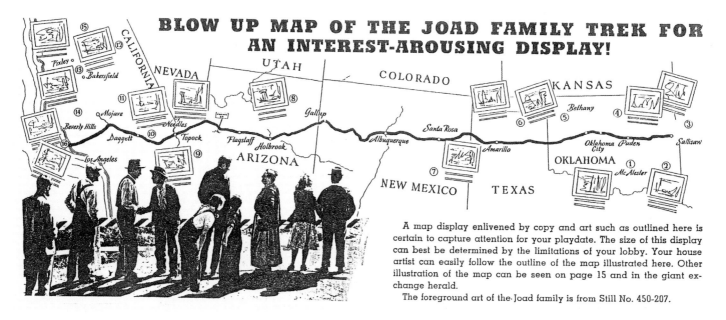

9.2. *The Grapes of Wrath,* lobby card, 1940. Twentieth Century-Fox's "Blow Up Map of the Joad Family Trek," showing the Highway 66 migration route from Sallisaw to Bakersfield as described in Steinbeck's novel. Courtesy of Center for Steinbeck Studies, San Jose State University.

and topical ballads. For a full week Guthrie and Lomax, with Lomax's wife Elizabeth Littleton, sat in the studio and recorded a wealth of material. On the last day of the session, March 27, Littleton asked Guthrie about the Dust Bowl refugees in California and his days in Oklahoma.[32] Guthrie responded with a song about "that sixty-six highway," the Will Rogers Road, rhyming the verses of the moment as he sang into the microphone:

There's a highway that goes from the coast to the coast
From New York town down to Los Angelese,

It's named Will Rogers that traveled that road,
From New York town down to Los Angelese.

That 66 Highway, the Will Rogers road,
it's lined with jalopies as far's you can see,
With a mighty hot motor and a heavy old load,
   —From Oklahoma to Los Angelese.[33]

During the summer of 1940, Guthrie traveled back to his childhood home of Okemah, Oklahoma, with folk singer Pete Seeger, a Harvard student from New York who had dropped out to work in union organizing. Returning to New York, Guthrie and Seeger composed the "66 Highway Blues" as a reprise to the "Will Rogers Highway" ballad.[34] Both Highway 66 songs remained isolated within the Guthrie song book, relatively unknown and commercially unrealized until well after World War II.[35] These Guthrie songs are among many that were composed by Dust Bowl migrants, most unknown outside the roadside camps, such as the California example reported by *Tent City News* in January 1940: "The Arkies and Okies in nineteen thirty-six,/Cranked up their flivvers and came west (on)/Sixty-six."[36]

Woody Guthrie's songs preserve the culture of Highway 66 as a road of trouble and sadness, a road far removed in spirit from the boosterism of America's Main Street. These traveling road blues remained outside the popular musical currents of the period, which were heard in the "Red River Valley" that John Ford had selected for the campfire scene in *The Grapes of Wrath*.[37] While even this cowboy ballad remained quite distant from the swing jazz sounds of New York, the guitar songs used in the film did capture the national mood of retrospect for the Dust Bowl period. As the European war drew closer, the familiar signs of U.S. 66 on the screen confirmed a democratic spirit of self-determined mobility. The movie literally projected the highway's numbers onto screens around the world, imagery that would mark the road to a mythical California in the new migration of prosperity that would follow in the wake of World War II.

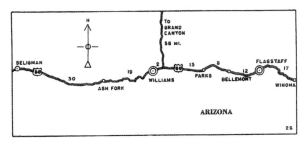

level plain. Unless you watch sharply, you will cross it before you are aware of it. It is over 100 feet deep and several hundred feet wide, although south of here it is deeper. Early wagon-train pioneers found it difficult to cross.

72 mi. (202 mi.) TOONERVILLE. A single building providing gasoline, groceries, and lunches. West of here, the plains end, and you soon enter the **COCONINO NATIONAL FOREST**. The first trees are rather scrubby, but they soon give way to tall yellow pines.

74 mi. (200 mi.) US 66 here crosses **PADRE CANYON**, which is quite similar to Canyon Diablo.

Now US 66 winds through the pines, which present a welcome relief from the parched desert. In this region, many ancient pueblos have been found, since the early Indians undoubtedly also enjoyed the timber and shade. Filling station operators between here and Flagstaff can direct you to some of these sites.

82 mi. (192 mi.) WINONA. (Alt. 6,005') **Winona Trading Post** offers cafe, gas, groceries, and several cabins.

US 66 now begins to climb more steeply, although there

are no difficult grades between here and Flagstaff. The pines become taller, and the road winds a bit.

At **86 mi.** (188 mi.) a road runs (L) to **WALNUT CANYON STATE PARK**, five miles south. This is one of the major prehistoric ruins easily reached from US 66. In a deep gorge, over 200 cliff dwellings cling to the sides of the steep rock. The village was busiest from 1000 to 1200 A. D., and the people were hunters, farmers, and traders. Open from 8 AM to 5 PM. No admission. Picnic area. Foot trails to many structures.

90 mi. (184 mi.) Gas station. Another at **91 mi.** (183 mi.).

93 mi. (181 mi.) Junction of US 66 and US 89. Camp Townsend Trailer Camp here, with garage and store. You can camp here in the pines.

96 mi. (178 mi.) Camp Elden. Another camping spot, with a garage and cafe.

99 mi. (175 mi.) FLAGSTAFF. (Pop. 8,089; alt. 7,000'; hotels: Monte Vista, Weatherford, Bank, Commercial; many courts, including: Arrowhead Lodge, El Pueblo, Flagstaff Motor Village, Rock Plaza, Vandevier Lodge, Nickerson's, Mac's, Motor Inn, Cactus Gardens, Dixon, and Sunset; garages: Cheshire, Babbitt, Waldhan's; curio shops; stores; cafes; all facilities.)

Flagstaff is the locale of the great **All-Indian Pow-Wow** each year for three or more days starting on July 4th and attended by thousands of Indians. Cowboys and Indians can be seen in their picturesque dress on Flagstaff streets

10.1 *A Guide Book to Highway 66* by Jack D. Rittenhouse, 1946. Sample pages of Rittenhouse's postwar guide book to Route 66, covering the stretch from Winona to Flagstaff. By permission of University of New Mexico Press.

Chapter Ten
(Get Your Kicks On)
Route Sixty-Six!

ONCE THE JAPANESE ATTACK ON PEARL HARBOR had thrust the U.S. into World War II, the strategic importance of U.S. 66 immediately became evident. The road had become a vital link between Midwest industrial centers and the port of Los Angeles, which had become a major war production center in its own right. The highway's significance was increased by the army training camps and air bases stretched along it. Once peace had been restored, tourists in increasing numbers flowed down U.S. 66. Among them were Bobby and Cynthia Troup, a Pennsylvania songwriter and his wife, who drove from their hometown in Lancaster in February 1946 to seek their fortune in Los Angeles. Along the way they wrote a jazz verse about their trip that became a postwar anthem, changing the name of the highway to Route 66.

JACK RITTENHOUSE

The rationing of rubber tires and gasoline imposed in 1942 greatly reduced travel on U.S. 66, and much of what remained was the transport of strategic materials between Chicago and California in military convoys. Most activity centered on the training bases in the desert where the warm temperatures and clear air permitted year-round exercises, but Army, Navy, and Marine facilities stretched along U.S. 66 from Missouri to Los Angeles.[1] Many were built as secret facilities omitted from road maps until the appearance of Jack Rittenhouse's *A Guide Book To Highway 66*. A Los Angeles advertising copywriter, Rittenhouse drove the highway from Los Angeles to Chicago in his tiny Bantam coupe in March 1946, enduring winter ice storms and twisting roads. Rittenhouse would go on to print 3,000 copies of his book (Fig. 10.1).[2]

The *Guide* located most of the military bases constructed along Highway 66. In the Ozarks near Waynesville, in Missouri, was Fort Leonard Wood, and in Oklahoma there were the Army Air Field at North Miami and Tinker Air Field in

Oklahoma City. Further west at El Reno was a German prisoner of war camp at the old Army fort, and there was a second German interment center at McLean, just over the line in Texas. Air fields were built in the panhandle at Foss, Oklahoma, and Amarillo, Texas, to protect the United States Helium Plant, a vital supply for the Navy surveillance blimps.[3]

In New Mexico a large tourist complex for military personnel developed on U.S. 66 along Central Avenue, near the Albuquerque Army Air Field. Here a host of highway motels and cafes also served the scientists from Los Alamos who were working on the Manhattan Project for the atom bomb.[4] Among these was a young Princeton graduate student, Richard Feynman, who took his ailing wife Arlene into Albuquerque for hospital treatments. As a respite, Feynman would grill steaks in the motel parking lot. Initially Feynman was embarrassed by the roadside exposure, but Arlene accepted the public display as part of the Western lifestyle. As Feynman recalled, "The hospital was right on Route 66, the main road across the United States! 'I can't do that,' I said. 'I mean with all those cars and trucks going by. I can't just go out there and start cookin' steaks on the lawn.'" Arlene suggested that he wear a chef's hat and that solved the problem.[5]

West of Albuquerque, in the mountains around Fort Wingate near Gallup, valuable uranium ore was mined for the Manhattan Project. Near Kingman a major Army Air Base was built for training night bomber pilots (many U.S. 66 motels were used as barracks).[6] Across the Colorado River was the Desert Training Center. During the spring and summer of 1942, General George Patton trained more than 60,000 troops here for Operation Torch, preparing for the British-American invasion of North Africa. Between Needles and the Daggett Air Field, tank maneuvers and night bivouacs studded the desert along U.S. 66 until October, when the troops shipped overseas. Other strategic installations included the Marine Corps Supply Depot at Barstow, the Army Air Field at Victorville, and the Kaiser steel mill at Fontana in the Pomona Valley.[7]

BOBBY TROUP

As Rittenhouse was traveling U.S. 66 east in early 1946 to write his guidebook, Captain Robert Troup, freshly discharged from the Marines, was making a similar trip westward with his wife, Cynthia, writing a song that would establish his name in the jazz clubs of Los Angeles. Like the Steinbecks' trip on U.S. 66 during the Depression, the Troups traveled quickly, and over time their trip has been similarly embellished. In this case, however, a record remains in photos and maps.

Troup was born in 1918 to a musical family in Lancaster, Pennsylvania, where his father ran a successful music store on West King Street. With his father's death in 1937, young Troup entered the University of Pennsylvania's Wharton Business School to train for the family business. There Troup became involved in the student theatricals of the Mask and Wig Club, writing for its 1940 production a song, "Daddy," that became a hit at the Philadelphia Embassy Club:[8]

Daddy! I want a brand new car,
Champaign and caviar,
Daddy! You want to get the best for me.[9]

116

The Embassy Club was fertile ground for musical talent. Here Troup met a young singer, Cynthia Hare, a society debutante with dreams of a theatrical career, who encouraged his writing.[10] In 1941, the Sammy Kaye Band recorded "Daddy," which spent nine weeks as #2 on the national Sunday Serenade radio hour.[11] The record's success took Troup to New York to write for the Tommy Dorsey Band and Harry James; the royalties bought him the new car his lyrics had asked for, a green Buick convertible, with a matching sedan for his mother.[12]

The attack on Pearl Harbor on December 7, 1941, altered any plans Troup might have made. He joined the Marines in March 1942, and married Cynthia in May before he was sent to Padre Island in South Carolina, and on to Saipan Island in the Pacific.[13] There he met a number of black soldiers with blues and jazz backgrounds that meshed with his own, and they formed a jazz band which included Johnnie Johnson, from St. Louis, who would join Chuck Berry after the war as pianist.[14] In 1945 Troup was given shore leave in Long Beach, and he went to see the hot jazz clubs in Hollywood along the Sunset Strip, an experience that was to have lasting effect in his postwar move to California.[15]

HOWARD JOHNSON'S

When Troup was released from his Marine unit in December 1945, he returned to his mother's house on West Wheatland Avenue in Lancaster, where Cynthia had raised two daughters born during the war.[16] While waiting for his discharge papers, Troup talked about returning to California to try his skills as a Hollywood songwriter. Although his mother urged him to stay on the East Coast, the lure of Los Angeles grew in the weeks after the New Year.[17] As Cynthia recalled: "Bobby just painted it, he was a dreamer. 'All the glamour and the studios, and you'll be in the sun!' Glamour: it just sounded exciting. When he came back from the war, that had a lot to do with it. He stopped here, and that's when he said, 'Oh, we've got to go to California.'"[18]

The Troups began plotting their route on AAA maps from the local Lancaster office (Fig. 10.2). They would take U.S. 40 to St. Louis where they would pick up U.S. 66 out to Los Angeles. They planned on ten days of driving to reach the coast.[19] After his discharge arrived on February 1, the Troups packed the green Buick convertible and, leaving the girls with his mother, drove to Harrisburg and on to the new Pennsylvania Turnpike at Carlisle in the mild winter air of Thursday, February 7, 1946.[20] The high-speed toll road had opened in 1940 before the war as the first modern expressway in the U.S., cutting through the Allegheny Mountains for 160 miles to Irwin, east of Pittsburgh.[21]

Once on the turnpike, the Troups enjoyed the peacetime euphoria of unrationed gasoline and the thrill of unlimited speed.[22] As they looked over the road map during lunch at a Howard Johnson's, Cynthia suggested they write a song about Route 40. Troup thought the idea silly since they would soon be on Route 66, their real road west.[23] Still, the germ of a highway lyric kept turning over in Cynthia's mind.

GET YOUR KICKS

At the Irwin exit, the Troups picked up U.S. 40, driving through West Virginia into Ohio where they stayed overnight with friends. They continued straight across Indiana and Illinois, trying to reach St. Louis by the weekend so

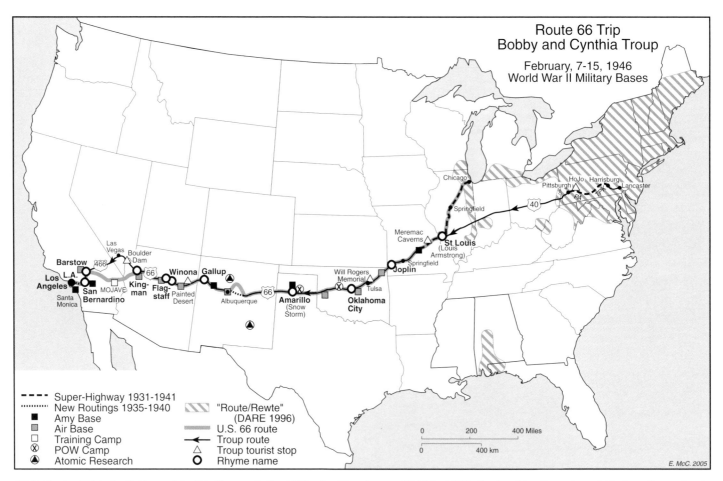

Route 66 Trip
Bobby and Cynthia Troup

February, 7-15, 1946
World War II Military Bases

Legend:

- – – – Super-Highway 1931-1941
- ········· New Routings 1935-1940
- ■ Amy Base
- ▨ Air Base
- □ Training Camp
- ⊗ POW Camp
- ▲ Atomic Research
- ▨ "Route/Rewte" (DARE 1996)
- ▬ U.S. 66 route
- ← Troup route
- △ Troup tourist stop
- ○ Rhyme name

Map labels: Las Vegas, Boulder Dam, Barstow, L.A., Los Angeles, San Bernardino, Santa Monica, MOJAVE, Kingman, 466, 66, Winona, Flagstaff, Painted Desert, Gallup, Albuquerque, Amarillo (Snow Storm), Will Rogers Memorial, Tulsa, Oklahoma City, Joplin, Springfield, Meremac Caverns, St Louis (Louis Armstrong), Chicago, Springfield, 40, Pittsburgh, HoJo, Harrisburg, Lancaster, PA

0 200 400 Miles
0 400 km

E. McC. 2005

10.2. Route 66 trip by Bobby and Cynthia Troup with World War II military bases, 1941 to 1946. Route of the Troups' road trip from Pennsylvania, through Oklahoma (shaded), to California in February 1946, showing the "rewte" (pronounced "root") dialect area and the locations along U.S. 66 of World War II military bases (after Rittenhouse 1946). By the author.

they could see Louis Armstrong at the Club Plantation club on Grand and Delmar.[24] In East St. Louis, U.S. 40 joined U.S. 66 (Fig. 10.3). With rising expectation, Cynthia began rhyming the new numbers in quick riffs, "Six, nix, picks, kicks," finally whispering to Bobby, "Get your kicks on Route Sixty-six," an alliteration of suggestive sexuality Troup instantly recognized as a winning lyric:[25] "That's a darling title! Goddam! That's a great title!"[26]

For Cynthia "kicks" referred to the excitement of reaching the western highway to Hollywood and the freedom of unlimited driving in those early peacetime months. Perhaps she was thinking about the champagne lyrics of Cole Porter's "I Get a Kick Out of You" from 1934, or the cool riffs of New York night clubs, rhyming the sixes jazz-style.[27] Whatever her source, in the swinging slang of the new postwar period, Cynthia had offered the key to their Highway 66 road song.

With the rhyme in mind, the Troups took U.S. 66 out from St. Louis southwest across the Missouri Ozarks, stopping at the Meramec Caverns near Stanton. Soon they entered cowboy country in Oklahoma, where they began taking snapshots of cattle ranches and small town cafes, and visited the recently dedicated Will Rogers Memorial in Claremore. Their photos show the Troups still in proper Eastern attire in the frontier landscape, proudly posing as tourists with their convertible against the bright glare of the winter sun (Fig. 10.4).[28]

10.3. *St. Louis and Vicinity*, ca. 1940. A Phillips 66 road map showing the use of U.S. 66 symbols in a commercial advertisement. Author's collection.

10.4. Bobby and Cynthia Troup, February 1946. Snapshots from the Route 66 trip to California showing the Troups at the Will Rogers Memorial in Claremore, Oklahoma, and the Buick convertible used on the trip. By permission of the Troup Family Collection.

By Monday the Troups had reached Oklahoma City and the open vistas of the plains, by now recovered from their Dust Bowl drought. Driving west across the Texas Panhandle, they hit a midnight snowstorm near Amarillo and took refuge in a highway motel. Once it cleared, they continued down U.S. 66, now a narrow, two-lane road passing through the drylands of eastern New Mexico. In Albuquerque they stopped for a haircut and rest. They followed the highway into the Indian lands at Gallup, and then into the Painted Desert of Arizona, where they stopped for more snapshots. At Kingman, they detoured north onto U.S. 466 to visit Boulder Dam and the Las Vegas casinos. When the Troups crossed the California line they registered the moment with more photos of highway signs, before recovering U.S. 66 at Barstow.[29]

For the Troups the trip over the Cajon Pass and down into the Los Angeles Valley was a welcome change, the fruit orchards and warm weather a reward for their long drive from the winter confines of Lancaster. That very day Los Angeles papers carried a photo of cars snowbound in a Chicago blizzard. Route 66 ran along the foothills into Pasadena and down the new Arroyo Seco Freeway into downtown "L.A.," as it was called by knowing natives. They took the last leg of U.S. 66 to Hollywood and a motel on Ventura Boulevard. It was now Friday, February 15, just seven days out from Pennsylvania, remarkable time on the narrow two-lane road that was U.S. 66 in that postwar winter of 1946.[30]

NAT KING COLE

Once settled, Bobby Troup was eager to see the musical sights, especially the Hollywood night clubs he recalled from his wartime shore leave. Most immediately he wanted to see the Nat King Cole Trio at the Trocadaro on Sunset Boulevard.[31] The jazz weekly, *Down Beat*, had announced the trio to its readers: "Bobby Ramos has a new 18-piece outfit at the Trocadaro, replacing Russ Morgan. Better news to hipsters is the King Cole Trio in the room named for them."[32]

Nat Cole was well known in Los Angeles jazz circles for his innovative swing piano style and a wartime hit on the local Capitol label, "Straighten Up and Fly Right," that had been inspired by his father's Alabama Baptist sermons.[33] Born Nathaniel Coles, he and his family had migrated north to Chicago after World War I, where young Coles showed early talent on the piano.[34] By his high school years he had formed a small band with his brother, imitating the local swing style of Earl "Fatha" Hines.[35] Fresh out of high school, in 1937 Coles joined a road show of Eubie Blake's *Shuffle Along* that folded, broke, in Los Angeles. Stranded in the city, Coles decided to make his way in the local jazz scene, changing his name to Cole and working with various small groups.[36] He developed an elegant keyboard technique, traveled east to New York, and absorbed the emergent Harlem bebop style. He returned to Los Angeles to form his own trio, with Oscar Moore on electric guitar and Johnny Miller on standup bass. During the war, the Nat Cole Trio had become the premier jazz group in Los Angeles, breaking the color barrier with its own "King Cole Room" at the Trocadaro (Fig. 10.5).[37]

Within days of his arrival Troup arranged to meet Cole through Bullets Durgom, the Trio's new manager, whom Troup knew through contacts with Tommy Dorsey.[38] Troup was introduced as the composer of the prewar hit "Daddy." When Cole asked about new songs, Troup played his latest ballad, "Baby, Baby All the Time." Cole then asked if Troup had anything more appropriate for his upbeat piano style.[39] Troup said that, driving out to Los Angeles with his wife, he had written half a song about Route 66, with the lyrics set to a twelve-bar blues beat:[40]

> If you ever plan to motor west, travel my way,
> Take the highway that's the best,
> Get your kicks on Route Sixty-six!
> It winds from Chicago to L.A.,
> More than two thousand miles all the way,
> Get your kicks on Route Sixty-six![41]

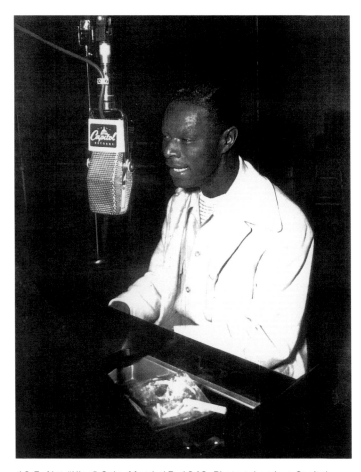

10.5. Nat "King" Cole, March 15, 1946. Photo taken in a Capitol Records studio in Los Angeles on the day of the original "Route 66!" recording, with Cole at the piano. By permission of Michael Ochs Archives.

The road song appealed to Cole, perhaps recalling his own experience when he had traveled west from Chicago. Cole sensed that the rhyming road numbers might be another novelty hit like his current "Frim Fram Sauce."[42] On instinct, Cole encouraged Troup to finish the song for a Capitol recording session in March, and Durgom arranged for Troup to use a CBS studio on Sunset Boulevard. Amid the distraction of rehearsing bands, Troup unfolded his AAA highway map and began composing a second verse, trying to rhyme the overnight place-names between St. Louis and Los Angeles to give the song a sense of rapid motion. Some names, such as Albuquerque, seemed impossible, but Troup finally worked out a lyric itinerary, with names about every 250 miles:[43]

Now you go through St. Louey, Joplin, Missouri,
Oklahoma City looks mighty pretty,
You'll see Amarillo, Gallup, New Mexico,
Flagstaff, Arizona, Don't forget Winona,
Kingman, Barstow, San Bernardino.[44]

For the final verse, Troup tried a riff in the latest hipster style that mimicked in *Down Beat* jive slang, even as it revealed his admiration for the cool L.A. scene:[45]

Won't you get hip to this timely tip,
When you make that California trip,
Get your kicks on Route Sixty-six![46]

A peculiarity of the verse lay in the pronunciation of "Route." Instinctively Troup assumed his eastern Pennsylvania accent, saying "rewte" instead of the Midwestern "rout."[47] This dialect boundary ran just west of Pittsburgh along the Ohio line, which marked the song's "Route" as Eastern speech (see Fig. 10.2).[48] More glaringly, Troup called the road "*Route* 66" instead of the "*Highway* 66" of Steinbeck and Guthrie who, among others, had always referred to the road by its Western name. Calling a highway a "route" was common in the East and, like the pronunciation, revealed the song as an outsider's description of 66 as a tourist road to California.[49] Troup's lyrics attuned the road to Eastern ears, and effectively dismissed the Dust Bowl "Highway 66" as a prewar Westernism. In this way, the song reset the symbolic quality of the highway, just as the Dust Bowl had, to make it once again meaningful for its times.

CAPITOL SESSIONS

Cole was satisfied with the lyrics and immediately logged the song for the Capitol recording session.[50] Cole's Trio recorded three versions of "Route 66" during March and April 1946. The first was for the CBS *Old Gold* radio broadcast on March 13, hosted by Frank Sinatra, who introduced Cole:

Sinatra: How about that brand new hit you're going to record any second, "Route 66"?
Cole: We'd be mighty proud to introduce it, Frank.
Sinatra: OK. "Route 66," America's All American Highway set to music and given that King Cole beat.[51]

Cole started off with a running blues beat on the keyboard that Oscar Moore chorded in jump time on his electric guitar. Then Cole sang out the opening verse with emphatic phrasing that pushed the lyrics in a fast rush of highway speed, extending the vowels to gain momentum:

If YOU/ever PLAN to motor west,
Travel MY way/the HIGHway that's the BEST,
Get your KICKS/on RO-OTE sixty-six.

It WINDS/from Chicago to L.A.,
More than TWO/thousand MILES/all the WAY,
Get your KICKS/on RO-OTE sixty-six.

Now you go through St. LOUEY/Joplin MissouRI,
And Oklahoma City/looks Mi-GHTY pretty,
You'll SEE AmaRILLO/Gallup New MexiCO,
Flagstaff Ari-ZONA/don't forget Winona,
Kingman/BARSTOW/San BernardinO.

Won't YOU/Get HIP to this TIMELY tip,
When you make/that Cal-I-fornia TRIP.
Get your KICKS/on RO-OTE sixty-six![52]

The official Capitol studio session two days later included a three-minute take of "Route 66" in the spirit of the *Old Gold* broadcast. Again, the fast-paced rhythm of Cole's piano and the hip, jazz-style delivery of the lyrics gave the recording the lively sound that signaled a hit. The success of this session led to a third take with the same timing on a V-Disc for Armed Forces Radio in early April, together with Troup's, "Baby, Baby All the Time."[53]

"Route 66" was released on April 22 as Capitol #256 with a B-side ballad, "Everyone's Saying Hello Again."[54] By

"ROUTE 66!---"

BY **BOB TROUP**

AS RECORDED FOR CAPITOL RECORDS BY KING COLE TRIO

BURKE & VAN HEUSEN INC.
Music Company

10.6. *Route 66!—*, 1946. Song sheet cover of Troup's hit showing the King Cole Trio and listing "Bob Troup" as the songwriter. Burke and Van Heusen, New York. Author's Collection.

mid-May, the national music weeklies had reviewed the release as a potential hit. *Down Beat* was cautious: "66 is well done, but no different than lots of other Cole records;" but *Billboard* enthused: "Despite its meatless make-up, 'Route 66' gets top-drawer treatment."[55] The song's popular appeal was immediately made evident by a Musiccraft cover with Georgie Auld and His Orchestra on April 30, and another by Bing Crosby and the Andrews Sisters on May 10.[56] The momentum climaxed in mid-summer when "Route 66" reached #3 on the *Billboard* Race Record Charts.[57] On August 12, *Newsweek* featured the King Cole Trio in its "Music Section," relating the success of its recent hits: "The latest is 'Get Your Kicks on Route 66,' a number Nat introduced at the Trocadaro."[58] In line with the Capitol recording, piano sheet music for *"Route 66!"* was published, featuring a cover photo of the King Cole Trio set against a bright yellow background (Fig. 10.6).[59]

SONG MAP

Within two weeks the royalties from the Capitol release allowed the Troups to make a down payment on a house in North Hollywood, their California dream realized beyond their wildest expectations. On their fourth wedding anniversary that May 2nd, the Troups moved into a small bungalow on Alcove Avenue, less than three months after leaving Lancaster. In celebration, Cynthia took from the glove compartment the AAA road map and pasted her snapshots of U.S. 66 signs on it, together with sections of the song sheet, to create a cartographic song collage. She circled the overnight place names: St. Louis, Joplin, Oklahoma City, Gallup, Flagstaff (and Winona), Kingman, Barstow, and San

Bernardino, and marked a black line from Chicago to St. Louis for the section they had missed in Illinois while on U.S. 40. In the center, she colored an animated U.S. 66 shield with a jazz trumpet, beside which she pasted pictures of the trio (Fig. 10.7).[60] Framed over the mantle, the Route 66 song map was a visual record of their journey, a literal icon of their Hollywood success. On the back Cynthia

10.7 *Route 66 Song Map*, 1946. Details from Cynthia Troup's collage of the American Automobile Association road map that the Troups used on their trip, together with snapshots taken of U.S. 66 road signs and pieces from the song sheet. Oklahoma and Texas are pictured on page 125; Illinois and Missouri on page 126; and Arizona and Calforina on page 127. By permission of Cynthia Troup Archive.

claimed her co-credit for the lyrics: "'Route 66' was written by Bobby Troup and Cynthia (1946) on their trip to California from Lancaster & Philadelphia, Pa."[61]

Once projected into the national culture, "Get Your Kicks on Route 66!" became a musical map of the highway for postwar travelers. The lyric cartography followed an ancient tradition of describing distant lands in metered verse traceable to the Homeric ballads of the *Odyssey*.[62] In such song cycles, the geography of unknown lands is revealed in repeated rhymes of distant places, just as the names in "Route 66" sounded a pathway from Chicago to California. Indeed, Troup was told that his song was used in just such a manner in the roadside cafes along Route 66: "They'd drop a nickel into the jukebox and plan the next day's drive through 'Saint Loo-ey and Joplin, Missouri.'"[63]

CHRISTMAS SONG

As Troup was enjoying the flush of popular success with "Route 66," Cole abandoned his upbeat jazz sound for more broadly appealing romantic ballads. That March, Cole announced a concert tour that would "Feature Serious Stuff," and by June he was in New York working on long piano pieces by Claude Debussy and George Gershwin.[64] Earlier, Cole and his trio had recorded "The Christmas Song," a holiday tribute written by Mel Tormé. To signal his turn from jazz to more popular music, Cole recorded it again once he returned from New York, this time backed by strings conducted by Nelson Riddle.[65] When released in November 1946, the lush arrangement became an instant Christmas classic, pointing Cole toward a wider, more romantic style.

In retrospect, the timing of the "Route 66" recording turned out to have been as fortuitous as that of Piepmeier and Avery's Springfield meeting in 1926, or that which found Lange and Taylor on the Canadian River bridge that August afternoon in 1938. If it had not been for the quicksilver trip to Los Angeles, Cole's need for a clever novelty that spring, and the corresponding pressure on Troup to finish the upbeat song, "(Get Your Kicks on) Route 66!" would never have become a national hit. Yet it was precisely the driving sound of immediate pleasure and the promise of the "Cal-I-fornia trip" that caught the ear of Eastern dreamers that first peacetime summer, urging them to try the open road and "motor west" for a new beginning after the decades of depression and war. The Troup song-map offered Route 66 as a highway of opportunity and pleasure; and in the rock and roll explosion that was to come, it became a road anthem that promoted Route 66 less as a highway than as a state of mind.

Chapter Eleven
Interstate Highways

THE EXPLOSION OF TRAVEL following World War II promoted a new commercial spirit along Route 66, together with federal improvements to the national highway system. With the postwar prosperity, U.S. 66 once again became the national tourist route to the Southwest and California. In 1947, the Highway 66 Association was revived, as new roadside businesses opened that advertised themselves with colorful postcards of the latest in roadside cafes and motels. The postwar revival was also expressed in federal planning for a national system of limited access expressways, realized in the Interstate and Defense Highway Program of 1956. From that point on, relocation and renumbering for the Interstate system gradually eliminated the original U.S. 66 routings and, bypassing small town centers across the Southwest, promoted a sense of nostalgia for the historic roadside landscapes of prewar Highway 66.

HIGHWAY 66 ASSOCIATION

After the war, Oklahoma again proved itself the center of Route 66 boosterism with a revival of the Main Street Association to promote local highway businesses. In October 1947, a meeting was held in Oklahoma City for the "Postwar Reorganization of the U.S. Highway 66 Association."[1] Among the various speakers was Ralph Jones, a New Mexico motel owner, who offered the vision of commercial profits from the promotion of U.S. 66 as a scenic highway to the Southwest: "We got it folks. All we have to do is go after it right. People must be sold on coming to 66 before they leave home. So let's set aside all the sectionalism and strive for the greatest good for the greatest number. Let's do it in the American way!"[2]

Among the many efforts to gain attention in the national press was the 1952 rededication of U.S. 66 as the "Will Rogers Highway." This was organized by Lyman Riley, owner of the Meramec Caverns in Missouri and president of the

Association. Using his connections with Will Rogers, Jr., star of the film biography, *The Story of Will Rogers,* Lyman got young Rogers to participate in the rededication ceremonies with the release of the film by Warner Brothers. The ceremony promoted U.S. 66 as a national highway to both the scenic wonders of the Southwest and Hollywood.[3]

POSTCARD MOTELS

In the flush of postwar travel, a network of overnight rest stops developed along Route 66 that advertised the highway as a scenic resort by using printed colored postcards. These were produced for local businesses by national printing companies and displayed the latest styles in highway facilities, especially the automobile tourist court and modern roadside motels which became identified with the exotic landscapes of the scenic Southwest.

The origins of the highway motel lay in the innovations of the Los Angeles architect, Arthur Heinmann, and his plans for suburban bungalow courts in the period following World War I.[4] Heinmann designed the first auto motor court in the "Mo-Tel Inn" along U.S. 101 in San Luis Obispo, registering the name with the Library of Congress in December 1925. The roadside auto "motel" remained a California phenomenon of the tourist highways of the Pacific Coast until World War II. Then it expanded eastward along Highway 66, across the Southwest, and after the war into the Midwest.[5] In 1949, the Duncan Hines's *Lodging for a Night* listed several such newly built motels along U.S. 66, including: the Manor Motel in Joliet, Illinois (opened in 1947); the Ranch Motel in Vinita, Oklahoma; the Ranch-O-Tel in Amarillo, Texas; the La Siesta Motel in Winslow, Ari-

zona; and Motel "66" in San Bernardino, California.[6] For Eastern travelers the exotic design and curious names gave these motels a unique Route 66 flavor, evoking the romance of Western movies against the dramatic landscapes of Arizona and New Mexico. By 1952, the highway motel achieved national attention with photo articles in the *New York Times*, *Business Week*, and *Newsweek*, as the concept reached the East Coast.[7]

The tourist postcards were sold in motel lobbies and service stations along the highway. Many were made by the Curt Teich Company of Chicago, which canvassed the hundreds of motor courts and motel cabins along U.S. 66 between Chicago and Los Angeles. A staff photographer filed a black-and-white print of the roadside setting, often including a motel room with a sample bedspread print, and a color reference sketch for printing. Then the Curt Teich artists would air-brush the photo before printing it on linen cardstock to produce the classic color postcard of the postwar era.[8] These were highly stylized in muted blues, reds, and greens, with painted clouds that set the Highway 66 motels in a Surrealist landscape, as in cards for the State Motor Lodge in Tucumcari, New Mexico, and Roy's Cafe Motel in Amboy, California (Fig. 11.1).

Except for the motels, little of the actual U.S. 66 roadway was depicted on the commercial postcards of the period. This reflected the lack of dramatic scenery along much of the route and the limited sales potential in long empty stretches. A few sites did capture the eye of postcard photographers, notably the express highway sections through the Missouri Ozarks near Rolla, and the Tijeras Canyon road cut through the Sandia Mountains east of Albuquerque

State Motor Lodge
Conveniently and Centrally Located on U.S. Highway 66
TUCUMCARI, NEW MEXICO

New Mexico Knotty Pine Interior
With the Finest of Furnishings

INNERSPRINGS
STEAM HEAT

STATE
MOTOR
LODGE

ROY'S
CAFE
MOTEL
AIR
COOLED
HU UNITS

Excellent Airport Adjoining
U.S. HIGHWAY 66 . . . Telephone #3 . . . AMBOY, CALIF.

AAA

DRIVE
SCENIC U S
66

11.1. Highway 66 motel postcards, ca. 1950-60.
Color postcards of the postwar period: State Motor
Lodge, Tucumcari, New Mexico, and Roy's Café
Motel, Amboy, California. Author's collection. Compare Roy's Cafe Motel sign with Jeff Brouw's 1987
photo of the same place on page 173.

11.2. Highway 66 roadside postcards of New Mexico, ca. 1950–60, showiing the ca. 1950 two-lane section (top) and ca. 1960 four-lane section (bottom) of Route 66 in Tijeras Canyon, east of Albuquerque. Author's collection.

(Fig. 11.2).[9] As with the views of the motels, they showed a scenic highway through the Southwest completely devoid of traffic. Such still life landscapes presented Route 66 as off the beaten trail, a trait that appealed to Easterners expecting the sunset horizons of movie Westerns. Despite their contrivance, the postcards do document crucial highway improvements along sections of U.S. 66 before the massive road building of the Interstate period.

TURNER TURNPIKE

Improvement of the U.S. 66 corridor had begun under the direction of various state highway departments before World War II. Several sections had been upgraded to limited access expressways in key urban areas. Examples include the 1932 Lindbergh Boulevard Beltway around St. Louis; the 1940 Arroyo Seco Freeway between Pasadena and Los Angeles; and the 1941 Joliet Road bypass from Chicago, built by local state highway departments (Fig. 11.3). To deal with wartime truck traffic along U.S. 66, Illinois also constructed four-lane segments around most of the major cities from Bloomington to Springfield. A similar roadway was constructed around Fort Leonard Wood in Missouri. Nevertheless Rittenhouse's *Guide* described much of U.S. 66 as a narrow, two-lane road without shoulders and often with sudden, sharp "Devil's Elbows" that made for dangerous driving.[10]

To improve this situation, several sections of U.S. 66 were relocated after the war. The most important projects were through the desert portions of Arizona and California. These included the rebuilding of the Red Rock Railroad bridge over the Colorado River to Needles in 1947 and the abandonment in 1952 of the treacherous switchbacks of the Oatman Gold Road through the Sitgreaves Pass in the Black Mountains for a level route along the Santa Fe Railroad tracks from Kingman to Topock.[11] This produced a relatively straight road from Kingman to Needles.[12]

The most significant postwar improvement was the opening of the Turner Turnpike between Oklahoma City and Tulsa, also in 1953.[13] Designed after the success of the Pennsylvania Turnpike as a high-speed toll road, the turnpike was named for Governor Roy J. Turner, who first proposed the project in 1947. The Turner Turnpike bypassed downtown sections of U.S. 66 through Edmond, Chandler, Bristow, and Supulpa, providing ninety miles of high-speed throughway.[14] Dedicated in May 1953, the Turner Turnpike was the first intercity regional bypass of U.S. 66, and it offered a vision of national toll roads paralleling the old alignment from Chicago to Los Angeles.[15] Oklahoma proposed additional tollways along the axis of U.S. 66, completing the Will Rogers Turnpike between Tulsa and the Missouri state line at Joplin in 1957. A western route from Oklahoma City to the Texas line, however, was opposed by local businessmen in Clinton and Elk City.[16]

MAGIC MOTORWAYS

The prospect of improving the federal highway system for high-speed traffic had been under discussion by the BPR (Bureau of Public Roads) since 1940. Two concepts for building the system had been proposed: one was a network of public toll roads, the other a federally financed freeway system, both of which would link the Atlantic and Pacific in a transcontinental grid. The BPR discussion was given momentum by the General Motors Futurama exhibition at

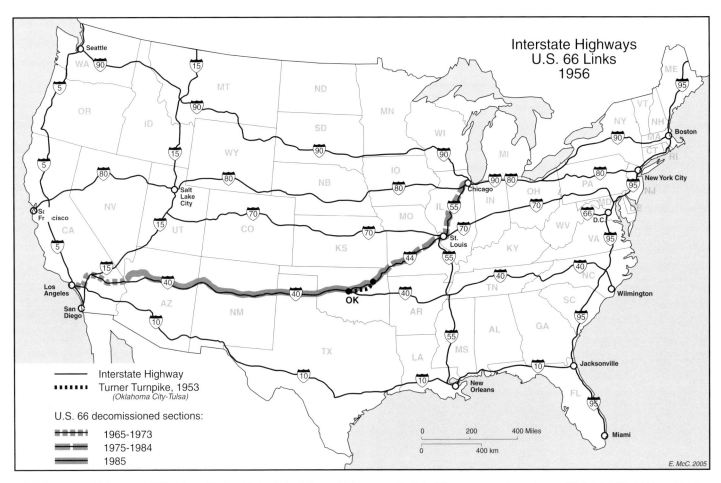

11.3. Interstate highways, 1956. Map of federal interstate defense highways, with U.S. 66 replacement numbers I-55, I-44, I-40, I-15, and I-10; also showing I-66 from Washington, D.C., to Strasburg, Virginia. By the author.

the 1939 New York World's Fair. Designed by architect Norman Bel Geddes and modeled on German autobahns opened in 1935, the miniature Magic Motorways model envisioned sweeping highway interchanges around towering city centers.[17] With its high-speed traffic lanes, the Geddes's model popularized the vision of transcontinental superhighways between the East and West coasts: "The motorways which stretch across the model are exact replicas, in a small scale, of motorways which may be built in America in the near future. They are designed to make automobile collisions impossible and to eliminate completely traffic congestion."[18]

While the Futurama Motorways offered the American public an enticing model for national superhighways, the BPR had developed its own working plan for new federal expressways. Director MacDonald had warned in 1935 of the increasing congestion, saying that, "we can no longer ignore the needs of traffic" on the existing road system.[19] The passage of the Federal Aid Highway Act of 1938 resulted in a planning report in 1939 by Herbert S. Fairbank of the BPR, *Toll Roads and Free Roads*, that discussed the merits of each type of system. A detailed traffic study was made of all major federal routes, with a proposed network of six major express toll roads, including the section of U.S. 66 from Chicago to Oklahoma City, and a larger system of freeways that likewise included the route of U.S. 66 from Chicago to Los Angeles, with a loop across Boulder Dam that led to Las Vegas, Nevada, on U.S. 466.[20]

INTERSTATE HIGHWAYS

During World War II, the strategic need for a national system of express highways became more apparent. President Roosevelt supported the planning of state expressway routes, realized in the Federal Aid Highway Act of 1944 for a "National System of Interstate Highways." After the war, the Fairbank proposal was presented in a map of *Interstate Highways* in 1947, which continued to indicate the route of U.S. 66 from Chicago to Los Angeles as a major

national superhighway (see Fig. 11.3).[21] National news articles remarked that, "No route designation has been selected yet similar to the familiar 'U.S. Route 1.' The P.R.A. [BPR] said the expressways would take the same general route as presently designated Federal highways and would probably have the same United States highway number."[22]

The interstate plan remained a paper project that lacked congressional funding of the massive construction costs until the presidency of wartime hero, Dwight D. Eisenhower. Drawing on his personal experience on the first transcontinental Army convoy from Washington, D.C., to San Francisco in 1919, and on his wartime knowledge of the German autobahns, Eisenhower favored such expressway construction. Yet, even with Eisenhower's inauguration in January 1953, the pressing problem of the Korean War deferred action for a year. With the passage of the Federal Highway Act of 1954, Eisenhower appointed General Lucius Clay to prepare a working plan for a national freeway system under the direction of Francis C. Turner at the BPR. The Clay report, presented to Congress in January 1955, recommended a 40,000-mile system of freeways funded by a Federal Highway Corporation that would pay ninety, rather than the traditional fifty, percent of the construction costs.[23] The President urged Congress to support the Clay Commission freeway plan with a direct appeal to House members in February 1955:

Our unity as a nation is sustained by free communication of thought and easy transportation of people and goods. The ceaseless flow of information throughout the republic is matched over a vast system of interconnected highways crisscrossing the country and joining at our national borders with friendly neighbors to the north and south.[24]

Despite Eisenhower's plea, the plan remained stalled in Congress. Senator Albert Gore of Tennessee offered a compromise bill in the spring of 1955, which was defeated by strong opposition to federal funding. Representative George Fallon of Maryland changed the name to the "National System of Interstate and Defense Highways," but again funding was denied.[25] Success was only achieved when Fallon added a federal gasoline tax to finance the program in January 1956. The bill was then further amended by Rep. Hale Boggs of Louisiana, finally to pass as the Federal Aid Highway Act in May 1956. On June 29, Eisenhower signed the bill for a federally financed system of 41,000 miles of national freeways that incorporated existing state toll roads, such as those of Oklahoma, into the system.[26]

INTERSTATE NUMBERING

Even before Eisenhower had appointed a director for the program, several states were eager to claim the first federal funds for expressway construction projects. In August, the Missouri Highway Commission awarded a contract to improve U.S. 66 in Laclede County, near Lebanon, as the "First project in the United States," of what would be later designated I-44. At the same time, the Kansas Highway Commission began construction on U.S. 40 near Topeka for what it called "Interstate Route No. 1," subsequently renumbered I-70. In October, Eisenhower appointed John A. Volpe of Massachusetts as the interim director of the Fed-eral Highway Administration until the President's first choice, B. D. Tallamy, then Chairman of the New York State Thruway, could take over the position.[27]

Volpe was eager to solve the problem of numbering the interstates. In January 1957, Volpe wrote to the president of AASHO (American Association of State Highway Officials) to urge "quick action on the development of Interstate sign-ing."[28] As with the original numbering meetings in 1925, AASHO appointed a Route Numbering Committee headed by A. E. Johnson of Arkansas and John O. Morton of New Hampshire. That spring, Johnson requested state highway departments to submit sample markers and numbering pro-posals for review.[29]

When Tallamy succeeded Volpe as Federal Highway Administrator that February, the matter of Interstate num-bering was still under discussion at AASHO. On June 26, the Executive Committee met in Seattle to work out a "num-bering method" from the wide range of state proposals.[30] While no detailed record survives, it appears that Johnson and Morton discussed the numbering problem informally, and they met again on July 9 to resolve the matter before the final AASHO meeting in August. A memo from Johnson summarized their position: "The matter of using an alpha-bet system to number the Interstate system was discarded by the Executive Committee. It appears now that the American system of route markers and route numbers will be used but altered so as not to conflict with the U.S. Numbered System."[31]

The committee's plan for Interstate route numbering and the design of shield markers was presented at the AASHO meeting on August 13 in LaSalle, Illinois. For the road markers, Johnson and Morton selected a reflective colored shield from samples submitted by Texas and Missouri highway engineers, lettered in white against a red background above large white route numbers on a blue field. For the numbers, Johnson simply reversed the pattern of the original federal numbering system (see Fig. 11.3). Thus, the major east-west transcontinental numbers began in the South, with I-10 between Jacksonville, Florida, and Los Angeles, paralleling U.S. 90, and moved north to I-90, paralleling U.S. 20 between Boston and Seattle. A similar reverse logic was used for numbering north-south highways, with I-95 paralleling U.S. 1 along the East Coast and I-5 paralleling U.S. 101 on the West Coast. The new numbering was designed to avoid using the same number in the same state for both the U.S. Route and Interstate Highway systems, although in some Midwest states the sets nearly collide, as U.S. 54 and I-55 do in central Illinois. On August 29, Johnson submitted the AASHO Interstate numbers and markers to Tallamy.[32] The system was finally approved on September 10, 1957.

INTERSTATE 66

With the new Interstate system in effect, the integrity of U.S. Route 66 was open to question. The single-numbered route from Chicago to Los Angeles established by Avery and Piepmeier in 1925 was now divided among five interstates.[33] These included I-55 as a north-south route from Chicago to St. Louis (and New Orleans); I-44 as an east-west diagonal from St. Louis to Oklahoma City, including the Will Rogers and Turner turnpikes; I-40 from Wilmington, North Carolina, through Oklahoma City to Barstow, California, via

Amarillo, Albuquerque, and Flagstaff; I-15 from Montana through Barstow over the Cajon Pass to San Bernardino; and I-10 from Jacksonville, Florida, through San Bernardino to Los Angeles and Santa Monica at the Pacific Ocean.

While the singular numbering of an Interstate route between Chicago and Los Angeles was abandoned, the distinctive signet of the double sixes was assigned to a new Interstate Highway connector, I-66, between Washington, D.C., and Strasburg, Virginia. This east-west route to the Shenandoah Valley had been selected by Fairbank as early as 1944, although with no assigned number, and was shown on the "Interstate Highway" map of 1947 as one of the primary national expressways.[34] The use of "66" plainly arose in the seriation of east-west connectors that included I-64 between Newport News, Virginia, and St. Louis (see Fig. 11.3). The assignment of the "66" with its historic associations to an expressway from the nation's capital to the historic Shenandoah Valley was doubtless purposeful. Whether the merits of selecting I-66 over other options, including I-62 and I-68, was debated before the final August 1957 meeting remains unknown, as AASHO records are silent on the matter.

ROUTE 66 IS DEAD! LONG LIVE ROUTE 66!

Even before Tallamy had given his final approval to the Interstate system, concern had emerged among members of the National U.S. Highway 66 Association. The division of U.S. 66 into five different interstate highways had raised serious questions about AASHO's decision to discard a through-route number from Illinois to California. On September 6, the Association's Executive Secretary, Jack Cutberth of Clinton, Oklahoma, wrote to AASHO Director

Johnson in Washington, expressing the Association's interest in maintaining the through route. Johnson took a month to respond, likely waiting for public reaction to the release of the Interstate map on September 24.[35] His reply expressed concern about disrupting the new Interstate numbering system, but at the same time demonstrated respect for the historical significance of Route 66 as a national highway: "It is impossible to have, for instance, a U.S. 66 marker and an Interstate marker going through the same state. The confusion to the public would be enormous because it is not standard practice on the part of the State or the highway user to refer to U.S. 66 or Interstate 66 but generally to 'Route 66'."[36]

The sense of AASHO and BPR's abandonment of U.S. 66 as a national highway number grew, following approval of the Interstate plan. At its annual meeting in 1962, members

11.5. *Route 66 Travel Guide*, 1965. Main Street Association's tourist guidebook showing the Interstate Highway shields for the U.S. 66 corridor. Author's collection.

of the Main Street Association passed a resolution noting that "the identity and historical significance of the name 'U.S. Highway 66' appears destined to cease to exist."[37] For a while this was belied by the use of Interstate shields together with U.S. 66 signs. The cover of the Main Street Association's *Route 66 Travel Guide* for 1965 shows I-40, I-44, and I-55 shields surmounted by a U.S. 66 marker (Fig. 11.5).[38] But, in fact, the physical identity of U.S. 66 was continuously eroded by widening and relocation throughout the 1960s construction of the Interstate system. As its physical identity was erased, nostalgia for Route 66 in the popular media grew, and the transformation of the route from physical road to national symbol accelerated. It was almost as if the more difficult it was to find the route on the land, the easier it was to locate its sense of unlimited opportunity in the mind. As the open road began to disappear in fact, it began to blossom as Route 66 in the mind of a youth generation that had never known it.

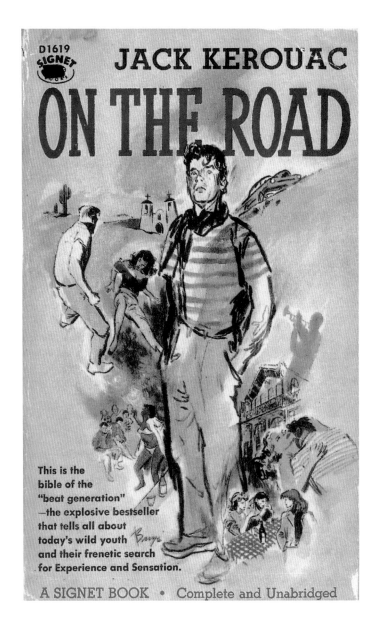

12.1. *On the Road*, jacket cover, 1958. This is the first Signet paper-back edition of "the bible of the 'beat generation'," Jack Kerouac's 1957 novel about his 1947 trip from New York to San Francisco along U.S. 66. Author's collection.

Chapter Twelve
Rock and Roll

THE BYPASSING OF ROUTE 66 engendered a popular fascination with the highway, one that increasingly transformed its identity as it was taken over by the electronic media of radio and television. In part, the transformation was fueled by efforts of media producers to profit from 66's appeal to suburban youth, most notably with CBS's weekly television show, *Route 66*. Yet Troup's song also played its part, propagating rhythm and blues images of Route 66 in versions by Chuck Berry and The Rolling Stones. The television series and rock lyrics fused a popular image of Route 66 as *the* highway of American youth culture, even as the road itself was disappearing from the landscape. It was through processes such as these that Route 66 was lifted from the land to become the iconic highway of the American spirit.

ON THE ROAD

The decade of prosperity that followed World War II, with its attendant conformity and homogenization, produced a rebellious youth culture that made itself felt in both literature and music. Among the landmark works was an autobiographical novel by a young New York writer, Jack Kerouac, who had attended Columbia University on a football scholarship. Hearing the Cole Trio's version of "Route 66!" in the spring of 1946 inspired Kerouac to plan his own trip to California for the following year.[1] Studying road maps, Kerouac decided to follow the "long red line called Route 6" that ran from Cape Cod into Nevada.[2] In the spring of 1947, he hitchhiked west from Patterson, New Jersey. Kerouac recalled the symbolic convergence of route sign sixes near Chicago that pointed the way west: "My first ride was a dynamite truck with a red flag, about thirty miles into great green Illinois, the truck driver pointing out the place where Route 6, which we were on, intersects Route 66 before they both shot west for incredible distances."[3]

When he returned that fall, Kerouac began writing a stream of consciousness travelogue-novel about his road trip, typing on a continuous 120-foot roll of pasted paper until he finished in 1951. When Viking published *On the Road* in 1957, the novel became the essential account of postwar wandering on the Western frontier, and the seminal masterwork of the new Beat generation culture.[4] Kerouac's impact exploded with the Signet paperback issued in September 1958. Its cover proclaimed it "the bible of the 'beat generation'" (Fig. 12.1).[5] With this, *On the Road* became the pocket guide to the routeways of the American West, fusing Routes 6 and 66 together into a single Beat roadway.

THE SEARCHERS

The expressive realism of Beat writing had parallels in the new medium of television and the realist dramas it brought into American homes. Early black-and-white television all but demanded exploitation of the film noir style of certain postwar films.[6] Among these stylized realist dramas was an evening series based on an earlier motion picture, *Naked City*, first broadcast by ABC in September 1958. Filmed on location in Manhattan, the series portrayed New York with gritty realism.[7] The series was written by two experienced television producers: Sterling Silliphant, who had written scripts for the *General Electric Theater*, and Herbert Leonard, who had produced the action series *Rin Tin Tin*.[8] Among the *Naked City* cast was a compelling young actor, George Maharis, who both Silliphant and Leonard felt had the potential to star in his own dramatic series.

In the spring of 1959, Silliphant and Leonard met in New York to discuss a project in which Maharis would play a young drifter from the slums of Hell's Kitchen, befriended by a rich playboy who wanders U.S. highways on a quest for adventure and self-discovery. The series, originally called *The Searchers*, was rejected by Columbia Screen Gems as too darkly written and lacking the "franchise" of familiar family forms. Despite this, the project continued to occupy Silliphant and Leonard, who finally self-produced a pilot episode in February 1960. The cast included Maharis, playing Buzz Murdock, and Martin Milner, as the playboy Tom Stiles. The two toured the back roads in a Corvette convertible, selected as the appropriately American sports car from General Motors, who would end up sponsoring the show. Although actually filmed in Covington, Kentucky, the pilot was set in Alabama. Entitled "Black November," this first episode set a precedent for locational realism that was to distinguish the new series, even when the story was set elsewhere.[9]

ROUTE 66

With the pilot completed in March, Silliphant and Leonard offered *The Searchers* to James Aubrey at CBS as a weekly drama. Aubrey found the pilot appealing, but apparently he requested a change in the title to compete more effectively with such ABC offerings as *77 Sunset Strip* and *Surfside 6*.[10] Silliphant changed the series title to *Route 66*. Leonard recalled the name arising as a generic symbol of the American road: "It just seemed right. We shot just a couple of dozen shows along Route 66 but it was a symbolic title . . . It's an expression of going somewhere . . . the best known American highway, cutting across America. It's the backbone of America."[11] It seems unlikely that a more concise statement of the iconic significance of Route 66 will ever be made: "It's an expression of going somewhere."

The producers wanted to use Troup's "Route 66!" behind the opening credits as the show's theme song, and they approached Troup's agent, Sydney Goldstein in Los Angeles. At the last moment, though, CBS Screen Gems asked Nelson Riddle to compose the theme, relieving them from paying royalties, but leaving Troup bitter.[12]

That summer, filming of *Route 66* was underway with location shooting in Louisiana and Los Angeles. In September, *TV Guide* put *Route 66* among the best new dramas in its "Fall Previews" issue, along with a Stone Age cartoon called *The Flintstones* (Fig. 12.2).[13] Reviewing the first episode, *Variety* was impressed by the show's realism: "The concept is different than anything that's been on before: the shooting is all-location and looks it; and the story values, at least in the opener, are adult and hard-hitting."[14]

The initial episode aired Friday, October 7, 1960, at 8:30 p.m., immediately following the Nixon-Kennedy debates which had preempted other programming. This was the second in the historic debates which had galvanized the American public. That the next two episodes of *Route 66* were also preceded by Nixon-Kennedy debates helped establish the series's success. Moreover, the hour-long drama overlapped ABC's *77 Sunset Strip* at 9:00, presenting the home viewer with two Friday night dramas with double-digit titles.[15]

Though few of *Route 66*'s episodes were filmed on U.S. 66, the series's concept was one of adventurous road travel, it was sponsored by Chevrolet, it featured the latest model Corvette convertible, and it cemented the connection of Route 66 to the idea of driving down the highway.[16] The opening shot was of a U.S. 66 shield beside a highway stretching into the distance (possibly filmed outside Los Angeles), accompanied by Riddle's jazz-inflected theme. Episodes shot in the Southwest to maintain the regional flavor included "Layout at Glen Canyon," at the new Colorado River dam in Arizona, and "An Absence of Tears," shot in Hollywood; but most of the second season's scripts were set in small towns far from Route 66: Reno, Nevada; Amity, Ohio; Gloucester, Massachusetts; and Carlisle, Pennsylvania.[17] Leonard recalled how locations were selected: "Sterling would pick locations from the map, interesting places where events were happening, like the big cattle auction in Reno or a major harvest . . . and he and I and a team would visit these places and check them out."[18]

By the third season, Maharis had become a problem. In April 1963, *TV Guide* described a "Blowout on 'Route 66,'" with Maharis walking off the set and leaving Milner to carry the script (Fig. 12.3).[19] Initially Maharis was written out of the series with an "illness," but in the final season of 1963-64 he was replaced by Glenn Corbitt as Lincoln Case. Despite this problem, *Route 66* remained a success for CBS, for its sponsor Chevrolet, and for Nelson Riddle, whose "Route 66 Theme" became a popular jazz hit (Fig. 12.4). The 116 episodes of the four seasons constituted a remarkable achievement for weekly television, with a quality of writing and location shooting that won respect among industry critics.[20]

Beyond these technical achievements, the show's success was ultimately due to its astute blending of existential Beat Generation wanderlust with the enlightened optimism of Kennedy's New Frontier.[21] The series projected an idealization of the highway into American homes as a symbol of both unfettered freedom and essential goodness, an updating of Whitman's "Song of the Open Road," and a Sixties myth for America.

FRIDAY

AN EVENING OF STONE-AGE

AND OTHER NEWCOMERS

ROUTE 66

Conlan Carter (1), Janet De Gore (2), James Whitmore (3), 'Law and Mr. Jones';
Quinn Redeker (4), Gogi Grant (5), Skip Homeier (6), 'Dan Raven'; Gary Clarke (7), Patricia
Donahue (8), Richard Denning (9), Jerry Paris (10), Herbert Rudley (11), 'Michael Shayne';

26

Pat O'Brien (12), Georgine Darcy (13), Helen Kleeb (14), Roger Perry (15), 'Harrigan and Son';
Noel Drayton (16), Kam Tong (17), Charles Quinlivan (18), Philip Ahn (19), 'Mr. Garlund';
Mr. and Mrs. Flintstone (20), 'Flintstones'; 'Route 66' marker (cast was on location).

12.2. *TV Guide, Fall Preview*, September 24, 1960. Friday program promotion, including *The Flintstones* and *Route 66* whose cast, it was noted, was on location. Courtesy of TV Guide Publications Group.

A KNOCK DEVELOPS ON 'ROUTE 66'

George Maharis (left) and Marty Milner tool along in their Corvette.

The trouble may be too much *GAS* and not enough *OIL*

CHUCK BERRY

12.3. "A Knock Develops on 'Route 66,'" *TV Guide*, January 26, 1963. Color location photo of George Maharis (left) and Martin Milner (right) in a Corvette convertible on Michigan Avenue in Chicago during the third season of the popular CBS series. Courtesy of TV Guide Publications Group.

At the same time as the television series, a new dance beat was propelling Route 66 into the world of rock and roll. Among the roots of this new beat was the progressive jazz that had evolved in Los Angeles during World War II. Among its innovators was "Slim Nadine," a stage name for Nat King Cole, who recorded several "blues" recordings with saxophonist Illinois Jacquet in 1946, just before Cole's trio recorded "Route 66!" The running blues beat of Cole's keyboard with the wailing Jacquet saxophone became the basis for an intense rhythm and blues that swept through dance clubs after the war.[22]

Among early rock musicians was St. Louis guitarist Chuck Berry, who had taken Cole's blues vocal style as an inspiration. In 1953, Berry formed a trio of his own with Johnny Johnson on piano and Ebby Harby on drums, who played the Cosmopolitan Club in East St. Louis.[23] Johnson had played in the jazz band Troup had put together on Saipan, while Berry styled his electric guitar after Johnny Moore, a member of Cole's trio. Berry was also influenced by Western swing dance bands with their quick riff chords.[24] Playing in local night clubs, Berry perfected an electric blues style that found an appreciative ear in Chicago bluesman, Muddy Waters. He suggested that Berry approach Chess Records on South Michigan Avenue, which in May 1955 produced Berry's first single, "Maybellene." The record was picked up by Alan Freed for his "Rock 'n Roll" radio show in Cleveland, and it became a summer hit, crossing over from black into white teen culture. Over the next two years, Berry produced a string of hits for Chess that climaxed in "Rock and Roll Music" in May 1957.[25]

Berry's success made him an easy target for harassment in the South, which resulted in Mann Act charges that he had transported a minor from El Paso to St. Louis in 1959.

12.4. *Route 66 Theme*, album cover, 1962. Cover of the Capitol Records album of TV show themes played by Nelson Riddle and his Orchestra, featuring Riddle's music for *Route 66*. The cover displays Jerry White's photo of a U.S. 66 sign on a California highway. Author's collection.

Now you go through St. Louey, Joplin, Missouri,
Oklahoma City looks *o-oh so* pretty,
You'll see Amarillo, Gallup, New Mexico,
Flagstaff, Arizona, Don't forget Winona.
Kingsman, *Bargstow*, San Bernardino.[27]

The changes in Berry's recording were not great, an uncalled for "s" in Kingman, a surprising "g" in Barstow, but they began a process that continues today in which, precisely as the symbolic Route 66 gets stripped from the land, so the song-map geography gets disconnected from the actual geography of the Southwest.

Chess released the Chicago session songs, including "Route 66," on the album *New Juke Box Hits* in June 1961, that received little attention (Fig. 12.5).[28] Berry was found guilty as expected, and he did two and a half years in the federal penitentiary in Terre Haute, Indiana.[29] Like Berry himself, the album was dismissed in the rush of summer hits; and "Route 66" was overlooked as filler, except in England where Chess records were sought after for their American blues sound.

THE ROLLING STONES

Rock and roll in England had found a wide audience among working class and university youth, an audience par-

Extended trials in 1960 took Berry from the stage to the courtroom and prompted Chess to consider recording a bank of songs in case he was imprisoned.[26] In January 1961, with his future in question, Berry went to Chicago and recorded four songs as insurance against his time in prison. Among these was an updated version of "Route 66!" sung to a pounding electric beat, with Johnny Johnson playing boogie-woogie on the piano and Willie Dixon on bass. The lyrics were familiar to Berry from his St. Louis boyhood, but some of the town names beyond Missouri were translated in free-form phonetics:

CHUCK BERRY
NEW JUKE BOX HITS

top tunes

12.5. Chuck Berry, *New Juke Box Hits*, album cover, 1961. Cover of the Chess Records Chuck Berry album that contained Berry's original "Route 66" recording. Author's collection.

ticularly fascinated by the blues music of American blacks. Among this audience was Mick Jagger, then at the London School of Economics, who had been ordering records from the United States and listening to the innovative electric blues.[30] Jagger's childhood friend, Keith Richards, recalled the surprise of running into Jagger on a London train around 1961 and discovering they were both listening to Berry and that Jagger had "been writing away to this, uh, Chess records in Chicago and got on a mailing list."[31] Out of their common interests, in May 1962 Jagger and Richards

formed a rhythm and blues band with friends Brian Jones, Bill Wyman, and Charlie Watts. Inspired by a Muddy Waters song, they called themselves The Rolling Stones and began filling London dance clubs with their energetic versions of American blues hits.[32]

At the same time, other English youth bands were also emerging with an American-style rock and roll beat, most notably The Beatles from the Merseyside clubs of Liverpool. In January 1962, The Beatles returned from a year in Hamburg, Germany, with a tight sound, playing Buddy Holly and Little Richard covers. In November 1962, they released the single, "Love Me Do." During the following year, the band aroused unknown heights of hysteria in England, climaxed by their appearance at the London Palladium in October 1963. American promoters arranged a Carnegie Hall concert and an appearance on the *Ed Sullivan Show* in February 1964 that brought the new British sound to American ears.[33] It was at this point that The Rolling Stones began to look across the Atlantic with dreams of matching the success of The Beatles.

ROUTE 66

Beginning in January 1963, The Rolling Stones recorded covers of Bo Diddley rhumba blues at London's Regent studios. During a second session in June, under their new manager, Andrew Oldham, they recorded the Chuck Berry song, "Come On," for Decca Records. This version became a hit that summer, which encouraged Oldham to complete an album by the new year.[34] During January and February 1964, the Stones returned to the Regent studios to cover American rock and roll songs that would display their energetic style as a British blues band distinct from The Beatles. Among the fifteen titles were the Willie Dixon hit, "I Just Want To Make Love To You," and "Route 66!" With Jagger on lead vocal, the Stones followed Berry's *New Juke Box Hits* version, with an intense driving beat that pushed the original twelve-bar jazz tune into primal rock.[35] The Troup lyrics were similarly energized, with the distant place names translated into unrecognizable sounds:

Well you go from *Senlouey, down* to Missouri,
Oklahoma City looks oh so pretty,
You oughta' see Amarillo, Gallup, New Mexico,
Flagstop, Arizona, Don't forget *Anona*,
Bigston, Bargstow, San Bernardino.[36]

Once on their playlist, "Route 66" became a standard for the Stones. On March 16, 1964, they performed a slow version for the *BBC Radio Hour* at the Camden Theater in London, with the place-names again translated into distorted sounds, only Oklahoma City and San Bernardino survived intact.[37] In April, Decca released *The Rolling Stones* album with "Route 66" as the lead track, thus giving the song signature cachet as raw blues in the style the band had perfected. When London Records released the album in the States in May, "Route 66" was shifted to track 2, still a singular cut on the opening side. The recording brought Troup's postwar hit to a new generation of American youth in a rock and

roll style that was immediately accepted as musical currency (Fig. 12.6).[38]

With the American album, Oldham arranged a June tour, hoping for the success that had been The Beatles, but the Stones aroused little interest in New York and flew directly to Hollywood. There they appeared on *Hollywood Palace,* hosted by Dean Martin, who was baffled by the band. At their San Bernardino concert, they opened with "Route 66" and got wild applause for the hometown lyrics. The band moved on to Chicago, where they made a pilgrimage to Chess Records and had the thrill of recording with their hero, Muddy Waters.[39] Although initially limited to a small following, the Stones established their pounding blues as a mark of British rock and roll and "Route 66" as a signature song which, with the passing years and the immense growth in the band's popularity, has introduced the postwar road lyric to every generation that rediscovers the Stones.

THEM

The Rolling Stones had more immediate impact within British working class culture, which found in the band's blues a source of inspiration. Van Morrison was a young musician from Belfast whose Irish father had brought back American jazz and blues records from his seaman's travels. Taking Jagger as his inspiration, Morrison formed his own rhythm and blues band called Them in the summer of 1964. That year Morrison's own song, "Gloria," made both British and American pop charts.[40] After the Stones released a live album from concerts in Liverpool and Manchester in June 1965, Morrison took their title "Route 66!" for his initial LP release.[41] Once again the place-names of

12.6. The Rolling Stones, *England's Newest Hit Makers,* album cover, 1964. Cover of the London Records Rolling Stones album that contained the London, January 1964 recording of "Route 66." Author's collection.

American towns were reshaped by the driving beat to form a new lyric for the song:

> *It winds* from St. Louey, *down to Missouri,*
> Oklahoma City looks mighty pretty,
> You'll see Amarillo, *Galluck,* New Mexico,
> Flagstop, Arizona, Don't forget Winona,
> *South Park* (!?), *Nine* (?), San Bernardino.[42]

The British blues beat continued to reverberate in American rock and roll with the rising success of the Stones and Them as popular touring bands. The association of "Route 66!" with the English groups remained intact, the song being performed in live concerts well through 1968.[43] The fact that the Troup place-names were now distorted beyond recognition was irrelevant. Many hearing the song for the first time had no idea it referred to a real road. In the hands of these rock musicians, "Route 66!"—and so Route 66 itself—became exactly what Leonard said it was, "an expression of going somewhere." What had been a nearly forgotten novelty hit of the postwar period had been transformed into a rock-and-roll classic that promulgated the identity of Route 66 and exported its free-spirited name wherever in the world rock and roll was heard.

13.1. *Twentysix Gasoline Stations*, 1962. Photo of a Phillips 66 station in Flagstaff from Edward Ruscha's *Twentysix Gasoline Stations*, taken by Edward Ruscha with Joe Goode on one of their Route 66 road trips between Oklahoma City and Los Angeles. By permission of Edward Ruscha.

Chapter Thirteen
Pop Art Highway

Around the time that Chuck Berry was recording "Route 66!" and Silliphant and Leonard were shooting *Route 66*, Los Angeles artists, including Edward Ruscha and Dennis Hopper, were beginning to make Route 66 the subject of a new American Pop Art, deploying a novel iconography of gas stations, motels, and hitchhikers on an endless highway. Ruscha did this in 1963 in his limited edition high-art book, *Twentysix Gasoline Stations;* Hopper in 1969 in his critically acclaimed and popular film, *Easy Rider.* In 1974, Stanley Marsh III and the Ant Farm, an art association, constructed Cadillac Ranch next to Route 66 near Amarillo, Texas, as a sculptural monument to the American automobile. As the old highway was being replaced by the new interstates, it was getting a whole new lease on life as a symbol.

TWENTYSIX GASOLINE STATIONS

Ed Ruscha (pronounced "Rew-shay") was a young artist who, after his high school graduation in 1956, had taken U.S. 66 from his hometown of Oklahoma City to Los Angeles to make his name in Hollywood.[1] He enrolled in the Disney-funded Chouinard Institute where he found Joe Goode, a hometown friend. Together Ruscha and Goode experimented with a realist art of the suburban landscape that would come to define the Southern California style. In 1961, Ruscha traveled to Europe, where he learned from the Dadaists about the power of the symbolic object. Returning to Los Angeles, Ruscha began to paint scenes of popular, everyday life, informed by his Polish Catholic heritage.[2]

Driving U.S. 66 in 1962 to visit family in Oklahoma City, Ruscha and Goode became fascinated by the symbolism of the highway scene. Ruscha conceived of a photo book that would treat the roadside filling stations like the stations of the cross, each allowed its own personality and meaning.[3] Starting from Los Angeles, Ruscha took snapshots in various locations, both night and day. He photographed Texaco and Phillips 66 stations, but more often independents and local trading posts. For the book, Ruscha arranged the photos in approximate sequence from California to Oklahoma, noting the location and the brand of gasoline.

Ruscha published *Twentysix Gasoline Stations* in January 1963, in an edition of 400, primarily sold to friends and Los Angeles art galleries.[4] The pioneering book captured the roadside architecture in simple snapshots, documenting the highway itself as part of the image (Fig. 13.1).[5] The imagery inspired Ruscha's most famous painting, *Standard Station, Amarillo, Texas*, which Hollywood actor and photographer Dennis Hopper purchased in 1963.[6] Both *Twentysix Gasoline Stations* and *Standard Station, Amarillo, Texas* became important icons in the art revolution called Pop Art, and they established Ruscha as an important West Coast proponent.[7] They also helped establish the modern American highway as a valid subject for art; and, although U.S. 66 was never named, its spirit, and the American spirit it was increasingly coming to symbolize, thoroughly pervaded Ruscha's project. Had Ruscha's gas stations not been, as they were, *on* U.S. 66, they would have been presumed to be there, given the character of the road Leonard had described as "the best known American highway" and "the backbone of America." *Any* highway, unless otherwise designated, was presumed to be U.S. 66.

EASY RIDER

A different realism found expression in Hollywood movies of the period that exploited California highways as settings in the tradition of *The Grapes of Wrath*. An early example of such neo-documentary road films was *The Wild One* of 1955, starring Marlon Brando as an outlaw biker. In this film, the motorcycle was a key element in script development, almost a character. Outlaw motorcycle films developed a cult following among cinema artists and laid a foundation for the work of a second generation that came of age during the 1960s. It was this generation that produced the modern motorcycle Western, *Easy Rider*.

The original idea for a biker film came from Peter Fonda, the son of Henry Fonda, the star of *The Grapes of Wrath*. In September 1967, the younger Fonda was in Toronto for a promotion of Roger Corman's motorcycle gang film, *The Wild Angels*. The film's poster inspired Fonda to think about producing his own motorcycle movie, one which would capture contemporary youth culture with biker heroes on an endless Western roadtrip. To further the project, he invited his friend Dennis Hopper. Fonda and Hopper had worked together on *The Trip*, Corman's film about LSD and hippie youth culture completed earlier that year. Hopper had established an acting career in films such as *Giant* with James Dean in 1955, and he had been photographing Los Angeles in the new Pop Art style along with Ruscha and David Hockney.[9] Fonda and Hopper discussed a hippie-biker Western they variously called *The Loners* or *Mardi Gras*. To help with the script, they called in Terry Southern, who had made his name reworking movies such as *Dr. Strangelove* and *Casino Royale*. With Southern in New York in November 1967, Fonda and Hopper taped a free-form dialogue about two characters, to be played by Fonda and Hopper: Captain America and Buffalo Billie, who would travel cross-country in search of self-revelation, smoking dope and dropping acid along the way. They called their radical story with its counter-culture heroes *Easy Rider*. With a script in hand, Hopper and Fonda found backers in Los Angeles by early December 1967.[10]

Filming began in New Orleans during Mardi Gras, February 1968. Hopper directed and played Cowboy Billie, and Fonda played Captain America with a U.S. flag stitched on his motorcycle jacket. Shooting was confused and Hopper and Fonda were hopelessly conflicted. The crew retreated to Los Angeles in March amid the sad news of Dr. Martin Luther King, Jr.'s assassination. Trying to restart the project, Fonda and Hopper began filming the road sequence from California to Louisiana, using old Los Angeles Police Department motorcycles cut as low riders. Fonda experimented with the rebuilt bikes around the city, as Hopper shot a sequence of billboards along Sunset Boulevard for the titles.[11] By mid-March, they were shooting in the Mojave Desert. Fonda later recalled shooting the crossing of the Colorado River bridge on the new Interstate 40: "We crossed the Colorado River many times for different lenses or camera angles, riding slowly, at twenty-five to thirty miles per hour so as not to make the background a blur."[12] This was, of course, the very spot where Fonda's father, Henry, had played Tom Joad in the 1939 *The Grapes of Wrath* (Fig. 13.2), a poignant revelation of U.S. 66's generation-spanning significance. [13]

The crew continued east into Arizona for the motorcycle scenes, using older, two-lane sections of U.S. 66 between Kingman and Flagstaff.[14] This location work was directed by Laszlo Kovacs, who had fled Budapest in the Hungarian uprising of 1956 and brought a sharp European perspective to the Western landscape. The crew headed north to Sacred Mountain and Sunset Crater National Monument, before returning to Route 66 and Taos, New Mexico, where Hop-

per had a vacation home. Shooting continued across the Texas panhandle in June, introducing a new character, George Hanson, played by Jack Nicholson, who had known Hopper from earlier Corman movies. In Texas, the news of Bobby Kennedy's assassination further shocked the cast. Filming wrapped in Louisiana by the end of July 1968.[15]

Easy Rider was edited by Fonda and Nicholson to a commercial length of two hours, overlaid with a soundtrack of contemporary rock songs by leading artists, including The Byrds, Jimi Hendrix, and Steppenwolf.[16] To tighten the film, the Sunset Boulevard billboard footage was replaced by a title sequence shot at the Los Angeles airport, LAX, from which the film cut to the opening sequence along Route 66 at the Colorado River. When shown at the Cannes Film Festival in May 1969, the film received standing ovations.[17] Similar applause greeted the New York premier. The *New York Times* review highlighted the motorcycle scenes with Fonda and Hopper along the unnamed Route 66: "They roll down macadam highways that look like black velvet ribbons, under skies of incredible purity, and the soundtrack rocks with oddly counterpointed emotions of Steppenwolf, the Byrds, the Electric Prunes, dark and smoky cries for liberation."[18]

When *Easy Rider* reached national distribution in August 1969, it became another touchstone for rebellious youth, especially in the wake of the traumatic events that had convulsed America in 1968.[19] The endless highway imagery, backed by psychedelic rock music, captured the existential search that Jack Kerouac had pioneered in *On the Road,* now presented as a rainbow-colored landscape of escape. Again, the absence of U.S. 66 shields was irrelevant. What other road could it be?

13.2. *Easy Rider*, 1968. Photographic still, Laszlo Kovacs, cinematographer, showing Peter Fonda (right) and Dennis Hopper (left) on the U.S. 66/I-40 Colorado River bridge at the California/Arizona state line. By permission of Columbia Pictures.

The concept of creating a monumental sculpture honoring Route 66 grew out of converging artistic interests in Texas in 1973. The proposal to bury classic, Cadillac tail-fin cars along the highway originated with San Francisco's Ant Farm, an association of art students and architects formed in 1968 to reinterpret American cultural icons in contemporary form.[20] Its founders, Chip Lord, Hudson Marquez, and Doug Michels, had become fascinated by the styling of postwar Cadillacs with their exaggerated rear fins. These postwar designs were credited to Harvey Earl, at General Motors, who had been inspired by World War II aircraft fighters. Earl first styled fins on the 1948 Cadillac, increasing their height each year until 1959, when the tail fin, fashioned like a rocket ship, almost reached a full foot.[21] In 1973, the Ant Farm discovered a book on these Cadillac designs and reworked the imagery for San Francisco-based *Rolling Stone* magazine, producing a circle of tail fins to honor Earl's achievement (Fig. 13.3):[22] "Rest in peace, Harvey Earl, with your wartime visions. And thank you Harley Earl, for leaving us this absurd, beautiful, obscene classic—the 1959 Cadillac."[23]

The Ant Farm's interest converged with that of Texas millionaire Stanley Marsh III. His fortune in natural gas had allowed him to indulge a taste for large-scale Pop Art installations at his Hidden Art Ranch west of Amarillo. In 1969, he had Claus Oldenburg's "Pool Table" of cut grass cleared on the ranch and, in 1973, had hired the famed earthworks sculptor, Robert Smithson, to build a monumental *Amarillo Ramp*, after Smithson's *Spiral Jetty* at the Great Salt Lake.[24] When the Ant Farm approached Marsh in May 1973 with the proposal for a Cadillac monument, it found him immediately receptive.[25]

Discussions dragged on through March 1974. The Ant Farm's first proposal was to bury the cars in a local Amarillo city park. Civic authorities objected, and Marsh decided to build the project at his Art Ranch on U.S. 66, recently widened to accommodate Interstate 40, eight miles west of the city.[26] Marsh placed ads in the *Amarillo Globe Times* offering to buy "Used Cadillacs" and found a number of willing sellers. During May, Marsh and the Ant Farm were able to acquire most of the classic, tail-fin Cadillacs they needed. Ultimately ten of the Cadillacs were buried twenty feet apart, nose first in the concrete, angled to match the inclination of the Great Pyramid at Cheops.[27] Set on the crest of a shallow ridge, they created an impressive silhouette when seen from traffic passing on Interstate 40.[28] Marsh was fully aware of the symbolism of setting the classic cars along the edge of the famous highway. As he quipped when interviewed by *Sports Illustrated*: "'I didn't want them to be haphazard,' he explains. No, he wanted Route 66 drivers to know for sure that the Cadillacs had been planted there by members of some highly intelligent civilization."[29]

The Cadillac Ranch was officially dedicated on June 21, 1974, with a champagne party on Marsh's spread.[30] Within a year, the Ant Farm installation had become an international sensation and a major tourist attraction. Newspapers from London to Rome cited Marsh as an eccentric collector and referred to his Art Ranch as the most notable museum in the Texas panhandle.[31] In 1976, the Ant Farm published an historical account of postwar design, *Automerica*, written by Lord. Cadillac Ranch graced the cover (Fig. 13.4), which brought further publicity.[32] Significantly, the association between the Cadillac Ranch and Route 66 was seen as the symbolic heart of the project, honoring both the dying

13.3. "The Cadillac Tail Fins–1948-59–have come full circle." *Rolling Stone*, August 29, 1974. Color collage by Chip Lord and the Ant Farm showing the development of the postwar Cadillac tail fins designed by Harvey Earl for General Motors. By permission of Chip Lord.

highway and these dated versions of the American automobile. Somehow the project marked the moment when the nation recognized that Route 66 had become a road of historic significance, and that its shields had become antique classics like the Cadillacs buried beside the new Interstate.

MICRO-SOFT

In the last decade of Route 66's life as a named highway, one final association was to link the road with the new age symbolized by the personal computer. In January 1975, *Pop-ular Electronics* ran an ad for a small electronics company called MITS, then located on Central Avenue along U.S. 66 in Albuquerque, which offered the Altair 8800 as the "World's First Microcomputer Kit."[33] At Harvard University, sophomore Bill Gates and his hometown Seattle friend, Paul Allen, saw the ad and recognized an opportunity to write a corporate-style computer program for the new home-built machine.[34] Gates and Allen called MITS to offer their programming services. Thinking them a Cambridge computer firm, MITS invited Allen to Albuquerque in Feb-

ruary.[35] Expecting an impressive office park, Allen was shocked by the roadside highway location:

> The word "unimposing" didn't begin to describe it. Just once-fabled and now fallen Route 66, the MITS

13.4. *Automerica,* 1978. Signet Press jacket cover by Bud Lee showing Chip Lord and the Ant Farm's original *Cadillac Ranch* installation for Stanley Marsh III along U.S. 66/I-40 in Amarillo, Texas. By permission of Bud Lee.

headquarters, which the company had occupied since its initial days of glory in the calculator business, on a nondescript storefront strip with an office supply shop and massage parlor.[36]

Much to Allen's surprise, the simple program he had quickly written at the airport actually worked on the Altair as it typed out its first command. The programming success immediately brought Gates down from Cambridge in March to work out details with MITS. He and Allen stayed at the Sundowner Motel on Central Avenue, still marked with its U.S. 66 shields.[37] The contract with MITS led Gates and Allen to form their own computer programming company in July 1975, which they registered as Micro-Soft, located at the Two Park Central Building, the company's first headquarters.[38] Gates soon dropped out of Harvard and hired a group of young computer programmers from the University of New Mexico. With increasing orders and limited access from Albuquerque, Gates and Allen decided to move their operation to their home base in Seattle in 1978, streamlining its name to Microsoft.[39] Though located on Central Avenue for but a brief moment, the presence of Micro-Soft on Route 66 foreshadowed that this road that had originated in the tourist-oriented boosterism of the Jazz Age was going to see its end in the era of the computer industry.

14.1. "End of Route 66," *Chicago Sun Times*, January 17, 1977. News photograph of U.S. 66 signs being taken down, Jackson Boulevard, downtown Chicago. Courtesy of Illinois State Historical Society.

Chapter Fourteen
Magical Road

WITH THE CONTINUAL DEVELOPMENT of the Interstate Highway System after 1956, original sections of U.S. 66 were gradually replaced by modern, limited-access freeways. The Interstate program proceeded on a state-by-state basis, with most of the early two-lane roadway upgraded by 1977. After this time, a feeling of historic nostalgia began to coalesce around the highway, with the final bypass of U.S. 66 in Williams, Arizona, completed in 1984, and the decommissioning of the federal number in 1985. A spirit of symbolic tribute grew in the national press, which fused the imagery of America's Main Street and the Dust Bowl, Bobby Troup and the Chevrolet Corvette Stingray. These elements constituted the core of a Route 66 iconography that continued to evolve after the decommissioning of the federal route in 1985. In the process, the historical events were stirred together into a national mythology of the American road; that is, the Open Road.

CHICAGO SIGNS

The replacement of Route 66 had begun with the opening of the Turner and Will Rogers turnpikes in Oklahoma, since they had been included as parts of I-44 when the federal Interstate numbers were assigned in 1957.[1] Within ten years, interstate construction programs had upgraded much of the Route 66 corridor to express highway standards (see Fig. 11.3).[2] From Chicago the roadway had been improved as a divided highway across central Illinois, with I-55 bypassing Bloomington and Springfield. Across the Mississippi, four-lane segments continued as I-44 through the Ozark Highlands of Missouri to Springfield and Joplin, connecting with the Will Rogers Turnpike in Oklahoma.

By 1969, Oklahoma sections of Route 66 had been improved as a divided highway with short bypass-segments of I-40 across western Oklahoma and the Texas panhandle to Amarillo.[3] West of Albuquerque into Gallup, U.S. 66

remained a narrow, two-lane road with only portions of limited access highway; in Arizona brief stretches of I-40 had been constructed near Flagstaff and Kingman, leaving much of the road in prewar alignment. After the highway crossed the Colorado River into California on the new span of I-40, it returned to the older U.S. 66 alignment across the Mojave Desert to Barstow. From this point, the highway had been upgraded to Interstate standards as I-15 over the Cajon Pass into San Bernardino, continuing into Los Angeles and the Pacific Ocean at Santa Monica as I-10.[4] For a brief moment, Route 66 had been assigned along the new Pasadena and Hollywood freeways through the four-level "stack" interchange, connecting to the new San Diego Freeway (I-405) in West Los Angeles in 1960.[5] With the opening of the Santa Monica Freeway (I-10) in 1965, however, signage for U.S. 66 was eliminated west of Pasadena, ten miles north of downtown Los Angeles; the federal signs were also removed from Santa Monica Boulevard, thereby disconnecting Route 66 from the Pacific Ocean.[6] This was the first historic section of U.S. 66 to disappear from state road maps, and it signaled a trend in other state highway departments (see Fig. 11.3).

With the completion of I-40 across the Mojave Desert from Needles to Barstow in 1974, the California Highway Department removed all U.S. 66 shields from the original highway alignment.[7] Surviving sections, such as Foothill Boulevard between San Bernardino and Pasadena, were then posted as State Route 66, leaving only relic portions intact.[8] The wholesale elimination of U.S. Route 66 in California was repeated by the Missouri and Illinois transportation departments. On January 17, 1977, Illinois DOT workers removed the federal shields on Jackson Boulevard in Chicago's Grant Park that had marked the "End of Route 66" at Lake Shore Drive (see Fig. 14.1).[9] Writing in the *Los Angeles Times*, Michael Seller acknowledged the passing of a "National Metaphor," recalling the landmarks in popular culture that had been defined by the highway:

> First, John Steinbeck's *The Grapes of Wrath* celebrated it. Then the song "Route 66" immortalized Gallup, Tucumcari [sic] and other unlikely places. Finally, there was the television show of the same name about two young drifters in a Corvette.[10]

As Route 66 was dismembered, so the final efforts of the Main Street Association aimed to forestall closure. In Clinton, Oklahoma, Association Secretary Jack Cutberth published a brochure in 1974 with the U.S. 66 shield depicted in Interstate colors to match the modern numbering of I-55 and I-10 from Illinois to California.[11] With Cutberth's death in 1978, however, the Main Street Association quietly disbanded and accepted the reality of the Interstate highways.[12] From this moment, the end of Route 66 became obvious and the survival of the last signed sections became a matter of historic curiosity. As Thomas Pew wrote in *American Heritage*:

> The Route 66 of memory is gone now, or most of it. Over the past two decades the freeway called Interstate 40 has taken away its name and its number, as well as obliterating much of the old roadbed, bypassing most of its little towns, leaving only isolated and poorly maintained stretches of the original highway.[13]

With Route 66 disconnected from Lake Michigan and the Pacific Ocean, only the interior portions remained marked from Joplin, Missouri, to the Colorado River in Arizona. As Interstate bypasses were completed, the dwindling number of surviving two-lane sections became the object of intense fascination. In 1981, *Arizona Highways* referred to Route 66 as "The Yellow Brick Road" of dreams between the glittering Oz of Chicago and the promise of Los Angeles, while the *New York Times*, quoting the Troup song lyrics, reported the sudden "silence of Route 66" with the completion of I-40 around Tucumcari, on July 4, 1981.[14] Two years later, *Life* magazine honored "the most famous highway in America" with a pictorial feature on Troup and his song map.[15] By 1984, only one original length of U.S. 66 remained signed through Williams, Arizona. On October 13, the last six miles of I-40 around Williams were officially completed, with ceremonies that included Bobby Troup singing his famous road song. The AP story likened the passing to an historic Western wagon trail (Fig. 14.2): "Route 66, the highway made famous in song, story and television, yesterday followed into history the pioneers and prospectors who once traveled the same route."[16]

With the completion of the Williams bypass, the American Association of State Highway and Transportation Officials (AASHTO), successor to AASHO, voted for the "Elimination of U.S. Route 66" at a meeting of the Route Numbering Committee in Duluth, Minnesota, on June 26, 1985.[17] Beyond the exceptional renumbering of U.S. 55 to U.S. 52 in Minnesota and Iowa in 1952, the decommissioning of U.S. 66 was the only federal highway of the original 1926 system to be eliminated from the national network.[18]

Examiner graphics

No more kicks on Route 66

WILLIAMS, Ariz. (AP) — Route 66, the highway made famous in song, story and television, yesterday followed into history the pioneers and prospectors who once traveled the same route.

A parade of vintage cars was scheduled as the last two-lane segment of U.S. 66, which once traversed eight states and three time zones from Chicago to Santa Monica, was bypassed by six miles of Interstate 40 around the north side of this northern Arizona town.

In its better days, the road was the setting for John Steinbeck's 1939 novel "The Grapes of Wrath" and a 1960s television series, "Route 66."

Bobby Troupe urged people to "Get your kicks on Route 66" in the song "Route 6f," which he wrote in the mid-1940s while driving from Pennsylvania to Los Angeles to try his hand in Hollywood.

Troupe was on hand for the elaborate ribbon-cutting ceremonies yesterday for the new stretch of I-40.

Much of the road followed a wilderness path toward California that was forged in 1857 by a caravan of camels commanded by Navy Lt. Edward Beale.

Wagon trains, cattlemen and finally trucks and cars followed, and the route was designated U.S. 66 in 1926.

The interstates began to replace Route 66 in the mid-1950s, and portions of Route 66 either were torn up as part of the interstate construction effort, reduced to frontage road or bypassed and abandoned.

14.2. "No More Kicks on Route 66," *San Francisco Examiner*, October 14, 1984. Graphic map showing the final section of U.S. 66 being replaced by I-40 in Williams, Arizona. By permission of *San Francisco Examiner*.

Reflecting the popular appeal of the highway, an AASHTO press release quoted the Troup song lyrics, "More than 2,000 miles all the way," while noting that the remaining mileage of the original highway would be marked as "Old U.S. 66" in New Mexico and by historic plaques in Oklahoma.[19] The chairman of the AASHTO Numbering Committee, Jack Freidenrich, acknowledged the historic symbolism of U.S. 66, but justified the decertification in the interest of progress: "'Nostalgia is an integral part of the American people,' he said. 'We like to cling to that kind of thing. If we were eliminating Route ABC, no one except local folks would care. I think this interest is kind of neat.'"[20]

MAGICAL ROAD

The vote to eliminate U.S. 66 from the federal highway system triggered an outpouring of reflective tributes from cultural historians who expanded the Route 66 iconography from the slender outlines given in the popular press. Among the most insightful was Phil Patton, who had completed his book, *Open Road,* the year following the AASHTO decision. In a chapter devoted to the "Myths of Route 66," Patton reviewed the power of the numbers themselves to promote the romantic legend of the highway as a transcontinental road:

> Sixty-six, of course, has always stood for a whole class of roads. The Okies didn't all take 66, they also took U.S. 54 and U.S. 80. Tourists took a number of roads to California. But 66, perhaps due to its mellifluous (and quite accidental) numbering, is the road that named the myth.[21]

The final closure of Route 66 in Arizona prompted local historians to preserve sections of the original highway within their state. In Kingman, the Historic Route 66 Association of Arizona was formed in November 1987 to mark the bypassed loop from Ash Fork to Seligman as State Highway 66, and to maintain the original Gold Road to Topock over the Sitgreaves Pass as an historic auto trail.[22] The Association produced a *Family Tour Guide* in 1989 for a "Fun Run" of antique autos over the 143-mile route.[23] The Kingman efforts also stimulated historic preservation of early sections of the National Old Trails Highway, near Williams through the Kaibab National Forest, and the discovery of original roadbeds of early U.S. 66 that required professional archeological analysis.[24] Such scholarly concern established precedents for the historic Route 66 surveys that followed in other states, from Oklahoma to Illinois, resulting in a National Park Service study of the highway in 1989, which proposed federal protection for the decertified federal routeway.[25]

In 1988, the historic retrospect of Route 66 was given formal confirmation by the University of Oklahoma Press, with publication of *Route 66: The Highway and Its People* by Quinta Scott of St. Louis and Susan Croce Kelly of Chicago.[28] Primary research into the early history of the highway resulted in oral interviews with key figures such as Ruth Seigler Avery, Gladys Cutberth, and Cynthia Troup, providing a basic chronology for understanding the development of Route 66 imagery in the national culture. In summarizing the symbolic elements, Kelly defined the context of Route 66 as a Western trail in the frontier tradition:

> The road that had been created by a Tulsa businessman and sent from the populated center of the

United States across the great wilderness of the Southwest had taken on a life of its own. There had been a book, a song, a television show and three generations of people who grew up and grew old with Route 66.[27]

Within two years of the Oklahoma Press study, the commercial market was opened by St. Martin's Press in New York with a companion pair of Route 66 books, including color printing and historic maps that presented the highway imagery in an attractive graphic style.[28] The larger volume, *Route 66: The Mother Road* by Michael Wallis of Tulsa, Oklahoma, offered a symbolic history where the factual elements dissolve into a magical world of memory:

Route 66. Just the name is magic. *Route 66.* It conjures

up all kinds of images. *Route 66.* An artery linking much of the nation. *Route 66.* An inspiration to literature, music, drama, art, and a nation of dreamers. *Route 66.* A highway fashioned from vision and ingenuity. *Route 66.* A broken chain of concrete and asphalt. *Route 66.* It has forever meant "going somewhere."[29]

The companion volume, *Route 66 Traveler's Guide* by Tom Snyder of California, adopted the format Rittenhouse had used in his *Guide Book to Highway 66*.[30] Original base maps from the Automobile Club of Southern California showed original alignments with an overlay of modern Interstate locations (Fig. 14.3). As Wallis had articulated the highway's magical power, so Snyder confirmed the evocative effect of the route name as an attraction:

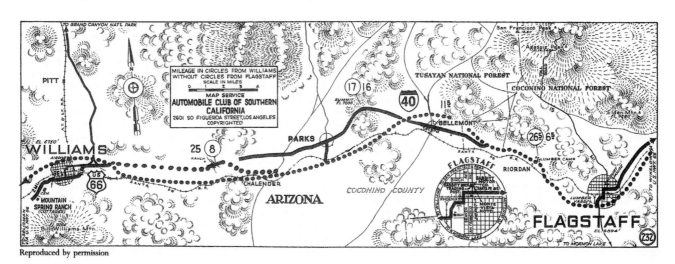

Reproduced by permission

14.3. *Route 66 Traveler's Guide,* 1990. Map from Tom Snyder's book showing the section of U.S. 66 from Williams to Flagstaff as portrayed in the Automobile Club of Southern California (1933) strip map, together with the modern I-40 alignments. Courtesy of St. Martin's Press.

But Route 66, ah, Route 66 was never ordinary. From its commissioning in 1926, the first highway to link Chicago and Los Angeles, US 66 was to townspeople along the route and travelers alike, something special. Soon it was even being called the "most magical road in all the world." And by any standard, that's what it became.[31]

Such magical imagery fused the specific elements of Route 66 into *the* iconic American highway, combining the tradition of the Western frontier trail with the modern memory of the automobile, where the Dust Bowl migrant and rock-and-roll travelers are part of the same pantheon of honor.[32] The final closure of Route 66 within the living memory of its travelers contributed to the sense of sudden loss, evoking the memory of the highway as a departed spirit. In this light, the profusion of books and mementos also relates to the popular nostalgia that has developed with the recollection of open-road travel in the pre-Interstate era.[33] The fascination with Route 66 since 1985 has not only shown a deep core of affection for the highway which has outlasted its decommissioning, but also transformed the words "Route 66" into a generic symbol of the American road with great power both at home and abroad.

Chapter Fifteen
Highway Icon Revisited

Route 66 was the American highway of the twentieth century, straddling it from Jazz Age to Computer Age, in gravel and concrete, in song and film, in television and Pop Art. Projected as an idea in the euphoria of the California Gold Rush, Route 66 endures as an idea in the euphoria of the Internet; but, between 1926 and 1985, the idea was a road, U.S. 66, a fact on the ground that did much to make one nation out of the United States. As the road was traveled, its meaning changed: initially the resolution of an ancient dream of a direct route to the Pacific, Route 66 became an incarnation of Walt Whitman's democratic ideal of the Open Road.

Its persistent power arose from its physical reality. The route connected two rich realms, the Mississippi River Basin and the Pacific Coast, across barriers of mountain and desert. Unlike more northerly alternatives, the 66 route offered an all-weather road that went *around* the mountains.

It is here, in these simple facts, that its power to evoke the idea of a frontier pathway to the Pacific had its roots, though the origin of the *idea* of a connection between the Atlantic and the Pacific lay elsewhere, in the dream of Western Europeans to reach the Orient by sailing west across the ocean. In this sense, the highway's origins lay in those desires that prompted Christopher Columbus to seek a direct route to the Indies which, frustrated by the surprise of the Americas, led to the explorations of the Spanish, and the French and Anglo-American quest for a Northwest Passage. The difficulty of crossing the Rockies saw the idea of the Northwest Passage evolve during the Gold Rush into a railroad to San Francisco, and finally into a railroad and auto highway south around the Rocky Mountains to Los Angeles. This centuries-long effort to find a level pathway across the continent underwrites Route 66's unique power to embody the westward propulsion of American culture.

That said, the history of U.S. 66 itself was a matter of conquering the desert void between the Mississippi and the Rio Grande, the *terra incognita* of Indian Territory, Oklahoma. Each incarnation of the route recast this journey across the Indian lands in its own terms, from the Pacific railroad through the Ozark Trails, to U.S. 66. Once established as a safe passage, U.S. 66 became an auto route for Main Street boosters, Dust Bowl migrants, and post-World War II travelers to California, in the process transcending its pavement to become a metaphor for self-exploration.

While the antecedents of Route 66 *are* to be found in the Gold Rush railroads of the nineteenth century and their predecessors, the modern highway was defined in the auto era of the twentieth century. Here the Bunion Derby and the Dust Bowl are fused with Corvettes and The Rolling Stones to constitute a singular icon that compresses historic time and recent memory in the popular myth called Route 66. Each generation of this image was projected into American culture through the popular media of its time.

Fueling this fusion was the essential populism of American society that saw, and continues to see, in Route 66 an appealing icon of its democratic freedom, expressed as the freedom to explore the American West as an individual dream. Through most of its history, most of the U.S. has been open to all its citizens without permission or passport, and this has been especially true since the advent of the automobile which has so encouraged free movement across the continent. This idea of personal travel constituted the essence of the "mother road" in *The Grapes of Wrath*, the song-map lyrics of "Get Your Kicks!," and the images of *Easy Rider*.

IMAGINARY LINES AND MAGICAL NUMBERS

In the beginning, Route 66 was a line drawn by the imagination. In giving substance to this linerality, Lewis and Clark demonstrated in 1805 that there was no natural waterway connecting the Mississippi and the Pacific. Line after line was subsequently projected over the mountains and across the desert to produce the series of proto-Route 66s that reoriented travel progressively farther south, from the Pacific Northwest to San Francisco and finally to Los Angeles. As these projected lines were attempted, they were refined under pressure from both the landscape and its travelers. In this way Route 66 ultimately realized the imaginary line of the Thirty-Fifth Parallel Railroad that Senator Gwin had proposed in 1853. This line held a compelling logic for those who saw in the 35° parallel an aspect of America's manifest destiny. It is this power of these successive lines across the void of the Southwest, and the dreams these lines embodied, that gave Route 66 its national currency as a special road destined to California by special forces. This was the attraction of the federal U.S. 66 route from Chicago to Los Angeles, which was to bring prosperity to the void called Oklahoma. This was one of the things that made Route 66 the Mother Road during the Dust Bowl and a magic road for postwar tourists. It was this power that encouraged it to be literally lifted from the map by the Beat writers and hippie bikers who once again made of 66 an imaginary line, but this time of *self*-exploration.

To claim that the root of the road's power lies in the simple physical facts is not to deny the power of the imagination, only to temper it. The role of the imagination in the history of Route 66 is enormous, and beyond the desires embodied in these lines projected across the West were the names, numbers, and images associated with them. The Northwest Passage was one such name, but another was the 35° parallel, understood not only as a line midway between the northern limits of American power in Canada and its southern limits in Mexico, but as a *number* whose simple definitiveness seemed to offer at least a mental security through the uncharted lands of New Mexico and Arizona.

This numerical power was transformed into the nominal power of named routes in the early auto era of the Ozark and National Old Trails highways; but once the possibility of numbering a new route was raised, the choice of the number became a paramount concern. Nothing more certainly illustrates the power of a name than the battle over U.S. 60 that took place between Oklahoma and Missouri on the one hand, and Kentucky on the other. The questions arising from the choice of the double sixes on April 30, 1926, are among the most vexing in the iconography of Route 66. Did Avery simply resurrect his sample 66 shields from 1925? Or did Page *choose* the number as a rational alternative to 68? Did any of them realize the alliterative power of 66? Did they understand the number's graphic strength? That such questions are still debated casts a mystical aura over the highway's iconography.

Once established, of course, 66 became a potent token not only for marking the new route, but also for advertising; first *of* the highway by the Main Street Association, then by association *with* the highway by Phillips 66. Once heard, the highway's name was unlikely to be forgotten, which is part of the reason the U.S. 66 shields became *the* signposts for the biblical exodus from the Dust Bowl. Writing the num-

bers might have saved Steinbeck time in composing *The Grapes of Wrath,* but, marching down the page, they also were powerful graphic symbols. A similar effect was realized by the Troups singing the route's name. When performed by the King Cole Trio, "Get Your Kicks" inspired Kerouac to take the trip that became *On the Road,* the Beat Generation's most significant road map. The numbers appealed to CBS producers as a primetime alternative to ABC's *77 Sunset Strip.* And they fueled the rock-and-roll renditions of the Troup lyrics in the 1960s by Chuck Berry and The Rolling Stones. It may also have been the appeal of the numbers that gave I-66 its special place from Washington, D.C., when the new Interstate highways were assigned in 1957, and aroused such concern when U.S. 66 was decommissioned in 1985. The history of Route 66 is fraught with this power of special numbers to bring meaning to the mundane.

AUTO RIVER

If questions of imaginary lines and magical numbers are put aside, further sources of Route 66's iconography may be found in its role as an automobile channel flowing between the Mississippi and the Pacific. In the prehistoric period, the separation between the Pueblo peoples on the Rio Grande and the pyramid centers on the Mississippi was reinforced by the lack of any kind of navigable waterway between the two civilizations. The Canadian River may well have been used as a trade route by the bison hunters, but it dried out in the Staked Plains of Texas well before reaching the Rio Grande. When Spanish explorers further discovered that the Colorado was entrenched in deep canyons, they became convinced that the only overland trail from Santa

Fe to Los Angeles was the circuitous loop north through the mesas to Las Vegas and so south over the Mojave Desert.

Trails worked out by American fur trappers confirmed the fact that no natural waterway connected the Great Plains and the Sierra Nevada Mountains. The Pacific Railroad surveys traced out possible pathways across the New Mexico Territory south of the Grand Canyon along the $35°$ parallel, but again provided no absolute assurance of a passable route to California. Moreover, the political realities of Indian Territory and the Missouri Compromise kept Northern emigrants from the Southern route across New Mexico.

The construction of the Santa Fe Railroad located an iron road between Albuquerque and Los Angeles in 1886. Nevertheless, the cultural barrier of Indian Territory discouraged the construction of a direct line from St. Louis, and indeed such a line remained unfinished at the time of Oklahoma statehood in 1907. It was at this moment that the National Old Trails, an auto highway, emerged as a practical road to California, although even this route followed the traditional Santa Fe detour around Oklahoma. The course of the new western auto route through Oklahoma was only established with the Ozark Trails Association and the western links to Santa Fe through Amarillo in 1917. From this point forward, the Ozark Trails began to divert traffic from St. Louis through Tulsa and Oklahoma City, directly across the Texas panhandle to Albuquerque and so on to California. Yet, as recently as the end of World War I, the Ozark Trails was merely a paper route on tourist maps.

The assignment of a federal highway route through Oklahoma in 1925 gave support to the direct diagonal that connected Chicago with Los Angeles through Tulsa as U.S. 60.

Even renumbered as U.S. 66, the federal route remained no more than a symbol on government maps. Only with the formation of the Highway 66 Association and the running of the Bunion Derby in 1928 was it demonstrated that this new transcontinental road was truly a shorter and more interesting course for California tourist traffic.

Ironically it was the Dust Bowl that ensured Highway 66 enduring fame as the primary westward channel from Oklahoma to the West. The mass movement of humanity inscribed the auto route in the minds of migrants and its direct way west became the most obvious course to California, fully paved only in 1937. During World War II, it became a strategic route between Chicago and Los Angeles, and after the war Route 66 became the natural way to go. The ascendance of Los Angeles as the center of California culture insured that Route 66 would become the reference road for the suburban cities developing in Southern California.

With the creation of the Interstate Highway System in 1956, Route 66 was established as *the* primary traffic artery across the Southwest. Like a natural river, this auto river had evolved smoother and smoother alignments for handling traffic. Former loops of abandoned highway litter the landscape like oxbows (Fig. 15.1). In this analogy, Route 66 had become the long-sought waterway to the West, perhaps not a Northwest but a Southwest passage which, like Mark Twain's Mississippi, offered ample opportunity for self-exploration, as *Route 66* and *Easy Rider* both made clear.

WESTERN HIGHWAY

The iconography of 66 draws on still more than imaginary lines, magical numbers, and the road as a river. Significant

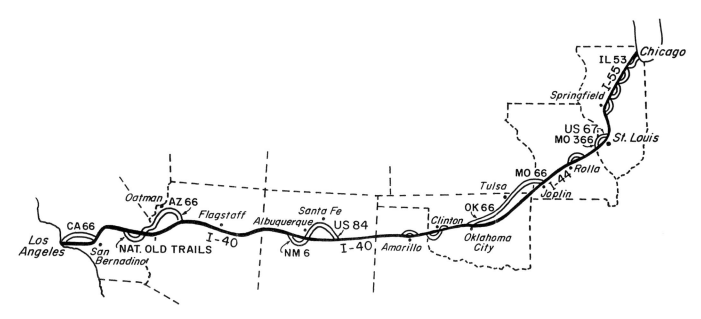

15.1. Locations of the original Route 66 that survive along the modern Interstate highways, showing the oxbows that are all that remain of the U.S. 66 auto river. Author's map; by permission of Iowa State Press.

imagery centers on regional landscapes that highlight the exotic appeal of Route 66 as a frontier path. Despite the size of Chicago and Los Angeles, these cities figure little in the popular descriptions of Route 66. Rather, it was the dry desert landscape of fantastic forms of the Southwest which made the highway a tourist attraction in its own right. The appeal centered on the scenery of New Mexico and Arizona, where the high mountain vistas and native Indian cultures combined to form a world exotic to Eastern travelers. The road's proximity to historic Santa Fe and the majestic Grand

Canyon, to sites such as Laguna Pueblo and the Painted Desert, made travel on Route 66 from Albuquerque to Kingman an exciting family adventure. It was this portion of Route 66 that Troup immortalized in his song-map.

In contrast, the Midwest segments formed little part of 66 imagery. The flat fertile farmlands of Illinois and the green rolling hills of Missouri were too familiar to Eastern travelers to excite comment. The crossing of the Mississippi River did constitute a notable boundary, and caverns and swimming holes in the Ozarks did catch travelers' attention, but it was the prairie horizon in Oklahoma that announced Route 66 as a highway of the American West. The experience of the endless prairie posed a new geography, complete with real Indians and real cowboys and cattle ranches, as the Troups discovered in February 1946. In fact, during the Depression, this had been the very center of the Dust Bowl, as it was also what remained of the almost-vanished idea of the Great American Desert. The real desert encountered in the Mojave was a whole other reality, and the contrast it provided with the lush valleys on the other side of the Cajon Pass made an impression Easterners only slowly forgot.

BRIEF MOMENTS

In retrospect, much of this Route 66 imagery was created under severe constraints. The numbering of U.S. 66, reached at a hastily convened meeting on a Friday afternoon on the last day of April 1926, is the essential example of how significant image elements were determined under stress. The political pressure being applied by Kentucky Governor Field and the Oklahoma Ku Klux Klan forced Avery and Piepmeier to a compromise over the route number in order to preserve a single coherent Chicago-to-Los Angeles route. A similar kind of temporal pressure is involved in John Steinbeck's creation of the "mother road" in *The Grapes of Wrath* that July 4th weekend of 1938, knowing that his Dust Bowl drama was being compromised by the war clouds in Europe. An even more apposite example was the press of history on the filming of John Ford's version of the book, when the German invasion of Poland in September 1939 appeared to overwhelm popular interest in the

Joad family saga. Only American isolationism permitted time for the Ford film to be released to popular acclaim, and for *The Grapes of Wrath* with its 66 signets to be published in Japan and Germany before the Pearl Harbor attack in 1941.

The Troups' story provides another example. Had the Troups left Lancaster later in February or had Capitol Records decided to delay the "Route 66" recording session in March, the creative moment would have been lost, especially given Cole's shift from jive rhymes to romantic ballads after the Capitol sessions. Surely the meeting of Troup and Cole immediately after Troup's days on the road contributed to the rush of rhyming that made this song such a hit that summer. Similar accounts show up in Leonard and Silliphant's story of the creation of *Route 66*, and in Peter Fonda's of *Easy Rider*.

POSTWAR MEMORY

The story of Route 66 is recent in a national memory three short centuries long. Its official birth date of 1926 and its decommissioning in 1985 offer no more than six decades of history proper. The myth of the road is not even that old. So recent indeed is the highway and its passing that its veneration could easily be regarded as a passing fad. The fascination with rock and roll and pop culture seems to be an attribute of the aging of the postwar generation, whose perspective may be no more than a passing interest in the preservation of their own childhood. Yet the innovations of the postwar period—the Interstate highway system, rock and roll, and tail-fin car design—do seem unique achievements that followed with the conclusion of World War II. In

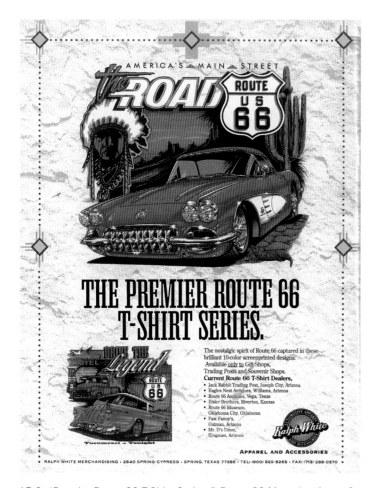

15.2. "Premier Route 66 T-Shirt Series," *Route 66 Magazine* 4, no. 2 (Spring 1997). Advertisement showing a classic Chevrolet Corvette from the *Route 66* television series as a t-shirt logo. By permission of Roger White Merchandising.

this light, Route 66 is *the* highway of postwar prosperity inaugurating the national nostalgia we are living through today.

Whatever the fate of these speculations, there is a substantial historical core around which the rest of our story wraps. It is that of the foundation of Route 66 in Oklahoma and the efforts of Cyrus Avery to connect Oklahoma to the rest of the nation. As the acknowledged father of Route 66, Avery's efforts and his transcontinental vision of the Ozark Trails can rightfully be credited as the conceptual heart of Route 66 iconography. The Oklahoma birthright sets the cultural tone on track toward the West as an effort by the new state boosters to tie the Indian Territory to the rest of the nation through the Good Roads movement and the populist promise of the automobile. Avery embodied the determination of Oklahoma Sooners to insure that a national route to California was directed through their state by whatever name could be invented, if not U.S. 60, then U.S. 66 or the Main Street of America.

The creation of a new highway in the new state of Oklahoma ultimately propelled the free-spirited drive that defined Route 66 in American culture (Figs. 15.2 and 15.3). As a recent highway in a recent region, U.S. 66 followed a tradition of Western trails into the expanding frontier, in this case the postwar suburban Sunbelt of the Southwest. Here Route 66 is most comfortably located among the natural wonders of the Grand Canyon in Arizona and the humanmade monuments of the Cadillac Ranch in Texas (Fig. 13.4). Route 66 is an Oklahoma road gone west, through Dust Bowl drought and the rock-and-roll rhythms of English blues bands. Its youth is its own iconography. It follows in the pioneer tradition of the Santa Fe Trail, the

15.3. "Route Beer 66," *Route 66 Magazine* 4, no. 2 (Spring 1997). Advertisement showing Route 66 as open-road background for a soda pop display. By permission of Route 66 Soda (815-458-2549).

Oregon Trail, and the Mississippi River tales of Mark Twain. Route 66 was a twentieth-century auto road that captured the thrust of the American westward energy, to California, to Los Angeles, to Hollywood, to the Pacific Ocean, to Japan and Asia. In its brief moment, Route 66 became an emblem of the American century's enduring booster optimism, human tragedy, and youth rebellion, the Apian Way of the auto generation.

SAYRE, OKLAHOMA, 1982

AMBOY, CALIFORNIA, 1987 (SEE PAGE 131.)

TUCUMCARI, NEW MEXICO, 1992

VEGA, TEXAS, 1991

15.4. Route 66 was decommissioned in 1985. In 1987, photographer Jeff Brouws became interested in the iconography of the American road, especially Route 66. These four photographs represent Route 66's emerging iconographic status, in the early post-decommissioning years, for fine-art photographers. They combine an awareness of new topographic imagery with an asute appreciation for America's changing cultural landscape. Photographs ©Jeff Brouws. Used by permission of the artist.

Notes

ABBREVIATIONS

AAA   American Automobile Association

AASHO   American Association of State Highway Officials

AASHTO   American Association of State Highway and
   Transportation Officials

AMPAS   Academy of Motion Picture Arts and Sciences,
   Beverly Hill, California

ASCAP   American Society of Composers, Authors, and Publishers

FHA   Federal Highway Administration

NHA   National Highway Association

NPR   National Public Radio

NRC   National Records Center, College Park, Maryland

WPA   Works Progress Administration

TERMINOLOGY

Throughout the book, New York refers to New York City; New York State is used to distinguish the city from the state.

INTRODUCTION

1. Douglas Penor [Infinity Outdoor Advertising], telephone conversation, 29 June 2001.

2. Aaron Barr, "Retailer Sets Course," *Adweek*, July 27, 1998, Midwest edition.

3. Tim Hawley [Campbell & Mithun], interview with the author, 10 November 2000.

4. Jan Bialostocki, "Iconography and Iconography," in *Encyclopedia of World Art*, vol. 7 (New York: McGraw-Hill, 1963), 770–82; William Lash, "Iconography and Iconology," in *The Dictionary of Art*, vol. 12 (New York: Grove, 1996), 89–98.

5. George Kattal, *Iconography of the Saints in Tuscan Painting* (Florence, Italy: Sansoni, 1952), xvii–xxxiii; Edwin Panofsky, *Early Netherlandish Painting*, vol. 1 (Cambridge: Harvard University, 1953), 1–20.

6. John A. Kouwenhoven, *The Columbia Historical Portrait of New York* (New York: Columbia University, 1953); Arthur Krim, "Imagery In Search of a City: The Geosophy of Los Angeles, 1921-1971" (Ph.D. diss., Clark University, 1980); idem, "Los Angeles

and the Anti-Tradition of the Suburban City," *Historical Geography* 18 (1992): 136n; I. N. Phelps Stokes, *The Iconography of Manhattan,* vol. 1 (New York: Dodd, 1915).

7. Alan Trachtenberg, *Brooklyn Bridge: Fact and Symbol* (New York: Oxford University, 1965), 167.

8. Ibid., 14.

9. J. W. Powell, *Report on the Lands of the Arid Region of the United States* (Washington, D.C.: Government Printing Office, 1878), 3.

10. Walter Prescott Webb, *The Great Plains* (Boston: Ginn, 1931), 7; Donald Worster, *Dust Bowl: The Southern Plains in the 1930s* (New York: Oxford University, 1982), 85.

11. Webb, *The Great Plains*, 18-19; WPA, *Illinois: A Descriptive and Historical Guide* (Chicago: A. G. McClure, 1947), 7–8.

12. J. Russell Smith, *North America: Its People and Resources* (New York: Harcourt, Brace, 1925), 290–91.

13. Allan P. Bennison, *Geological Highway Map of the Great Lakes Region* (Tulsa: American Association of Petroleum Geologists, 1978); D. Q. Bowen, *Quarternary Geology* (Oxford: Pergamon, 1978), 52; E. C. Pielou, *After the Ice Age* (Chicago: University of Chicago, 1991), 10; WPA, *Illinois*, 9–12. Elevations cited from Jack Rittenhouse, *A Guide Book to Highway 66* (1946; Albuquerque: University of New Mexico, 1989).

14. Bennison, *Geological Highway*; Donald Jorgenson, *United States Geological Survey: Paleohydrology of the Central United States* (Washington, D.C.: Smithsonian Institution, 1989), 5–6; WPA, *Missouri: A Guide to the Show Me State* (New York: Duell, Sloan and Pearce, 1941), 408.

15. John R. Borchert, "The Climate of the Central North American Grassland," *Annals of the Association of American Geographers* 40 (1950): 1–39; J. Russell Smith, "The Drought-Act of God and Freedom," *Survey Graphic* 23 (1934): 412–14; WPA, *Missouri*, 20.

16. Martyn J. Bowden, "The Great American Desert in the American Mind" in *Geographies of the Mind*, ed. David Lowenthal and Martyn J. Bowden (New York: Oxford University, 1975), 119–48; Holdon, *The Great American Desert* (New York: Oxford University, 1966), 11–15; Webb, *The Great Plains*, 152.

17. Bennison, *Geological Highway* ; WPA, *Kansas: A Guide to the Sunflower State* (New York: Viking, 1939), 439–40; WPA *Missouri*, 235–36.

18. Bennison, *Geological Highway*.

19. James N. Gregory, *American Exodus: The Dust Bowl Migrations and Okie Culture in California* (New York: Oxford University, 1989), 3–6; John Steinbeck, *The Grapes of Wrath* (New York: Viking, 1939); Worster, *Dust Bowl*, 54–56, 69–71.

20. Dan E. Feray, *Geological Highway Map of the Pacific Southwest* (Tulsa: American Association of Petroleum Geologists, 1968); W. A. Renfro, *Geological Highway Map of Texas* (Tulsa: American Association of Petroleum Geologists, 1973); Webb, *The Great Plains*.

21. Grant Foreman, ed., *Adventures on Red River by Cpt. Randolph R. Marcy* (1852; Norman: University of Oklahoma, 1938) 151; D. W. Meinig, *Southwest* (New York: Oxford Unviersity, 1971), 4-5; WPA, *Texas: A Guide to the Lone Star State* (New York: Hastings House, 1940), 10–11.

22. Feray, *Pacific Southwest*; Diana J. Kleiner, "Helium Production" in *The Handbook of Texas*, vol. 3, ed. Ron Tyler (Austin: Texas State Historical Association, 1996), 545–46; Renfro, *Map of Texas*; United States Department of Interior, Bureau of Mines, "Amarillo-Helium Capitol of the World" in *Amarillo*, ed. Clara T. Hammond (Amarillo, TX: George Autry, 1971), 199–201; WPA, *Texas*, 249.

23. A. W. Kuchler, "A Physiographic Classification of Vegetation," *Annals of Association of American Geographers* 39 (1949): 201–10; WPA, *New Mexico: A Guide to the Colorful State* (New York: Hastings House, 1940), 10.

24. Jerry McClanahan, "Rock, Scissors, Pavement," *Route 66 Magazine* 4, no. 1 (1996): 24–26; Rittenhouse, *Guide Book*, 77.

25. W. Scott Baldridge and Kenneth H. Olsen, "The Rio Grande

Rift," *American Scientist* 77 (1989): 240–47.

26. Warren T. Finch, *Uranium Provinces of North America* (Washington, D.C.: United States Geological Survey, 1996), 6-7; Jill Schneider, *Route 66 Across New Mexico* (Albuquerque: University of New Mexico, 1991), 67–69.

27. Phillip Oetking, *Geological Highway Map, Southern Rocky Mountain Region* (Tulsa: American Association of Petroleum Geologists, 1967); WPA, *New Mexico*, 10–11.

28. Halka Chronic, *Roadside Geology of Arizona* (Missoula, MT: Mountain Press, 1983), 202–05; Rittenhouse, *Guide Book*, 89.

29. Chronic, *Roadside*, 285-87; Wendell A. Duffield, *Volcanoes of Northern Arizona* (Grand Canyon, AZ: Grand Canyon Association, 1997); WPA, *Arizona: A State Guide* (New York: Hastings House, 1940), 15.

30. Smith, *North America*, 472–74.

31. Chronic, *Roadside*, 84–86; Richard M. Tosdal, "The Jurassic Arc in the Sonoran and Southern Mojave Deserts" in *Guidebook for Field Trips*, ed. V. W. McKelvey (Washington, D.C.: United States Geological Survey, 1994), 3–5.

32. Smith, *North America*, 467.

33. Cheri Rae, *East Mojave Desert: A Visitor's Guide* (Santa Barbara, CA: Olympus, 1989), 126; Rittenhouse, *Guide Book*, 109–10; Marshall Trimble, *Roadside History of Arizona* (Missoula, MT: Mountain Press, 1986), 290–91.

34. WPA, *Arizona*, 338.

35. Feray, *Pacific Southwest*.

36. Rae, *East Mojave*, 82–83; WPA, *California: A Guide to the Golden State* (New York: Hastings House, 1939), 602–03.

37. Rittenhouse, *Guide Book*, 113.

38. Rae, *East Mojave*, 101; Clifford J. Walker, *Back Door to California: Mojave River Trail* (Barstow, CA: Mojave River Museum, 1986), 36–67.

39. Les Brown, *Encyclopedia of Television*, 3rd ed. (Detroit: Gale Research, 1992); WPA, *California*, 613–14.

40. WPA, *California*, 616–19.

41. Harry R. Bailey, *The Climate of Southern California* (Berkeley: University of California, 1966), 17–19.

CHAPTER ONE

1. "Arrowheads Found with New Mexico Fossils," *Science* 76 (November 25, 1932): 12–13; Stuart J. Fiedel, *Prehistory of the Americas* (London: Cambridge University, 1987), 48; F. H. Roberts, "Folsom Find," *El Palacio* 23 (1927): 510–12.

2. Johnnie Johnson, telephone conversation with author, November 20, 1991; Michael J. O'Brien and W. Raymond Wood, *Prehistory of Missouri* (Columbia: University of Missouri, 1998), 55–58; R. E. Taylor, R. E., et al., "Clovis and Folsom Age Estimates," *Antiquity* 70 (1996): 515–25.

3. Karl Butzer, "This Is Indian Country," *Geographical Magazine* 52, no. 11 (1979): 140–48.

4. Carol Karasik, *The Turquoise Trail* (New York: Abrams, 1993); Phil C. Weigand and Gorman Harbottle, "The Role of Turquoise in Ancient Mesoamerican Trade Structure," in *The American Southwest and Mesoamerica*, ed. J. E. Erikson and T. C. Baugh (New York: Plenum, 1993), 155–77.

5. Fiedel, *Prehistory*, 201–14. *Anasazi* is a Navajo term, and the Navajo are not Pueblo people. Thus, *Anasazi* is currently being reconsidered by a growing number of scholars and National Park Service personnel as the appropriate term for these perhistoric indigenous citizens of the Southwest.

6. Kendrick Frazier, *People of Chaco* (New York: Norton, 1986), 182–85.

7. John R. Stein, "The Chaco Roads," *El Palacio* 94, no. 1 (1989): 8–15.

8. Richard I. Ford, et al., "Three Perspectives on Puebloan Prehistory" in *New Perspectives on the Pueblos*, ed. A. Ortiz (Albuquerque: University of New Mexico, 1972), 19–39.

9. Claudine Marie Gilbert, *Oklahoma Prehistory* (Norman: University of Oklahoma, 1980), 40–41; Christopher Lintz, "Texas Panhandle-Pueblo Interactions" in *Farmers, Hunters, and Colonists*, ed. K. A. Spielman (Tucson: University of Arizona, 1991), 89–106.

10. Melvin L. Fowler, "A Pre-Columbian Urban Center on the Mississippi," *Scientific American* 233, no. 8 (1975): 92–101; William R. Iseminger, "Mighty Cahokia," *Archeology* 49, no. 3 (1996): 30–37.

11. Fiedel, *Prehistory*, 94; Stuart Struever and Felicia A. Koster, *Americans in Search of Their Past* (New York: Doubleday, 1979).

12. Brian M. Fagan, *People of the Earth* (Boston: Little, Brown, 1986), 297; Francis Jennings, *The Founders of America* (New York: Norton, 1993), 50.

13. James A. Brown, "Spiro Exchange Connections" in *Southeastern Natives and Their Pasts*, ed. D. G. Wycoff and J. L. Hoffman (Norman: Oklahoma Archeological Society, Cross Timbers Association, 1983); Gilbert, *Oklahoma*, 47–54; Dennis A. Peterson, et al., *An Archeological Survey of Spiro Vicinity* (Norman: University of Oklahoma, 1993).

14. David LaVere, *The Caddo Chiefdoms* (Lincoln: University of Nebraska, 1998).

15. Susan C. Verik and Timothy G. Baugh, "Prehistoric Plains Trade" in *Prehistoric Exchange*, ed. Timothy G. Baugh and J. Erikson (New York: Plenum, 1994), 249–67.

16. John R. Swantl, *Source Materials on the History of the Caddo Indians* (Washington, D.C.: Smithsonian Institution, 1942), 37; Gene Weltfish, "The Plains Indians" in *North American Indians*, ed. E. Burke and N. O. Lurie (New York: Random House, 1998), 200–13.

17. William H. Goetzmann and Glynder Williams, *The Atlas of North American Exploration* (New York: Prentice-Hall, 1992), 36–37.

18. Henry Walker and Don Bufkin, *Historic Atlas of Arizona* (Norman: University of Oklahoma, 1986), 12–13.

19. William F. Zornow, *Kansas: History of the Jayhawk State* (Norman: University of Oklahoma, 1957), 21–23.

20. B. S. Dodge, *The Road West* (Albuquerque: University of New Mexico, 1980), 8–9; Myra E. Jenkins and Albert H. Schroeder, *A Brief History of New Mexico* (Albuquerque: University of New Mexico, 1974), 20–23.

21. John Galvin, ed., *A Record of Travels in Arizona and California, 1775–1776, Fr. Francisco Garcés* (Los Angeles: John Howell, 1963), 63.

22. Walker and Bufkin, *Historic Atlas*, 72–73, 76–79.

23. Goetzmann and Williams, *North American Exploration*, 60–65.

24. Ibid., 94–95, 98–99.

25. Henry Folmer, "The Mallet Expedition of Santa Fe," *Colorado Magazine* 16, no. 5 (1939): 161–73.

26. D. W. Meinig, *The Shaping of America*, vol. 1, *Atlantic America* (New Haven: Yale University, 1986), 334–35; idem, vol. 2, *Continental America* (New Haven: Yale University, 1993), 60–62, 138–40.

27. Goetzmann and Williams, *North American Expedition*, 144–45.

28. Milo Milton Quaiff, *The Southwest Expedition of Zebulon Pike* (Chicago: Donnelley, 1925), 155–56; Hobart E. Stocking, *The Road to Santa Fe* (New York: Hastings House, 1971), 7–8.

29. Goetzmann and Williams, *North American Expedition*, 144–45.

30. Grant Foreman, *A History of Oklahoma* (Norman: University of Oklahoma, 1942), 66; Martyn J. Bowden, "The Great American Desert in the American Mind" in *Geographies of the Mind*, ed. David Lowenthal and Martyn J. Bowden (New York: Oxford University, 1975), 121; George J. Goodman and Cheryl A. Lawson, *Retracing Major Stephen H. Long's 1820 Expedition* (Norman: University of Oklahoma, 1995), 111–12.

31. Larry M. Beachum, "To the Westward, William Becknell and the Santa Fe Trade," *Journal of the West* 28, no. 4 (1989): 9, 11; Thelma S. Guild and Harvey L. Carter, *Kit Carson* (Lincoln: University of Nebraska, 1984), 12–15; Jenkins and Schroeder, *Brief History*, 31–33; Leo E. Oliva, *Soldiers on the Santa Fe Trail* (Norman: University of Oklahoma, 1967), 7–10.

32. Hilde Heun Kagan, ed., *The American Heritage Atlas of the United States* (New York: American Heritage, 1966), 148–49; Meinig, *Shaping*, vol. 2, 92–95.

33. Elmo Ingethron, *Indians of the Ozark Plateau* (Point Lookout, MO: Ozark Press, 1970), endmap; Kagan, *Heritage Atlas*, 148.

34. Foreman, *History of Oklahoma*, 71–72; Maurice G. Fulton, *Diary and Letters of Josiah Gregg* (Norman: University of Oklahoma, 1941); M. L. Moorhead, ed., *Josiah Gregg, "Commerce of the Prairies"* (Norman: University of Oklahoma, 1954).

CHAPTER TWO

1. D. W. Meinig, *The Shaping of America*, vol. 1, *Atlantic America* (New Haven: Yale University, 1986), 30–35.

2. Henry S. Drago, ed., *"The Oregon Trail" by Francis Parkman* (New York: Dodd, Mead, 1964), v–vi; David Lavender, *The Overland Migrations* (Washington, D.C.: National Park Service, 1980), 28–31; Henry Walker, *The Wagon Masters* (Norman: University of Oklahoma, 1966), 16–17; WPA, *The Oregon Trail* (New York: Hastings House, 1939), 1–3.

3. Hubert Howe Bancroft, *History of California*, vol. 7 (San Francisco: The History Company, 1890), 500–01; Hilde Haun Kagan, ed., *The American Heritage Atlas of the United States* (New York: American Heritage, 1966), 202–03; George Rogers Taylor, *The Transportation Revolution, 1815–1860* (New York: Holt, Rinehart, and Winston, 1951), 80–85; James E. Vance, Jr., *The North American Railroad: Its Origin, Evolution, and Geography* (Baltimore: Johns Hopkins University, 1995), 148–49.

4. William M. Meigs, *The Life Of Thomas Hart Benton* (New York: Lippincott, 1924), 418.

5. William H. Goetzmann and Glynder Williams, *The Atlas of North American Exploration* (New York: Prentice-Hall, 1992), 158–59; Allan Nevins, *Frémont, Pathfinder of the West* (New York: Longmans, Green, 1955), 211.

6. Thomas Frederick Howard, *Sierra Crossing* (Berkeley: University of California, 1998), 12–33; Lavender, *Overland*, 60–65; WPA, *California, A Guide to the Golden State* (New York: Hastings House, 1939), 46–51.

7. Carol Christensen and Thomas Christensen, *The U.S.-Mexican War* (San Francisco: Bay Books, 1998), 96–104; Fairfax Downey, *Texas and the War with Mexico* (New York: American Heritage, 1961), 87–88.

8. Christensen and Christensen, *U.S.-Mexican War*, 106–15; Downey, *War with Mexico*, 140–43; D. W. Meinig, *The Shaping of America*, vol. 2, *Continental America* (New Haven: Yale University, 1993), 147–50.

9. Ralph K. Andrist, *The California Gold Rush* (New York: American Heritage, 1961), 10–19; Marcia Eymann, "Introduction" in *Silver and Gold: Cased Images of the California Gold Rush*, ed. D. H. Johnson and M. Eymann (Ames: University of Iowa, 1998), xiii–xxxi; Gerald Thompson, *Edward F. Beale and the American West* (Albuquerque: University of New Mexico, 1983), 29–31.

10. Andrist, *Gold Rush*, 124–32; Eymann, "Introduction," xxv; Mel Scott, *The San Francisco Bay Area* (Berkeley: University of California, 1959), 27–31.

11. Grant Foreman, *Marcy and the Gold Seekers* (Norman: University of Oklahoma, 1939), 8–10; William H. Goetzmann, *Army Exploration in the American West* (New Haven: Yale University, 1959), 212–16; W. Eugene Holdon, *Beyond the Cross Timbers: Travels of Randolph Marcy* (Norman: University of Oklahoma, 1955), 56–62.

12. Holdon, *Cross Timbers*, 74.

13. Kendrick Frazier, *People of Chaco* (New York: Norton, 1986), 23–25; Goetzmann, *Army*, 240–44.

14. James A. Coombs, "Exploration and Mapping of the Southwest Route" in *Exploration and Mapping of the American West*, ed. D. P. Koepp (Chicago: Speculum Orbis, 1986), 61–99; B. S. Dodge, *The Road West* (Albuquerque: University of New Mexico, 1980), 57–58; Goetzmann, *Army*, 244–46.

15. Marshall Trimble, *Roadside History of Arizona* (Missoula, MT: Mountain Press, 1986), 228–30.

16. Howard, *Sierra Crossing*, 107–108; Captain L. Sitgreaves, *Report of an Expedition Down the Zuñi and Colorado Rivers* (1853; Chicago: Rio Grande Press, 1962), end map; David J. Weber, *Richard H. Kern, Expeditionary Artist* (Albuquerque: University of New Mexico, 1985), 211–13.

17. Dan E. Fehrenbacher, *The South and Three Sectional Crises* (Baton Rouge: Louisiana State University, 1980), 9–15; Glover Moore, *The Missouri Controversy, 1819–1821* (Lexington: University of Kentucky, 1967), 100–16; Allan Nevins and Henry Steele Commager, *A Short History of the United States*, 3rd ed. (New York: Modern Library, 1956), 165, 204–05; Arthur Quinn, *The Rivals: William Gwin, David Broderick and the Birth of California* (New York: Crown, 1994), 82–91.

18. Robert G. Cleland, *A History of California: The American Period* (New York: Macmillan, 1922), 350–51; William H. Ellison, "Memoirs of the Hon. William H. Gwin," *California Historical Society Quarterly* 9 (1940): 1–3; Quinn, *The Rivals*, 91–93.

19. Hubert Howe Bancroft, *History of California*, vol. 2 (San Francisco: The History Company, 1888), 726; Coombs, "Mapping," 90; Ellison, "Memoirs," 173; Meigs, *Life of Thomas*, 420–22; Nevins and Commager, *Short History*, 350–71; Goetzmann, *Army*, 266–69.

20. Bill Gilbert, *Westering Man: The Life of Joseph Walker* (New York: Atheneum, 1983), 236–42; Howard, *Sierra Crossing*, 109; Weber, *Richard Kern*, 329–30.

21. Cleland, *History of California*, 496–502.

22. Ellison, "Memoirs," 173; Goetzmann, *Army*, 276; [William H.] Gwin, *On the Bill to Establish a Railway to California* (Washington, D.C.: Congressional Globe, 1853); D. W. Meinig, *The Shaping of America*, vol. 3, *Transcontinental America* (New Haven: Yale University, 1998), 11–14.

23. Bancroft, *California*, 520; Lewis H. Haney, *A Congressional History of Railways* (Madison: University of Wisconsin, 1910), 51–55; Howard, *Sierra Crossing*, 109; Robert R. Russell, *The Improvement of Communication With the Pacific Coast* (Cedar Rapids, IA: Torch Press, 1948), 97–108.

24. Bancroft, *California*, 521; Cleland, *History of California*, 374–75; Goetzmann and Williams, *North American Exploration*, 166–67; Haney, *Congressional History*, 56; Hudson Strode, *Jefferson Davis: American Patriot* (New York: Harcourt, Brace, 1955), 261–62.

25. Grant Foreman, ed., *A Pathfinder in the Southwest: Itinerary of Lieutenant A. W. Whipple* (Norman: University of Oklahoma, 1941), 6–10, 19; H. Craig Miner, *The St. Louis-San Francisco Transcontinental Railroad: The Thirty-Fifth Parallel Project, 1853–1890* (Lawrence: University of Kansas, 1972), 1–4; Vance, *North American Railroad*, 163.

26. Donald Chaput, *François Aubry* (Glendale, CA: Arthur H. Clark, 1975), 133–36; Lavender, *Overland*, 54–55; Frank C. Lockwood, "Arizona Pioneers: 1854 to 1864," *Arizona Historical Review* 5, no. 4 (1933): 320; Walker D. Wyman, "F. X. Aubry: Santa Fe Freighter and Explorer," *New Mexico Historical Review* 7, no. 1 (1932): 8–9.

27. Foreman, *Pathfinder*, 10–11.

28. Ibid., 20.

29. Miner, *Parallel Project*, 12–13; Lt. A. W. Whipple, *Report of Exploration for a Railway Route North of the Thirty-Fifth Parallel, House Document*, no. 129 (Washington, D.C.: Government Printing Office, 1854), 32–33.

30. Goetzmann, *Army*, 284–85; Goetzmann and Williams, *North American Exploration*, 166–67; Vance, *North American Railroad*, 166–67.

31. Coombs, "Mapping," 84–85; Lewis Burt Lesley, ed., *Uncle Sam's Camels* (Cambridge: Harvard University, 1929), 1–18; Thompson, *Edward Beale*, xi, 29–31, 104–13, 122–23.

32. Phil Patton, *Open Road: A Celebration of the American Highway* (New York: Simon and Schuster, 1986), 37; Albert C. Rose, *Historic American Roads* (New York: Crown, 1976), 57; Thompson, *Edward Beale*, 123.

33. Ralph J. Roske, *Everyman's Eden: A History of California* (New York: Macmillan, 1968), 363; Robert L. Thompson, *Wiring a Continent* (Princeton: Princeton University, 1947), 38–40.

34. Nevins and Commanger, *Short History*, 311–12; Vance, *North American Railroad*, 169–73.

35. H. L. Conrad, ed., *Encyclopedia of the History of Missouri*, vol. 5 (St. Louis: Southern History Company, 1901), 108–10; George S. Scott, *History and Directory of Springfield* (Springfield, MO: Patriot Advertiser, 1878), 67–68.

36. Mary E. Brantley, *John S. Phelps and the Public Domain* (Columbia: University of Missouri, Western Historical Manuscript Collection, c. 1935), 29–35; Goetzmann, *Army*, 248.

37. Brantley, *Public Domain*, 35; John S. Phelps, "Letter," *Missouri Republican*, June 7, 1853; idem, "Speech of Hon. John S. Phelps," *Missouri Republican*, January 30, 1853.

38. Brantley, *Public Domain*, 35; Goetzmann, *Army*, 113; Miner, *Parallel Project*, 19–21.

39. John W. Million, *State Aid to Railways in Missouri* Chicago: University of Chicago, 1986), 133; Milton D. Rafferty, *Missouri: A Geography* (Boulder, CO: Westview, 1980), 58; Carl O. Sauer, *The Geography of the Ozark Highlands of Missouri* (Chicago: University of Chicago, 1920), 139–44.

40. Sauer, *Ozark*, 144–45; Scott, *Directory of Springfield*, 67–69; WPA, *Missouri: A Guide to the Show Me State* (New York: Duell, Sloan and Pearce, 1941), 331.

41. Miner, *Parallel Project*, 44–51; Rafferty, *Missouri*, 117; P. E. Rose,

"The Old Wire Road," *Ozark Mountaineer*, August 1953; Scott, *Directory of Springfield*, 108–09.

42. Emily J. Harris, "Introduction" in *Prairie Passage: The Illinois and Michigan Canal Corridor*, ed. E. Ranney, E. J. Harris, et al. (Urbana: University of Illinois, 1998), 37–43; Harol M. Mayer and Richard C. Wade, *Chicago: Growth of a Metropolis* (Chicago: University of Chicago, 1969), 28. The I&M Canal opened in 1848.

43. Theodore Pease, *Story of Illinois*, 3rd ed. (Chicago: University of Chicago, 1967), 102–03; WPA, *Illinois: A Descriptive and Historical Guide* (Chicago: A. G. McClure, 1947), 29–30.

44. Paul M. Anole, *"Here I Have Lived:" A History of Lincoln's Springfield* (Springfield, IL: Abraham Lincoln Association, 1935), 162–63; WPA, *Illinois*, 385–86.

45. William K. Ackerman, "Early Illinois Railroads," *Chicago Historical Society* 20, no. 2 (1883): 99–108.

46. W. W. Belcher, *The Economic Rivalry Between St. Louis and Chicago* (New York: Columbia University, 1947), 72–73; William Cronon, *Nature's Metropolis: Chicago and the Great West* (New York: Norton, 1991), 296–97.

47. Ackerman, *Early Illinois*, 50–51.

48. Cronon, *Metropolis*, 68–71; Mayer and Wade, *Chicago*, 24–30.

49. Belcher, *Rivalry*, 55–56.

50. Carrol D. Harding, *George M. Pullman* (New York: Newcomen Society, 1951), 10–11; WPA, *Illinois*, 62.

CHAPTER THREE

1. Zoeth S. Eldredge, *History of California*, vol. 4 (New York: Century History, 1915), 267–69.

2. David F. Myrick, *Railroads of Nevada and Eastern California*, vol. 2 (Reno: University of Nevada, 1961), 762–64; Allan Nevins, *Frémont, Pathfinder of the West* (New York: Longmans, Green, 1955), 587–89.

3. Stuart Daggett, *Chapters on the History of the Southern Pacific Railroad* (New York: Ronald, 1922), 121–24; Eldredge, *California*, 403.

4. Grant Foreman, ed., *A Pathfinder in the Southwest: Itinerary of Lieutenant A. W. Whipple* (Norman: University of Oklahoma, 1941), 21–22; Robert E. Reigel, "William Jackson Palmer" in *Dictionary of American Biography*, vol. 8, ed. D. Malone (New York: Scribner's Sons, 1934), 195–96.

5. William J. Palmer, *Report of Surveys Across the Continent in 1867–'68* (Philadelphia: W. B. Selheuner, 1869), 1; "William H. Greenwood," *National Cyclopedia of American Biography*, vol. 18 (New York: James T. White, 1920), 364.

6. William H. Goetzmann, *Army Exploration in the American West* (New Haven: Yale University, 1959), 243.

7. Palmer, *Report*, 185.

8. Ibid.

9. Daggett, *Chapters*, 122–23.

10. Eldredge, *California*, 403–404; Neil C. Wilson and Frank J. Taylor, *Southern Pacific* (New York: McGraw-Hill, 1952), 50–51.

11. Remi Nadeau, *City-Makers* (Los Angeles: Trans-Angelo Books, 1965), 127–47.

12. Glenn D. Bradley, *The Story of the Santa Fe* (Boston: Robert G. Baeder, 1920), 141–43; Myrick, *Railroads*, 762–63.

13. Keith L. Bryant, *History of the Atchison, Topeka and Santa Fe* (New York: Macmillan, 1974), 60–61; idem, "William B. Strong" in *Railroads in the Nineteenth Century*, ed. R. L. Frey (New York: Facts on File, 1988), 382–84; Myra E. Jenkins and Albert H. Schroeder, *A Brief History of New Mexico* (Albuquerque: University of New Mexico, 1974), 64; James Marshall, *Santa Fe: The Railroad That Built an Empire* (New York: Random House, 1945), 93–94, 132–34.

14. Bryant, *Atchison*, 60; Fred G. Gurley, *New Mexico and the Santa Fe Railway* (New York: Newcomen Society, 1950), 14; Marshall, *Santa Fe*, 134–35.

15. Gurley, *New Mexico*, 19.

16. Bryant, *Atchison*, 185; Myrick, *Railroads*, 763.

17. Bradley, *Story*, 220; Marshall, *Santa Fe*, 163.

18. Marshall, *Santa Fe*, 163, 354–355; Marshall Trimble, *Roadside History of Arizona* (Missoula, MT: Mountain Press, 1986), 288.

19. Marshall, *Santa Fe*, 171; Myrick, *Railroads*, 769.

20. Myrick, *Railroads*, 764–65; "William Hood," *National Cyclopedia of American Biography*, vol. 20 (New York: James T. White, 1929), 12–13.

21. Daggett, *Chapters*, 133–34; Marshall, *Santa Fe*, 189; Myrick, *Railraods*, 765, 767; Walter C. Schuiling, *San Bernardino County* (Woodland Hills, CA: Windsor, 1984), 65.

22. Myrick, *Railroads*, 766.

23. Ibid., 770; Schuiling, *Bernardino County*, 66.

24. Bryant, *Atchison*, 102–103; Nadeau, *City-Makers*, 154–55.

25. Robert G. Cleland, *A History of California: The American Period* (New York: Macmillan, 1922), 442; Nadeau, *City-Makers*, 155; Wilson and Taylor, *Southern Pacific*, 86.

26. Bryant, *Atchison*, 186; J. Donald Hughes, *The Story of the Man in the Grand Canyon* (Grand Canyon, AZ: Grand Canyon Natural History Association, 1967), 89–90; Steve Schmollinger, "Hot Sand and Drifting Snow," *Pacific Rail News*, November 1988.

27. Warren J. Belasco, *Americans on the Road: From Auto Camp to Motel* (Cambridge: MIT, 1979), 9; Winfield Hogaboom, "1902, To the Grand Canyon on an Automobile," in *Essays on the Grand Canyon*, ed. P. Schullery (Boulder: Colorado Associated Press, 1981), 57–69; J. Donald Hughes, *In the House of Stone and Light* (Grand Canyon, AZ: Grand Canyon Natural History Association, 1978), 70–71.

28. Preston George and Sylvan R. Wood, *The Railroads of Oklahoma*, bulletin 60 (Boston: Railway and Locomotive Historical Society, 1943), 10; H. Craig Miner, *The St. Louis-San Francisco Transcontinen-*

tal Railroad: The Thirty-Fifth Parallel Project, 1853–1890 (Lawrence: University of Kansas, 1972), 78–79.

29. H. Craig Miner, "The Struggle for an East-West Railway in Indian Territory," Chronicles of Oklahoma 47(1969): 564.

30. George and Wood, Railroads of Oklahoma, 10–12; Miner, Parallel Project, 123; Miner, "Struggle," 123, 567–68, 575–79.

31. WPA, Arkansas: A Guide to the State (New York: Hastings House, 1941), 54–55.

32. William E. Hayes, Iron Road to Empire: History of the Rock Island Lines (New York: Simmons-Boardman, 1953), 160–61.

33. George and Wood, Railroads of Oklahoma, 43; Hayes, Iron Road, 160–61.

34. Byron B. Price and Frederick W. Rathjew, The Golden Spread: Illustrated History of Amarillo and the Texas Panhandle (Northridge, CA: Windsor, 1986), 75.

35. L. P. Gilvin, "Highways," in Amarillo, ed. Clara T. Hammond (Amarillo, TX: George Autry, 1971), 280–82.

36. Bryant, Atchison, 94–96, 192–93; David F. Myrick, New Mexico's Railroads (Albuquerque: University of New Mexico, 1970), 22–25.

CHAPTER FOUR

1. Frank Donovan, Wheels for a Nation (New York: Crowell, 1965), 39–44; Warren T. Finch, Uranium Provinces of North America (Washington, D.C.: United States Geological Survey, 1996), 27, 37–39; James J. Flink, The Car Culture (Cambridge: MIT, 1975), 13–14; John B. Rae, American Automobile Manufacturers (Philadelphia: Chilton, 1959), 24–25.

2. Mindy Bingham, Berta Benz and the Motorwagen (Santa Barbara, CA: Advocacy Press, 1989), 46; Flink, Car Culture, 11–13; T. R. Nicholson, The Wild Roads: Transcontinental Motoring (New York: Norton, 1969), 1–2, 12–13.

3. Albert B. Bochroch, American Automobile Racing (New York: Viking, 1974), 12–16; Flink, Car Culture, 14–15; Richard Mathison, Three Cars in Every Garage: A History of the Automobile Club in Southern California (New York: Doubleday, 1968), 6.

4. William Craige and James R. Hulbert, A Dictionary of American Regional English, vol. 1 (Chicago: University of Chicago, 1938), 98; "The Horse Will Be Forgotten," Boston Transcript, May 17, 1897; J. A. Simpson, and E. S. Weiner, Oxford English Dictionary, vol. 1, 2nd ed. (New York: Oxford University, 1989), 806.

5. Flink, Car Culture, 15; John B. Rae, The Road and the Automobile in American Life (Cambridge: MIT, 1971), 54.

6. Rae, The Road, 35, 50.

7. "An American Appian Way," Good Roads, August 1906, 57–58; Flink, Car Culture, 30–31; Drake Hokanson, The Lincoln Highway: Main Street Across America (Ames: University of Iowa, 1988), 7; Bellany Partridge, Fill'er Up! Fifty Years of Motoring (New York: McGraw-Hill, 1952), 183; Rae, The Road, 35.

8. Nicholson, Wild Roads, 6–7; Rae, The Road, 34.

9. Nicholson, Wild Roads, 145–56, 162–63; Antonio Scarfoglio, Round the World in a Motor-Car (London: Grant Richards, 1909), 141–43.

10. Scarfoglio, Round the World, 145.

11. Nicholson, Wild Roads, 163–75.

12. Bochroch, Racing, 25–28.

13. Flink, Car Culture, 30–31; Mathison, Three Cars, 3–4.

14. Finch, Uranium, 67–73, 158; Virginia Scharff, Taking the Wheel: Women and the Coming of the Motor Age (New York: Free Press, 1991), 25; Louise C. Smith, "Long Island Motor Parkway, 1908–1930," Nassau County Historical Journal 22, no. 2 (1961): 14–27; Rae, The Road, 35, 50; Fred J. Wagner, "Long Island's Motor Parkway," House Beautiful 36, no. 8 (September 1914): xiv–vi.

15. Donald J. Hughes, The Story of the Man in the Grand Canyon

(Grand Canyon, AZ: Grand Canyon Natural History Association, 1967), 107–13; Albert D. Manchester, "A Marco Polo of the Motor Age," *Car Collector* 11 (June 1989): 50–51; A. L. Westgard, *Tales of a Pathfinder* (New York: A. L. Westgard, 1920), 13.

16. "17,000 Miles Trip by Motor Car in 1913: Westgard, Man of Many Miles," pamphlet (New York: NHA, 1913), 1–7.

17. "17,000 Miles"; Richard F. Weingroff, "When Highways Had Names," *SCA Journal* 14, no. 1 (1996): 2–5; A. L. Westgard, "From Coast to Coast by Automobile," *Collier's* 47 (January 14, 1911): 1–3.

18. Dave Cole, "Magazines for Early Motorists," *SCA Journal* 14, no. 1 (1996): 7.

19. Westgard, "Coast to Coast," 1911.

20. Albert C. Rose, *Historic American Roads* (New York: Crown, 1976), 86.

21. "17,000 Miles," 2; *Strip Maps of the "Trail to Sunset,"* (New York: AAA, 1911).

22. W. C. Davidson, "The Missouri Cross State Highway-Old Trail Road," *Better Roads* 2, no. 12 (1911): 80–86; Richard F. Weingroff, "The National Trails Road," typescript, FHA, Washington, D.C., 1989, 2–4.

23. Weingroff, "Old Trails," 4–6; "The Women's National Old Trail Roads Association," *Southern Good Roads* 3 (December 1911): 19.

24. Elizabeth B. Gentry, *The Old Trail Roads* (Kansas City, KS: Missouri Daughters of the American Revolution, 1911), 5–8.

25. "Ocean-To-Ocean Transcontinental Highway," *Good Roads* 12 (January 13, 1912): 45; Weingroff, "Old Trails," 15–17.

26. "National Old Trails Road Convention," *Better Roads* 4, no. 5 (1912): 66–67; Weingroff, "Old Trails," 10–11.

27. Elizabeth B. Gentry, "National Old Trails Road," *Better Roads* 2, no. 8 (1912): 55.

28. "Coast to Coast," *Better Roads* 4, no. 9 (1912): 46–47; Weingroff, "Old Trails," 20–21.

29. Weingroff, "Old Trails," 15–17.

30. "National Old Trails Road Association," *Better Roads* 5, no. 6 (1913): 24–27; Weingroff, "Old Trails," 15–17, 24–25.

31. Arizona Good Roads Association, *Illustrated Road Maps and Tour Book* (1913; Phoenix: Arizona Highways Magazine, 1987), 115; Jack Rittenhouse, *A Guide Book to Highway 66* (Albuquerque: University of New Mexico, 1989), 110.

32. Judge J. M. Lowe, "Permanently Sign-Posting the Old Trails Road," *Better Roads and Streets* 4, no. 10 (1914): 14–15; Mathison, *Three Cars*, 32.

33. O. T. Parker, "National Old Trails Road," *Better Roads and Streets* 5, no. 3 (1915): 18–20; Weingroff, "Old Trails," 29–30.

34. Weingroff, "Old Trails," 30–31; A. L. Westgard, "Motor Routes to the California Expositions," *Motor* (March 1915): 1–8.

35. R. Robinson Rowe, "Red Rock Bridge on U.S. 66," *California Highways and Public Works* 26, no. 7–8 (1947): 20–22.

36. Donald C. Jackson, *Great American Bridges and Dams* (Washington, D.C.: Preservation Press, 1988), 249; Michael Wallis, *Route 66: The Mother Road* (New York: St. Martin's, 1990), 209.

37. Weingroff, "Old Trails," 24.

38. Richard Hofstadter, "'Coin's Financial School' and the Mind of 'Coin' Harvey" in *"Coin's Financial School" by William H. Harvey*, ed. R. Hofstadter (Cambridge: Harvard University, 1963), 9–12; Arthur Krim, "The Ozark Trails: The Original Mother Road," *SCA Journal* 14, no. 1 (1996): 22; Jeannette P. Nichols, "William Hope Harvey" in *Dictionary of American Biography*, ed. R. L. Schulyer (New York: Scribner's, 1958), 288–89.

39. WPA, *Arkansas*, 112; Nan Marie Lawler, "The Ozark Trail Association" (master's thesis, University of Arkansas at Fayetteville, 1991), 8–9.

40. "Coin Harvey," *Southern Good Roads* 3 (June 1911): 20; Lawler, "Ozark Trail," 9.

41. Clara B. Kennan, "The Ozark Trail and Coin Harvey," *Arkansas Historical Quarterly* 7 (1948): 301–02; Krim, "Ozark Trails," 22; Lawler, "Ozark Trail," 11; [Ozark Trails map], *Gravette* [Arkansas] *News Herald*, May 9, 1913.

42. Kennan, "Coin Harvey," 302; Krim, "Ozark Trail," 2; "Ozark Trail Association," *Good Roads* 13 (July 26, 1913): 39.

43. Ruth Singer Avery, "Cyrus Stevens Avery," *Chronicles of Oklahoma* 45 (1967): 88; "Cyrus S. Avery," *History of Oklahoma*, vol. 3, ed. Joseph B. Thoburn (Chicago: American Historical Society, 1916), 981; "The Ozark Trails," *Good Roads* 14 (June 6, 1914): 32.

44. Avery, "Cyrus Stevens Avery," 85; Quinta Scott and Susan Croce Kelly, *Route 66: The Highway and Its People* (Norman: University of Oklahoma, 1988), 10–11; Thoburn, *History of Oklahoma*; Wallis, *Mother Road*, 6–7.

45. Lawler, "Ozark Trail," 36–37 ; "Oklahoma," *Southern Good Roads* 6 (December 1916): 20–21.

46. "Amarillo Given Trail Convention," *Daily Oklahoman*, November 23, 1916; "Convention Notice," *Daily Oklahoman*, November 21, 1916; Krim, "Ozark Trails," 21–26; Lawler , "Ozark Trail," 46–54.

47. "Oklahoma, The Ozark Trail," *Better Roads and Streets* 9, no. 1 (1917): 25.

48. Neil Goble, "End of the Trail for Monte Ne," *Highway* (February 1962): 40–43; Krim, "Ozark Trails," 24; Lawler, "Ozark Trail," 43, 46–54; Henry Miller, *The Air-Conditioned Nightmare* (San Francisco: New Directions, 1945), 134–39.

49. Kennan, "Coin Harvey," 315; Krim, "Ozark Trails," 23; *Ozark Trails Route Book* (Monte Ne, AR: Arkansas Ozark Trails Association, 1919).

50. Krim, "Ozark Trails," 24–25; Lawler, "Ozark Trail," 64–70.

51. "St. Louis Man is Elected Head of Ozark Trail Assn.," *Duncan* [Oklahoma] *Banner*, August 29, 1924.

CHAPTER FIVE

1. *America's Highways, 1776–1976: A History of the Federal-Aid Program* (Washington, D.C.: FHA, 1976), 17–18; Albert C. Rose, *Historic American Roads* (New York: Crown, 1976), 27; Joseph S. Wood, "The Idea of a National Road" in *The National Road*, ed. Karl Raitz (Baltimore: Johns Hopkins University, 1996), 115–17.

2. Billy Joe Peyton, "Surveying and Building the Road" in *The National Road*, ed. Karl Raitz (Baltimore: Johns Hopkins University, 1996), 133–47; Rose, *Historic Roads*, 36; Gregory S. Rose, "Extending the Road West" in *The National Road*, ed. Karl Raitz (Baltimore: Johns Hopkins University, 1996), 164–67. Two western extensions from Vandalia were constructed by 1853 to the Mississippi River at East St. Louis and upriver twenty miles at Alton, Illinois.

3. Peirce Lewis, "Landscape of Mobility" in *The National Road*, ed. Karl Raitz (Baltimore: Johns Hopkins University, 1996), 17–18.

4. FHA, *History*, 24–26; Phil Patton, *Open Road: A Celebration of the American Highway* (New York: Simon and Schuster, 1986), 37; Rose, *Historic Roads*, 57.

5. Rose, *Historic Roads*, 73–76, 91; Bruce E. Seely, *Building the American Highway System* (Philadelphia: Temple University, 1987), 16–17; Weingroff, "When Highways Had Names," *SCA Journal* 14, no. 1 (1996): 1–5.

6. FHA, *History*, 108, 192; Richard F. Weingroff, "Broader Ribbons Across the Land," *Public Roads*, June 1996, 1–16, 32–39.

7. FHA, *History*, 108–109; Weingroff, "Broader Ribbons," 7; idem, "From Names To Numbers," *AASHTO Quarterly* 76, no. 2 (1997): 6–8.

8. A. H. Hinkle, "Standard Highway Signs," *Good Roads* 66, no. 4 (1924): 95–97; A. R. Hirst, "Marking and Mapping the Wisconsin Trunk Line Highway System," *Good Roads* 55, no. 2 (1919): 1–3; Weingroff, "Names to Numbers," 8.

9. AASHO Staff, "The U.S. Route Numbered System," in *Golden Anniversary* (Washington, D.C.: AASHO, 1964), 140–41; Ruth Singer Avery, "Cyrus Stevens Avery," *Chronicles of Oklahoma* 45 (1967): 87; FHA, *History*, 109; A. H. Hinkle, "How Shall Interstate

Highways Be Named and Marked?" *American Highways* 5, no. 1 (1925): 21–22; Rose, *Historic Roads*, 98; Quinta Scott and Susan Croce Kelly, *Route 66: The Highway and Its People* (Norman: University of Oklahoma, 1988), 14–15; Weingroff, "Names to Numbers," 8–9.

10. "Origin of U.S. Route Markers," *Public Roads* 2, no. 7 (1956): 5; Scott and Kelley, *Route 66*, 13–14; "Standard Signs Adopted for Federal Highways," *American City*, October 1925 ; "Tulsa Linked With Nation," *Tulsa Tribune*, May 31, 1925; Weingroff, "Names to Numbers," 9.

11. "Tulsa Linked"; Scott and Kelley, *Route 66*, 11–12; Jim Ross, "'Proud of What It Means,' Route 66," *Chronicles of Oklahoma* 73 (1995): 262–63.

12. "Tulsa Linked."

13. Ibid.; Scott and Kelley, *Route 66*, 14–17.

14. Arthur Krim, "Numbering Route 66," typescript, Society for Commercial Archeology, Pittsburgh, October 1990, 3–4.

15. Cyrus S. Avery to Mr. E. W. James, 16 June 1925, BPR Collection, NRC.

16. "Interesting Folks," *Studebaker Wheel* (February 1926): 13.

17. AASHO Staff, "U.S. Route," 142; Frederick W. Cron, "Touring by Numbers, Why and How," *Public Works* (February 1968): 80–82; E. W. James, "Making and Unmaking a National System of Marked Routes," *American Highways* 13, no. 10 (1935): 16–18; M. A. O'Brien, "History of United States Numbered Highways," *California Highways and Public Works* 31, no. 3–4 (1952): 54–55; Transcript of interview with E. W. James, 1967, BPR Collection, NRC, 9; Transcript of the 2nd full meeting of the Joint Board on Interstate Highways, 3–4 August 1925. BPR Collection, NRC; Weingroff, "Names to Numbers," 9, 11.

18. Cron, *Touring*, 81; Telegram from B. H. Piepmeier to W. C. Markham, 8 February 1926, BPR Collection, NRC; Weingroff, "Names to Numbers," 1.

19. AASHO Staff, "U. S. Route," 142; Seely, *Building*, 78; Weingroff, "Names to Numbers," 11.

20. Joint Board, 3–4 August 1925, 30

21. Krim, "Numbering," 5; Ross, "Proud," 262; Scott and Kelly, *Route 66*, 14; Weingroff, "Names to Numbers," 14.

22. Joint Board, 3–4 August 1925; O'Brien, "Numbered Highways," 55.

23. Krim, "Numbering," 6; Ross, "Proud," 263; Scott and Kelly, *Route 66*, 14–15; Richard F. Weingroff [FHA] to author, 6 January 1999, 13–14.

24. "Kentucky Will Ignore Roads Named by U.S. as Highways," *Frankfort* [Kentucky] *Journal*, December 8, 1925.

25. "Governor W. J. Fields," [Kentucky State Historical Society] *Register* 22, no. 64 (1924): 1; Lowell H. Harrison, ed., *Kentucky's Governors* (Lexington: University of Kentucky, 1985): 132–33; John E. Pearce, *Divide and Dissent: Kentucky Politics* (Lexington: University of Kentucky, 1987), 26–27.

26. Krim, "Numbering," 6; Weingroff, "Names to Numbers," 14.

27. Piepmeier to Markham, 8 February 1926.

28. Scott and Kelly, *Route 66*, 15; Krim, "Numbering," 6; Weingroff, "Names to Numbers," 14.

29. Cyrus S. Avery to Frank Page, 22 March 1926, BPR Collection, NRC.

30. Avery, "Cyrus Stevens Avery," 87; Bob L. Blackburn, "Martin Edwin Trapp" in *Oklahoma's Governor, 1907–1929*, ed. L. H. Fischer (Oklahoma City: Oklahoma Historical Society, 1981), 156; Edwin McReynolds, *Oklahoma: A History of the Sooner State* (Norman: University of Oklahoma, 1954), 350; Ross, "Proud," 261–62; James Scales and Danny Goble, *Oklahoma Politics: A History* (Norman: University of Oklahoma, 1982), 189; Joseph B. Thoburn and Muriel Wright, *Oklahoma: A History of the State and Its People,* vol. 2 (New York: Lewis Historical Publishing, 1929), 699; "Tulsa Man Will Get State Highway Post," *Daily Oklahoman*, February 16, 1924.

30. David C. Boles, "The Effects of the Ku Klux Klan on the Election of 1926," *Chronicles of Oklahoma* 55 (1977): 426; Victor E. Harlow, *Oklahoma* (Oklahoma City: Harlow, 1950), 368; Scales and Goble, *Oklahoma Politics*, 135; Thorburn and Wright, *Oklahoma*, 700.

32. Charles C. Alexander, *The Ku Klux Klan in the Southwest* (Lexington: University of Kentucky, 1965), 154–55; Boles, "Effects," 425–26; Arnel Morgan Gibson, *Oklahoma: A History of Five Centuries* (Norman: University of Oklahoma, 1981), 217; Scales and Goble, *Oklahoma Politics*, 128.

33. "About Politics and Politicians," *Harlow's Weekly*, January 9, 1926.

34. Alexander, *Ku Klux*, 228; Boles, "Effects," 425; "Johnston Leading for Governor," *Harlow's Weekly*, March 30, 1926; Scales and Goble, *Oklahoma Politics*, 130; Kenneth L. Tracy, "Henry Simpson Johnston" in *Oklahoma's Governors, 1907–1929*, ed. L. H. Fischer (Norman: University of Oklahoma, 1981), 177–78.

35. "Election Board Hears Eligibility Question," *Harlow's Weekly*, May 8, 1926.

36. Cyrus S. Avery to Mr. W. C. Markam, 17 May 1926, BPR Collection, NRC; Ross, "Proud," 264.

37. Scott and Kelly, *Route 66*, 15–17; Weingroff, "Names to Numbers," 14.

38. Krim, "Numbering," 6.

39. Thomas H. MacDonald to Cyrus Avery, 14 April 1926, BPR Collection, NRC.

40. Arthur Krim, "Highway Reports: First Numbering of Route 66 in Missouri," *SCA News Journal* 11, no. 2 (1990): 10.

41. "Glenstone is Designated as State Highway," *Springfield* [Missouri] *Leader*, April 30, 1926, 1.

42. "Boulevard Proposed," *Springfield* [Missouri] *Republican*, May 1, 1926, 1; "District 8 Open House, April 19," pamphlet, State Highway Commission, Springfield (Missouri), 1975.

43. Cyrus S. Avery, "History of U.S. Highway 66," typescript, c. 1927, Ruth Sigler Avery (private) Collection, Tulsa, Oklahoma, 1; "Engineers Will Give Chamber Program," *Tulsa Tribune*, March 20, 1924; "John Page, Division Engineer for Texas," *News in Public Roads*, July 1961; Obituary of John M. Page, *FHWA News*, August 19, 1969; J. M. Page, *Annual Report of the State Highway Commission* (Oklahoma City: Oklahoma Highway Commission, 1925); Scott and Kelly, *Route 66*, 17.

44. Krim, "Numbering," 7–8; Ross, "Proud," 264; Weingroff, "Names to Numbers," 14.

45. Avery, "History of U.S. Highway 66," 1927.

46. Joint Board, 3–4 August 1925; Krim, "Numbering," 7; Scott and Kelly, *Route 66*, 15; Weingroff, "Names to Numbers," 14.

47. Arthur Krim, "The 66th Anniversary of Route 66," *SCA News Journal* 12, no. 2 (1992): 21–26.

48. Telegram from [Cyrus S.] Avery and [B. H.] Piepmeier to Thomas H. MacDonald, 30 April 1926, BPR Collection, NRC.

49. Avery to Markam, 17 May 1926.

50. Thomas H. MacDonald to Cyrus Avery, 11 June 1926, BPR Collection, NRC.

51. Cyrus S. Avery to Mr. Thos. H. MacDonald, 15 June 1926, BPR Collection, NRC.

52. "Election Board Hears"; "Election Board Holds Trapp Is Eligible," *Harlow's Weekly*, May 15, 1926.

53. Boles, "Effects," 426; *Fitzpatrick v. McAlister*, 17513 Oklahoma Sup. Ct. at 1; Arnel Morgan Gibson, *Oklahoma: A History of Five Centuries* (Norman: University of Oklahoma, 1981), 218; Harlow, *Oklahoma*, 368; "Judge Zwick Holds Trapp Is Eligible," *Harlow's Weekly*, June 12, 1926; Krim, "Numbering," 9–10; Ross, "Proud," 264; Scales and Goble, *Oakahoma Politics*, 135–36; Thorburn and Wright, *Oklahoma*, 700.

54. Thomas H. MacDonald to Cyrus Avery, 23 July 1926, BPR Collection, NRC.

55. Cyrus S. Avery to Mr. E. W. James, 26 July 1926, BPR Collection, NRC; Ross, "Proud," 265.

56. Frank T. Sheets to Mr. E. W. James, 30 July 1925, BPR Collection, NRC.

57. E. W. James to Cyrus Avery (unsigned), 7 August 1926, BPR Collection, NRC.

58. [W. C.] Markham, "Memorandum to AASHO Members," 11 August 1926, BPR Collection, NRC; Scott and Kelly, *Route 66*, 17.

59. AASHO Staff, "Route 66," 143; Ross, "Proud," 265; Michael Wallis, *Route 66: The Mother Road*, 8; Weingroff, "Names to Numbers," 14.

60. "United States Numbered Highways," *American Highways* 3 (October 1925): 3–17; *United States Numbered Highways* (Washington, D.C.: AASHO, 1927), 24–27.

61. "Get Acquainted with Arizona: Condition Map," *Arizona Highways* 2 (October 1926): 14.

62. "U.S. and State Markers Being Erected," *New Mexico Highway Journal* 4 (March 1927): 12.

63. Cyrus S. Avery, *Report to the State Highway Commission* (Oklahoma City: Oklahoma Highway Commission, 1927), 192.

64. "About Politics and Politicians," *Harlow's Weekly*, August 7, 1926; idem, November 6, 1926; Boles, "Effects," 430–32; Scales and Goble, *Oklahoma Politics*, 137–38; Thorburn and Wright, *Oklahoma*, 700–01; Tracy, "Henry Simpson Johnston," 178–80.

65. Gibson, *Five Centuries*, 218; Harlow, *Oklahoma*, 369; Ross, "Proud,"265; Thorburn and Wright, *Oklahoma*, 702; Tracy, "Henry Simpson Johnston," 181–82.

66. "Close of Road," *Tulsa Tribune*, January 27, 1927.

67. "Political Blasts in Oklahoma," *Springfield* [Missouri] *Daily News*, February 4, 1927.

68. "Mandigo Will Succeed Page," *Blackwell* [Oklahoma] *Morning Tribune*, May 17, 1927.

69. "Piepmeier Expected to Resign," *St. Louis Globe-Democrat*, November 28, 1926.

70. Arthur Piepmeier, "Father Was an Engineer: A Story of Bion Harmon Piepmeier," privately printed booklet, Nashville, 1992, v–1; "Piepmeier Resigns," *Jefferson City* [Missouri] *Capitol News*, December 14, 1926; Mari Ann Winters [Missouri Highway Commission, Jefferson City] to author, 27 December 1989.

71. Harrison, *Kentucky's Governors*, 135.

72. Thorburn and Wright, *Oklahoma*, 703; Harlow, *Oklahoma*, 271–72; Von Russell Creel, "Court in Peril: The Legislative Judicial Struggle of 1927–1929," *Chronicles of Oklahoma* 52 (1974): 220–36; Tracy, "Henry Simpson Johnston," 184–93.

73. Krim, "Numbering," 10–11; Ross, "Proud," 265.

CHAPTER SIX

1. Quinta Scott and Susan Croce Kelly, *Route 66: The Highway and Its People* (Norman: University of Oklahoma, 1988), 23–24; "Political Blasts in Oklahoma," *Springfield* [Missouri] *Daily News*, February 4, 1927; "Uniform Marking for U.S. Highways," *New York Times*, January 2, 1927.

2. "John T. Woodruff Elected to Head '66' Association," *Springfield* [Missouri] *Daily News*, February 5, 1927; "Plan U.S. 66 as Widest Highway," *Motorist* (April 1927): 14; Lon Scott, "The Greatest Highway Project in America," *The Nation's Highways* (June 1927): 1.

3. "Unified Effort in Building of Roads Urged," *Springfield* [Missouri] *Leader*, May 2, 1927.

4. "U.S. 66 Highway Association Holds Conference," *Good Roads* 27 (August 1927): 1.

5. Drake Hokanson, *The Lincoln Highway: Main Street Across America* (Ames: University of Iowa, 1988), 93; Lincoln Highway Association, *The Lincoln Highway* (New York: Dodd, Mead, 1935), 228;

"Topics of the Times," *New York Times*, June 18, 1927; Richard F. Weingroff, "From Names to Numbers," *AASHTO Quarterly* 76, no. 2 (1997): 14.

6. Michael Wallis, *Route 66: The Mother Road* (New York: St. Martin's, 1990), 12.

7. Scott and Kelly, *Route 66*, 33; James H. Thomas, *The Bunion Derby* (Oklahoma City: Southwest Heritage, 1981), 14–15; Wallis, *Mother Road*, 12–13.

8. "Quamowaha, Hopi Indian, Enters Coast-to-Coast Race," *New York Times*, February 17, 1928; Thomas, *Bunion*, 15; Wallis, *Mother Road*, 12–13.

9. Thomas, *Bunion*, 23–25, 30–45; "Three New York Runners Lead in Marathon," *New York Times*, March 5, 1928; Wallis, *Mother Road*, 13–14.

10. Thomas, *Bunion*, 56–57.

11. "Grange Quits, Payne Still Leads Marathon," *New York Times*, April 11, 1928; "Payne Regains Lead in Home Town Dash," *New York Times*, April 18, 1928.

12. "Pyle's Guarantee Attached in West," *New York Times*, April 14, 1928.

13. Thomas, *Bunion*, 63–69.

14. Ibid., 20

15. "Marathon Runners Arrive in Chicago," *New York Times*, May 6, 1928; "Payne Regains"; Thomas, *Bunion*, 87–89, 95–98, 100–03.

16. "55 Reach Goal Here," *New York Times*, May 27, 1928.

17. "Directors of 66 Split After Avery is Double-Crossed," *Tulsa Tribune*, May 29, 1928; Scott and Kelly, *Route 66*, 36, 197; Thomas, *Bunion*, 120–26.

18. R. L. Davee, "Another '66' Spasm," *Georgia Highways* (September 1928): 17.

19. Thomas Hart Benton, *An Artist in America* (New York: Robert McBride, 1937), 201–03; Patricia Junker, "Thomas Hart Benton: 'Boomtown'" in *Memorial Art Gallery*, ed. S. D. Peters (Rochester: University of Rochester, 1988), 211; Karal Ann Marling, "Thomas Hart Benton's 'Boomtown'" in *Prospectus 6*, ed. J. Salzman (New York: Burt Franklin, 1981), 73–77; Michael Wallis, *Oil Man: The Story of Frank Phillips* (New York: St. Martin, 1988), 190–93, 236–44.

20. Hannah Campbell, *Why Did They Name It?...* (New York: Fleet, 1964), 175–77; "Route 66, Past, Present. No Future," *Shield* 7, no. 4 (1982): 17; Wallis, *Oil Man*, 245–46; *Why 66?* (Bartlesville, OK: Phillips Petroleum, [1983]), 7–8.

21. Campbell, *Name It?*, 177.

22. Wallis, *Oil Man*, 247–48.

23. *Why 66?*, 12.

24. WPA, *Los Angeles: A Guide to the City* (New York: Hastings, 1941), 136–37.

25. "U.S. Highway 66 From Chicago to Los Angeles," *St. Louis Post-Dispatch*, December 15, 1929.

26. Main Street of America, *Map of U.S. 66 Highway* (1932; Kingman, AZ: Mojave Chamber of Commerce, 1988).

27. Arthur Krim, "Mapping Route 66, A Cultural Cartography" in *Roadside America*, ed. J. Jennings (Ames: Iowa State University, 1990), 201–02; *Sectional Road Map, Los Angeles, California, to Flagstaff, Arizona*, no. 36 (Los Angeles: Automobile Club of Southern California, 1937; Tom Snyder, *The Route 66 Traveler's Guide* (New York: St, Martins, 1990), xx–xxi.

28. "U.S. Highway 66 to the Olympics," *Saturday Evening Post*, July 17, 1932.

CHAPTER SEVEN

1. "Great Drought," *Nation* 131, no. 20 (August 1930): 195; "Great Drought of 1930," *Literary Digest* 106 (August 16, 1930): 5–6; "Wide Area in Southwest Hit by Drought in Heat Wave," *New York*

Times, April 13, 1930; David Worster, *Dust Bowl: The Southern Plains in the 1930s* (New York: Oxford University, 1982), 10–11.

2. Donald Day, *Will Rogers: A Biography* (New York: David McKay, 1962), 267; "Will Rogers Raises $90,000 for Relief," *New York Times*, February 9, 1931; Worster, *Dust Bowl*, 11.

3. Will Rogers Memorial Commission, ed., *Radio Broadcasts of Will Rogers* (Stillwater: Oklahoma State University, [1990]), 66.

4. R. Douglas Hurt, *The Dust Bowl: An Agricultural and Social History* (Chicago: Nelson, 1981), 33–34; Russell J. Smith, "The Drought, Act of God and Freedom," *Survey Graphic* 23 (1934): 412–14; Worster, *Dust Bowl*, 13, 92–94.

5. R. Douglas Hurt, "Dust!" *American Heritage* 28, no. 5 (1977): 34–35; Worster, *Dust Bowl*, 18–20.

6. Robert Geiger, "If It Rains . . . ," *Washington Evening Star*, April 15, 1935; Mencken, H. L., *The American Language*, supplement 1 (New York: Knopf, 1945), 329.

7. Hurt, *Dust Bowl*, 1–4; Milton Meltzer, *Dorothea Lange: A Photographer's Life* (New York: Farrar, Strauss, 1978), 102; Worster, *Dust Bowl*, 28–31, 42.

8. William R. Brown, *Imagemaker: Will Rogers and the American Dream* (Columbia: University of Missouri, 1970), 255; Donald Day, *Will Rogers: A Biography* (New York: David McKay, 1962), 257–61; Dixon Wecter, "Will Rogers" in *Dictionary of American Biography*, supplement 1, ed. H. E. Starr (New York: Scribner's, 1944), 635–37; Ben Yagort, *Will Rogers: A Biography* (New York: Knopf, 1993), 229–30.

9. "Names Highway for Rogers," *New York Times*, January 6, 1936; Yagort, *Will Rogers*, 322.

10. Jerry McClanahan, "Rock, Scissors, Pavement," *Route 66 Magazine* 4, no. 1 (1996): 24; "Minutes of the [AASHO] Executive Committee," typescript, BPR Collection, NRC, 39, 44; Schneider, *Route 66 Across New Mexico* (Albuquerque: University of New Mexico, 1991), 172; Scott and Kelly, *Route 66*, 68–69.

11. Raymond Fielding, *The March of Time* (New York: Oxford University, 1978), 3–4; Arthur Krim, "Filming Route 66: Documenting the Dust Bowl Highway" in *Place, Power, Situation and Spectacle: A Geography of Film*, ed. S. C. Aitken and L. E. Zonn (Lanham, MD: Rowan and Littlefield, 1994), 185.

12. Pare Lorentz, *FDR's Moviemaker* (Reno: University of Nevada, 1992), 36–37; Meltzer, *Dorothea Lange*, 102; Robert L. Snyder, *Pare Lorentz and the Documentary Film* (New York: Oxford University, 1968), 24–25.

13. Book review of *The Roosevelt Year, News-Week* (April 14, 1934): 39; Krim, "Filming," 186; [Pare Lorentz] "Agriculture," *News-Week* (March 30, 1935): 3–4; idem, "Agriculture," *News-Week* (June 9, 1934): 3–4; idem, "Drought," *News-Week* (August 18, 1934): 3–4; idem, *Moviemaker*, 28–31; idem, *The Roosevelt Year, 1933* (New York: Funk and Wagnall's, 1934); Richard Dyer MacCann, *The People's Films: A Political History of U.S. Government Motion Pictures* (New York: Hastings House, 1973), 61–63; Snyder, *Lorentz*, 19–25.

14. Lorentz, *Moviemaker*, 36–38; Synder, *Lorentz*, 24.

15. Russell Campbell, *Cinema Strikes Back: Radical Filmmakers in the United States, 1930–1942* (Ann Arbor: UMI Research, 1982), 124–27; Calvin Tomkins, *Paul Strand* (New York: Aperture, 1976), 158.

16. Campbell, *Cinema*, 127; MacCann, *People's Films*, 63; Snyder, *Lorentz*, 29.

17. Krim, "Filming," 187; Meltzer, *Dorothea Lange*, 104–05; Snyder, *Lorentz*, 30–32.

18. Eric Barnouw, *Documentary: A History of the Non-Fiction Film* (New York: Oxford Unversity, 1974), 114, 118; "Cinema: Tormented Dust," *Time* (May 25, 1936): 47; "Dust Storm Film," *Literary Digest* (May 16, 1936): 22–23; Lorentz , *Moviemaker*, 39–40; "The Plow That Broke the Plains," *McCall's* (July 21, 1936); Snyder, *Lorentz*, 33.

19. Lorentz, *Moviemaker*, 48–50; Virgil Thompson and Pare

Lorentz, *The Plow That Broke the Plains: Suite for Orchestra* (New York: Music Press, 1942), 28.

20. Barnouw, *Documentary*, 117–18; "Tormented Dust."

21. Therese Thau Heyman, *Celebrating a Collection: The Work of Dorothea Lange* (Oakland, CA: Oakland Museum, 1978), 53–57; Meltzer, *Dorothea Lange*, 28–31, 71–76, 93–99; Beaumont Newhall, *The History of Photography* (New York: Museum of Modern Art, 1964), 146.

22. Meltzer, *Dorothea Lange*, 105; Paul Taylor, "Again By Covered Wagon," *Survey Graphic* 24 (1935): 348–51.

23. Dorothea Lange [writing as Lucretia Penny], "Pea-Picker's Child," *Survey Graphic* 24 (1935): 352–53; Meltzer, *Dorothea Lange*, 105.

24. Paul Taylor, "Again By Covered Wagon," *Survey Graphic* 24 (1935): 348.

25. Heyman, *Collection*, 60–61, 71–72; Lange, Dorothea, "Dragin-Around People," *Survey Graphic* 25 (1936): 524–25; Meltzer, *Dorothea Lange*, 103–06, 132–34; Newhall, *Photography*, 143–46.

26. Arthur Krim, "Right Near Sallisaw," *Steinbeck* 12, no. 1 (1999): 1–4; Paul S. Levin and Katherine Northrup, eds., *Dorothea Lange: Farm Security Administration Photographs*, vol. 1 (Glencoe, IL: Text-Fiche, 1980), 199; Meltzer, *Dorothea Lange*, 141–48.

27. Levin and Northrup, *Farm Security*, vol. 1, 199.

28. "New Heat Wave: Oklahoma Asks More Aid," *New York Times*, August 9, 1936.

29. Scott Donaldson and R. H. Winnick, *Archibald MacLeish: An American Life* (Boston: Houghton Mifflin, 1992), 271; D. G. Kehl, "Steinbeck's 'String of Pictures' in *The Grapes of Wrath*," *Image* 17, no. 1 (1974): 4; Archibald MacLeish, *The Land of the Free* (New York: Harcourt, Brace, 1938), 52; Meltzer, *Dorothea Lange*, 184.

30. Levin and Northrup, *Farm Security*, vol. 2, 8.

31. Robert Coles, "*An American Exodus* As a Documentary Milestone" in *Perpetual Mirage: Photographic Narratives of the Desert West*, ed. Mary Castlebury (New York: Abrams, 1996), 135; Heyman, *Collection*, 41; Meltzer, *Dorothea Lange*, 186.

32. Robert Coles, *Dorothea Lange: Photographs of a Lifetime* (New York: Aperture, 1982), 178; Dorothea Lange and Paul Taylor, *An American Exodus: A Record of Human Erosion* (New York: Reynal and Hitchcock, 1939), 61; Levin and Northrup, *Farm Security*, vol. 2, 161.

33. Arthur Krim, "Mother Road, Migrant Road, Dorothea Lange on U.S. 66," *Landscape* 31, no. 2 (1991): 16; Lange and Taylor, *American Exodus*, 56–57; David Lopez [Department of Transportation, Oklahoma City] to author, 10 July 1991; Jim Ross, "Ghost Bridge of the Canadian," *Route 66 Magazine* 4, no. 2 (1997): 32–35.

34. David Zinman, *50 Classic Motion Pictures* (New York: Limelight Editions, 1992): 251–55.

35. Heyman, *Collection*, 69; Lange and Taylor, *American Exodus*, 57.

36. Jefferson Hunter, *Image and Word* (Cambridge: Harvard University, 1997), 101–02; Quinta Scott and Susan Croce Kelly, *Route 66: The Highway and Its People* (Norman: University of Oklahoma, 1988), 58.

37. Krim, "Mother Road," 16; idem, "Oklahoma Route 66: American Highway Icon" lecture, May 9, 1997, Oklahoma Preservation Conference, Clinton, OK, 11–12.

38. Lange and Taylor, *American Exodus*, 103.

39. Levin and Northrup, *Farm Security*, vol. 2, 161.

40. Meltzer, *Dorothea Lange*, 185–86; Sam Stourdzé, "Introduction" in Lange and Taylor, *An American Exodus*, ii.

41. Meltzer, *Dorothea Lange*, 203; Stourdzé, op. cit., p. ii–iv.

42. Lange and Taylor, *American Exodus*, 102.

43. Ibid., 104; Arthur Krim, "Mapping Route 66, A Cultural Cartography" in *Roadside America*, ed. J. Jennings (Ames: Iowa State

University, 1990), 202; Paul Taylor, *Adrift on the Land* (New York: Public Affairs Committee, 1940), 4.

44. Lange and Taylor, *American Exodus*, 102.

45. Meltzer, *Dorothea Lange*, 204.

46. Ibid., 229; Coles, "Documentary Milestone," 133–34; Stourdzé, op. cit., iv–v.

CHAPTER EIGHT

1. Jackson J. Benson, *The True Adventures of John Steinbeck* (New York: Viking, 1984), 113–15, 255–56; Robert DeMott, "Introduction" in *Grapes of Wrath* by John Steinbeck (New York: Penguin, 1992), xx–xvi; Warren French, *John Steinbeck* (New York: Twayne, 1961), 20–21, 294–95; Harry Thorton Moore, *The Novels of John Steinbeck* (New York: Normandie House, 1939).

2. Benson, *True Adventures*, 296–97; Jackson J. Benson and Anne Loftis, "John Steinbeck and Farm Labor Unionization," *American Literature* 52 (1980): 200–01; Roy Hammet, telephone conversation with author, August 19, 1997; Moore, *Novels*, 41; "Right Near Sallisaw," *Steinbeck* 12, no. 1 (1999): 1–4.

3. Benson, *True Adventures*, 27–77; Moore, *Novels*, 53.

4. Benson, *True Adventures*, 293–95; French, *Steinbeck*, 22–23, 81; R. S. Hughes, *John Steinbeck: A Study of the Short Fiction* (Boston: Twayne, 1989), 48–49.

5. Benson, *True Adventures*, 297–301; French, *Steinbeck*, 23; Moore, *Novels*, 40–41; John Steinbeck, *Working Day: The Journals of* The Grapes of Wrath, ed. Robert DeMott (New York: Viking, 1989), xxxiv.

6. Jackson J. Benson, "'To Tom, Who Lived It': John Steinbeck and the Man from Weedpatch," *Journal of Modern Literature* 5 (1976): 155; idem, *True Adventures*, 332; French, *Steinbeck*, 24; Anne Loftis, "John Steinbeck and the Federal Migrant Camps," *San Jose Studies* 16, no. 1 (1990): 78–79; Alice Barnard Thomsen, "Eric Thompson

and John Steinbeck," *Steinbeck* 3, no. 2 (1990): 2.

7. Benson, "'To Tom,'" 154–56, 200–01; idem, *True Adventures*, 332–39; DeMott, "Introduction," xxvii; Loftis, "Migrant Camps," 79–80; Milton Meltzer, *Dorothea Lange: A Photographer's Life* (New York: Farrar, Strauss, 1978), 203.

8. John Steinbeck, "Dubious Battle in California," *The Nation* (September 12, 1936: 302–05.

9. Benson, "'To Tom,'"200; idem, *True Adventures*, 347; DeMott, "Introduction, xxvii; Robert J. Doherty, "Introduction" in *Dorothea Lange: Farm Security Administration Photographs*, vol. 1, ed. Paul Levin and Katherine Northrup (Glencoe, IL: Text-Fiche, 1980), 32; Charles Wollenberg, "Introduction" in *The Harvest Gypsies* by John Steinbeck (Berkeley: Heyday, 1988), v–xvii.

10. "Harvest Gypsies," *San Francisco News*, October 5, 1936.

11. Benson, "'To Tom,'"200; idem, *True Adventures*, 333, 335; Steinbeck, *Working Days*, xxviii.

12. Arthur Krim, "Steinbeck, Lorentz and Lange," *Steinbeck* 6, no. 2 (1993): 8–9; Levin and Northrup, *Farm Security*, vol. 1, 207–08; Loftis, "Migrant Camps," 88.

13. Benson, "'To Tom,'"204; idem, *True Adventures*, 358–59; French, *John Steinbeck*, 24; Moore, *Novels*, 88.

14. Moore, *Novels*, 54, 88; Benson, "'To Tom,'"153; idem, *True Adventures*, 360; Arthur Krim, "John Steinbeck and Highway 66," *Steinbeck* 4, no. 2 (1991): 8; Jay Parini, *John Steinbeck: A Biography* (New York: Henry Holt, 1995), 192–93.

15. Benson, *True Adventures*, 362–63; Parini, *Biography*, 194–95.

16. Benson, "'To Tom,'" 203–04; idem, *True Adventures*, 375, 378; DeMott, "Introduction," xxix–xxx; French, *John Steinbeck*, 24; Susan Shillinglaw, "Local Newspapers Report on 'The Oklahomans,'" *Steinbeck* 2 (Summer 1989): 4–5; Steinbeck, *Working Days*, xxxvi.

17. Benson, *True Adventures*, 369–70; French, *John Steinbeck*, 24; Steinbeck, *Working Days*, xxxvii.

18. Benson, "'To Tom,'" 204; idem, *True Adventures*, 370–71; Dean Briely, "Horace Bristol, Eye on an Era," *Photo Metro* 11 (August 1993): 6–8; Horace Bristol, "Documenting 'The Grapes of Wrath,'" *The Californians* 6, no. 1 (1988): 47; Ken Conner and Debra Heimerdinger, *Horace Bristol: An American View* (San Francisco: Chronicle, 1996), 55; DeMott, "Introduction," xxxiii; William Howarth, "The Mother of Literature: Journalism and *The Grapes of Wrath*" in *New Essays on* The Grapes of Wrath, ed. D. Wyatt (New York: Cambridge University, 1990), 76–77; Arthur Krim, review of *Horace Bristol* in *Steinbeck* 10, no. 2 (1997): 20.

19. "The Wrath Hasn't Left Steinbeck," *London Daily Mail*, September 18, 1961.

20. Benson, *True Adventures*, 371; Bristol, "Documenting," 47; Krim, review; Steinbeck, *Working Days*, lv.

21. Benson, *True Adventures*, 371–72; French, *John Steinbeck*, 96; Steinbeck, *Working Days*, 9–11.

22. Howarth, *Mother*, 90; Roy S. Simmonds, "The Original Manuscript," *San Jose Studies* 16, no. 1 (1990): 121.

23. John Steinbeck, *Grapes of Wrath* (New York: Penguin, 1939), 103.

24. "Crime" Floyd Flushed," *Time* (October 22, 1934): 18; "Milestones," *Time* (October 29, 1934): 68; "'Pretty Boy Floyd,' Notorious Bandit, Killed by U.S. Agents," *San Francisco Examiner*, October 23; "'Pretty Boy' Floyd Shot!" *San Francisco Examiner*, October 22, 1934; Steinbeck, *Working Days*, 20; Michael Wallis, *Pretty Boy* (New York: St. Martin's, 1992), 350–51.

25. Arthur Krim, "Right Near Sallisaw," *Steinbeck* 12, no. 1 (1999): 1–4; Steinbeck, *Grapes*, 291; Steinbeck, *Working Days*, 31.

26. D. G. Kehl, "Steinbeck's 'String of Pictures' in *The Grapes of Wrath*," *Image* 17, no. 1 (1974): 2.

27. Erwin G. Gudde, *California Place Names* (Berkeley: University of California, 1969), 277–78; Krim, "Sallisaw"; WPA, *Oklahoma: A Guide to the Sooner State* (Norman: University of Oklahoma, 1941), 262.

28. Parini, *Biography*, 205; Steinbeck, *Working Days*, 36–37.

29. Steinbeck, *Working Days*, 37.

30. Ibid., 152.

31. Krim, "Steinbeck and Highway 66," 8.

32. Holograph manuscript of *The Grapes of Wrath* by John Steinbeck, 1938, John Steinbeck Collection, Barrett Library, University of Virginia, Charlottesville.

33. Manuscript, *Grapes*.

34. Krim, "Steinbeck and Highway 66," 8; Steinbeck, *Working Days*, 152.

35. Manuscript, *Grapes*.

36. Manuscript, *Grapes*.

37. Steinbeck, *Working Days*, 31; Loftis, "Migrant Camps," 78–79; Simmonds, "Original," 123.

38. James N. Gregory, *American Exodus: The Dust Bowl Migrations and Okie Culture in California* (New York: Oxford Unviersity, 1989), 100; Steinbeck, *Grapes*, 280.

39. Benson, *True Adventures*, 379; Parini, *Biography*, 207; Steinbeck, *Working Days*, 46–48, 58–59, 65; Elaine Steinbeck and Robert Wallsten, *Steinbeck: A Life in Letters* (New York: Viking, 1975), 170–71.

40. Benson, *True Adventures*, 390–91; DeMott, "Introduction," xliii.

41. See the manuscript of *Grapes*, compared to Steinbeck, *Grapes*, 228.

42. Arthur Krim, "Elmer Hader and *The Grapes of Wrath* Book Jacket," *Steinbeck* 4 (1991): 1–3; "Paintings: Auction, June 27," brochure for Sotheby's, New York, 1989, Lot 95; Steinbeck, *Working Days*, 97.

43. Benson, *True Adventures*, 394–95; Susan Shillinglaw, "Introduction" in *The Grapes of Wrath: A Fifty Year Bibliographic Survey*, ed. R. E. Harmon (San Jose, CA: Steinbeck Research Center, 1990), 2.

44. Parini, *Biography*, 226.

45. Charles Poore, "Books of the Times," *New York Times*, April 14, 1939.

46. George Stevens, "Steinbeck's Uncovered Wagon," *Saturday Review of Literature* 15 (April 15, 1939): 2–3.

47. Warren French, *Filmguide to* The Grapes of Wrath (Bloomington: Indiana University, 1973), 16; Robert E. Harmon, ed., *The Grapes of Wrath: A Fifty Year Bibliographic Survey* (San Jose, CA: Steinbeck Research Center, 1990), 217.

48. "Library Bans Steinbeck Book," *New York Times*, August 19, 1939; "Orders Steinbeck Book Burned," *New York Times*, November 15, 1939; Steinbeck, *Working Days*, 78; David Wyatt, "Introduction" in *New Essays on The Grapes of Wrath*, ed. David Wyatt (New York: Cambridge University, 1990), 2.

49. Benson, *True Adventures*, 453–54; Shillinglaw, "Introduction," 2.

50. Adrian H Goldstone and John R. Payne, *John Steinbeck, Bibliographic Catalogue* (Austin: University of Texas, 1974), 44–47; James Johnson, *John Steinbeck*, catalogue 6 (Carmel, CA: James Johnson, 1991), 68.

51. Helmut Liedloff, *Steinbeck in German Translation* (Carbondale: Southern Illinois University, 1965); Arthur Krim, "*Fruchte des Zornes*: *The Grapes of Wrath* in Wartime Germany," *Steinbeck* 7 (1994): 2.

52. Goldstone and Payne, *Bibliographic Catalogue*, 152, 187.

53. Harmon, *Bibliographic Survey*, 20; Liedloff, *German Translation*, 97.

54. Krim, "Wartime Germany," 2–4; Liedloff, *German Translation*, 90–93.

55. John Steinbeck, *Fruchte des Zornes*, trans. Klauss Lambrecht (Zurich: Humanitas, 1940), 182.

56. Krim, "Wartime Germany," 3; Liedloff, *German Translation*, 97.

57. John Steinbeck, *Fruchte Des Zornes*, trans. Karen Von Schab (Berlin: Vorwerk, 1943), 170.

58. Zuoya Coa, "The Chinese Translation of *The Grapes of Wrath*," *Steinbeck* 10, no. 2 (1997): 11; Goldstone and Payne, *Bibliographic Catalogue*, 149, 168; Gregory, *Okie Culture*, 58; Harmon, *Bibliographic Survey*, 24; Kiyoshi Nakayama, "'The Grapes' Transplanted to Japan," *San Jose Studies* 16, no. 1 (1990): 92; John Steinbeck, *Ikari No Budo*, trans. Itari Nii (Tokyo: Shigen Sha, 1939); WPA, *California*, 60–61, 409.

59. John Steinbeck, *Grazdya Gneva*, trans. N. Volzhinya (Moscow: State Publisher, 1940), 130; Harmon, *Bibliographic Survey*, 29; Susan Shillinglaw, "Five Steinbeck Specialists Visit the USSR," *Steinbeck* 3 (Winter, 1990): 2–3.

CHAPTER NINE

1. Jackson J. Benson, *The True Adventures of John Steinbeck* (New York: Viking, 1984), 372–73, 408–09; "Fox Gets Steinbeck Book," *New York Times*, April 21, 1939; Warren French, *Filmguide to* The Grapes of Wrath (Bloomington: Indiana University, 1973), 16, 23; Mel Gussow, *Don't Say "Yes" Until I've Finished Talking*, Darryl Zanuck (Garden City, NY: Doubleday, 1971), 90–91; Robert E. Harmon, ed., *The Grapes of Wrath: A Fifty Year Bibliographic Survey* (San Jose, CA: Steinbeck Research Center, 1990), 217; Joseph Millichan, *Steinbeck on Film* (New York: Frederick Unger, 1983), 26; John Steinbeck, *The Grapes of Wrath* (New York: Viking, 1939).

2. French, *Filmguide*, 16–17; Millichap, *Steinbeck on Film*, 30–31; Aubrey Soloman, *Twentieth Century-Fox: A Corporate History* (Metuchen, NJ: Scarecrow, 1988), 39–41, 58–59.

3. Ruby Behlmer, *Memo From Darryl F. Zanuck* (New York: Grove, 1993), 22–23; Peter Bogdanovich, *John Ford* (Berkeley: University of California, 1968), 72–74; Henry Fonda with Howard Teichman, *Fonda: My Life* (New York: New American Library, 1981), 133–36; Millichap, *Steinbeck on Film*, 32.

4. Behlmer, *Memo*, 33–34; Benson, *True Adventures*, 80–82, 409; Gussow, *Don't Say*, 91; Millichap. *Steinbeck on Film*, 43–44; Tom Stempel, *Screenwriter: The Life and Times of Nunnally Johnson* (San

Diego: A. S. Barnes, 1980), 59–61, 78–80, 84, 212–14.

5. Bogdanovich, *John Ford*, 69–70; Edward Buscombe, *Stagecoach* (London: British Film Institute, 1992), 39–40; Fonda, *My Life*, 139.

6. French, *Filmguide*, 78; Stempel, *Screenwriter*, 79, 196; Harmon, *Bibliographic Survey*, 218.

7. Nunnally Johnson, "The Grapes of Wrath" in *Twenty Best Screen Plays*, ed. J. Gassner and D. Nichols (New York: Crown, 1943), 346.

8. Horace Bristol, "Documenting 'The Grapes of Wrath,'" *The Californians* 6, no. 1 (1988), 47; Ken Conner and Debra Heimerdinger, *Horace Bristol: An American View* (San Francisco: Chronicle, 1996), 56; Louis Owens, *The Grapes of Wrath: Trouble in the Promised Land* (Boston: Twayne, 1989), 99; "The Grapes of Wrath," *Life* 3 (June 5, 1939): 66–67.

9. Jackson J. Benson, "'To Tom, Who Lived It': John Steinbeck and the Man from Weedpatch," *Journal of Modern Literature* 5 (1976): 206.

10. Stempel, *Screenwriter*, 87; Fonda, *My Life*, 237; David Zinman, *50 Classic Motion Pictures* (New York: Limelight, 1992), 237.

11. French, *Filmguide*, 18; Stempel, *Screenwriter*, 84–85.

12. Behlmer, *Memo*, 17–19; "Biography of Otto Brower," typescript, c. 1938, AMPAS Archive; Stempel, *Screenwriter*, 75.

13. Mimeograph of negative and positive stock film material from John Ford's *Grapes of Wrath*, 1940, Grinberg Film Library, Los Angeles. Typed logs of Brower's work are now preserved in the Grinberg Film Libraries as well. *Other sources*: Arthur Krim, "Filming Route 66: Documenting the Dust Bowl Highway" in *Place, Power, Situation and Spectacle: A Geography of Film*, ed. S. C. Aitken and L. E. Zonn (Lanham, MD: Rowan and Littlefield, 1994), 192; Stempel, *Screenwriter*, 84.

14. Buscombe, Edward, *Stagecoach*, British Film Institute, 1992, 39–41; Krim, "Dust Bowl Highway," 192; idem, "Highway Film Footage Found in Hollywood," *SCA News Journal* 12, no. 3 (1992): 29; Mimeograph, film stock, 2, 4–6.

15. Benson, "'To Tom,'" 406; Fonda, *My Life*, 137; Krim, "Footage Found."

16. F. Condon, "The Grapes of Rap," *Colliers* 15 (January 27, 1940): 23; Krim, "Dust Bowl Highway," 194.

17. Fonda, *My Life*, 137.

18. Ibid.

19. D. Ford, *Paddy: The Life of John Ford* (Englewood Cliffs, NJ: Prentice-Hall, 1979), 145.

20. French, *Filmguide*, 20; *The Grapes of Wrath*, DVD, directed by John Ford (1940; Beverly Hills: Fox Studio Classics, 2004); Krim, "Footage Found"; Mimeograph, film stock; Stempel, *Screenwriter*, 84.

21. Krim, "Dust Bowl Highway," 195.

22. Elaine Steinbeck and Robert Wallsten, *Steinbeck: A Life in Letters* (New York: Viking, 1975), 195.

23. Behlmer, *Memo*, 34–36; French, *Filmguide*, 20; Ford, *Paddy*, 145–46; Stempel, *Screenwriter*, 88.

24. Buscombe, *Stagecoach*, 84; Krim, "Dust Bowl Highway," 197–98; Pare Lorentz, "The Grapes of Wrath" in *Lorentz on Film: Movies 1927–1941* (Norman: University of Oklahoma, 1986), 183–86.

25. Lorentz, "Grapes,"185.

26. Harmon, *Bibliographic Survey*, 5; Krim, "Dust Bowl Highway," 195–96.

27. Woody Guthrie, *Bound for Glory* (1943; New York: New American Library, 1971), 191–225; Joe Klein, *Woody Guthrie: A Life* (New York: Random House, 1980), 75–98.

28. James N. Gregory, *American Exodus: The Dust Bowl Migrations and Okie Culture in California* (New York: Oxford University, 1989), 228; Klein, *Guthrie*, 83–84, 96–97; David Worster, *Dust Bowl: The Southern Plains in the 1930s* (New York: Oxford University, 1982), 48–49.

29. Klein, *Guthrie*, 43–45; H. R. Stoneback, "Rough People . . . Are the Best Singers" in *The Steinbeck Question*, ed. D. R. Noble (New York: Whitson, 1990), 159.

30. H. R. Stoneback, "Woody Sez: Woody Guthrie and 'The Grapes of Wrath,'" *Steinbeck* 2 (Summer 1989): 8.

31. Klein, *Guthrie*, 145–46, 163–64; Stoneback, "Woody Sez," 9.

32. Woody Guthrie, *Library of Congress Recordings*, Rounder Records, #1043, LP; Klein, *Guthrie*, 154–55, 159.

33. Guthrie, *Library of Congress*; Manuscript for "Will Rogers Highway," by Woody Guthrie, [March] 1940, Woody Guthrie Archives, New York City.

34. Woody Guthrie and Pete Seeger, *Hard Hitting Songs for Hard Hitting People* (1940; New York: Oak, 1967), 62–63; Klein, *Guthrie*, 156, 165–68; Pete Seeger and R. Santelli, "Hobo's Lullaby" in *Hard Travelin'*, ed. R. Santelli and E. Davidson (Hanover, NH: Wesleyan University, 1999), 22–25.

35. Gregory, *Okie Culture*, 232; Stoneback, "Rough People," 168–69.

36. W. J. Stein, *California and the Dust Bowl* (Westport, CT: Greenwood, 1973), 19.

37. French, *Filmguide*, 20; Stoneback, "Rough People," 159.

CHAPTER TEN

1. Norman Polmar and Thomas B. Allen, *World War II: America at War* (New York: Random House, 1991), 678–79; Quinta Scott and Susan Croce Kelly, *Route 66: The Highway and Its People* (Norman: University of Oklahoma, 1988), 75–80.

2. Jack Rittenhouse, *A Guide Book to Highway 66*, v–vi; Michael Wallis, *Route 66: The Mother Road*, 19–25.

3. Jim Edwards and Hal Ottaway, *Vanished Splendor II: A Postcard Album of Oklahoma City* (Oklahoma City: Abalache Book Shop, 1984), No. 390; Clara Hammond, ed., *Amarillo* (Amarillo, TX: George Autry, 1971), 203; Rittenhouse, *Guide Book*, 41, 56–67; Scott and Kelly, *Route 66*, 76–77; WPA, *Oklahoma: A Guide to the Sooner State* (Norman: University of Oklahoma, 1941), 170.

4. Stephanie Groueff, *Manhattan Project* (Boston: Little Brown, 1967), 203–09; Edith C. Truslow and Ralph C. Smith, *Project: The Los Alamos Story* (Los Angeles: Thomas, 1983), 58–59; Rittenhouse, *Guide Book*, 77–78; Tom Snyder, *The Route 66 Traveler's Guide* (New York: St. Martin's, 1990), 75–77.

5. Richard Feynman with Ralph Leighton, *What Do You Care What Other People Think?* (New York: Norton, 1988), 46.

6. Rittenhouse, *Guide Book*, 107; Jill Schneider, *Route 66 Across New Mexico* (Albuquerque: University of New Mexico, 1991), 67; Scott and Kelly, *Route 66*, 79–80.

7. Carlo D'Este, *Patton: A General for War* (New York: Harper Collins, 1995), 408–09, 417–27; Rittenhouse, *Guide Book*, 112, 121–23.

8. ASCAP, *Biographical Dictionary* (New York: R. R. Bower, 1980), 511; Don Heckman, "Bobby Troup, Writer of Classic Song 'Route 66,' Dies," *Los Angeles Times*, February 9, 1999; Arthur Krim, "'Get Your Kicks on Route 66!' A Song Map of Postwar Migration," *Journal of Cultural Geography* 18 (1998): 51; "Route 66: The Lyric Lingers On," *Arizona Highways* 57, no. 7 (1981): 6–14; Tom Teague, *Searching for 66* (Springfield, IL: Samizdat House, 1991), 229–31; Wallis, *Mother Road*, 9–11.

9. Sammy Kaye, *Sammy Kaye and His Orchestra, 1940–41*, Hindsight Records, #HSR-158, LP; Teague, *Searching*, 231.

10. Wydham Chow, "Getting Our Kicks with Bobby Troup," *Tiki News* 7 (1996): 5; Scott and Kelly, *Route 66*, 149; Teague, *Searching*, 235.

11. ASCAP, *Dictionary*, 511; Chow, "Our Kicks," 4–5; "Machine Records," *Billboard* 53 (September 30, 1941): 42; Teague, *Searching*, 236; Wallis, *Mother Road*, 11.

12. Scott and Kelly, *Route 66*, 149; Teague, *Searching*, 236; Bobby

Troup, "Introduction" in *Route 66 Traveler's Guide and Roadside Companion* by Tom Snyder (New York: St. Martin's, 2000), ix–x; Bobby Troup, telephone conversation with author, 20 May 1989.

13. ASCAP, *Dictionary*, 511; "Lyric Lingers," 11; Troup, conversation, 20 May 1989 and 15 February 1991; Wallis, *Mother Road*, 11.

14. Troup, conversation, February 15, 1991; John E. Brown, "Letters: Bobby Troup," *Los Angeles Times*, February 13, 1999.

15. Scott and Kelly, *Route 66*, 148; Troup, conversation, 8 April 1989 and 6 December 1998.

16. *Polk's Lancaster* [Pennsylvania] *Directory* (Boston: Polk, 1944), 485; Troup, conversation, 8 April 1989 and 16 October 1995; Wallis, *Mother Road*, 11.

17. Scott and Kelly, *Route 66*, 149; Wallis, *Mother Road*, 11; Teague, *Searching*, 229.

18. Scott and Kelly, *Route 66*, 146.

19. Scott and Kelly, *Route 66*, 149; Troup, conversation, 11 February 1989; Teague, *Searching*, 228–29; Krim, "Song Map," 59.

20. Scott and Kelly, *Route 66*, 149; Troup, conversation, 20 May 1989; Wallis, *Mother Road*, 11; "Weather Calendar," *Intelligencer Journal* [Lancaster, PA], February 7, 1946.

21. Dan Cupper, *The Pennsylvania Turnpike: A History* (Lebanon, PA: Applied Arts, 1990), 18–19; WPA, *Pennsylvania: A Guide to the Keystone State* (New York: Oxford University, 1940), 483–84.

22. Polmar and Allen, *World War II*, 679; Bobby Troup, interview by Robert Roth, *All Things Considered*, NPR, 6 May 2000.

23. Drew Greenland, "Route 66," *Life* (June 1983): 73; "Lyric Lingers," 11; Scott and Kelly, *Route 66*, 149; Teague, *Searching*, 229–30; Troup, interview; Wallis, *Mother Road*, 11, 13.

24. "Everyday Magazine," *St. Louis Post-Dispatch*, February 9, 1946; Scott and Kelly, *Route 66*, 149.

25. Arthur Krim, "Lyric Cartography of Route 66," typescript, Newberry Library, Chicago, 1996, 13; William Stage, "Americans and the Automobile," *SCA News Journal* 10, no. 1: 1, 6–7; Wallis, *Mother Road*, 14; Teague, *Searching*, 236.

26. Teague, *Searching*, 230.

27. Robert Kimball, ed., *Cole* (New York: Holt, Rinehart and Winston, 1971), 122; Arthur Krim, "Mapping Route 66, A Cultural Cartography" in *Roadside America*, ed. J. Jennings (Ames: Iowa State University, 1990); *Oxford English Dictionary*, vol. 8 (New York: Oxford University, 1989), 417; Charles Schwartz, *Cole Porter: A Biography* (New York: Dial, 1977), 134–36.

28. Scott and Kelly, *Route 66*, 149; Troup, conversation, 9 October 1994; Wallis, *Mother Road*, 13; WPA, *Oklahoma*, 223; Rittenhouse, *Guide Book*, 43.

29. Krim, "Mapping," 207; Scott and Kelly, *Route 66*, 149; Troup, conversation, 9 October 1994; Wallis, *Mother Road*, 13.

30. Rayner Banham, *Los Angeles: The Architecture of Four Ecologies* (New York: Penguin, 1970), 88; Otis Ferguson, "NY to LA," *New Republic* (July 14, 1941): 49–52; David Gebhard and Harriette Von Breton, *L.A. in the 30's* (Layton, UT: Peregrine Smith, 1975), 32; Krim, "Song Map," 50–51; Troup, conversation, 20 May 1989; Mat Weinstock, *My L.A.* (New York: Current, 1947), 47–53.

31. Teague, *Searching*, 231; Wallis, *Mother Road*, 1990, 13.

32. Hal Holly, "Los Angeles Band Brief," *Down Beat* 13 (February 11, 1946): 6.

33. Maria Cole with Louie Robinson, *Nat King Cole* (New York: William Morrow, 1971), 47; Leslie Gourse, *Unforgettable: The Life and Mystique of Nat King Cole* (New York: St. Martin's, 1991), 61–65; James Haskins and Kathleen Benson, *Nat King Cole* (New York: Stein and Day, 1984), 25; Colin Larkin, "Nat King Cole," *The Guinness Encyclopedia of Popular Music* (London: Guinness, 1993), 229; "Nat King Cole, 45," *New York Times*, February 16, 1965; Nat King Cole Trio, *Jumpin' at Capitol*, Classic Records, #RZ-71009, LP; Gunter Schuller, *The Swing Era, 1930–1945* (New York: Oxford University, 1989), 819.

34. "Cole, 45,"; Cole and Robinson, *Nat King Cole*, 36–40; Larkin, *Guinness*, 229.

35. "Cole, 45"; Stanley Dance, *The World of Earl Himes* (New York: Scribner's, 1977), 150; Haskins and Benson, *Nat King Cole*, 21; Schuller, *Swing*, 817; Barry Ulanow, *The Incredible Cosby* (New York: McGraw-Hill, 1948), 229.

36. Cole and Robinson, *Nat King Cole*, 39; Gourse, *Unforgettable*, 61; Haskins and Benson, *Nat King Cole*, 21; Larkin, *Guinness*, 291; Ulanow, *Cosby*, 229.

37. Cole and Robinson, *Nat King Cole*, 39–41; Scott DeVeaux, *Birth of Bebop* (Berkeley: University of California, 1997), 329; Ralph Eastman, "'Pitchin' Up a Boogie,' African-American Musicians in Los Angeles, 1930–1945," in *California Soul*, ed. J. C. DjeDje and E. S. Meadows (Berkeley: University of California, 1998), 85; Gourse, *Unforgettable*, 67; Haskins and Benson, *Nat King Cole*, 33–37; Schuller, *Swing*, 817–18; Lee Young, telephone conversation with author, 19 April 1989.

38. "King Cole's Managers Three," *Down Beat* 13 (May 20, 1946): 5; Teague, *Searching*, 231; Troup, conversation, 8 April 1989.

39. Chow, "Our Kicks," 5; "Lyric Lingers," 1981; Teague, *Searching*, 231; Troup, interview.

40. Scott and Kelly, *Route 66*, 150; Troup, conversations, 11 February and 8 April 1989; Wallis, *Mother Road*, 13–15; Troup, interview.

41. Teague, *Searching*, 230–31.

42. Maria Cole, telephone conversation with Arthur Krim, 13 April 1989; Nat King Cole, *Nat "King" Cole, 1946*, Classic Records, #1005, LP; Cole and Robinson, *Nat King Cole*, 164; Gourse, *Unforgettable*, 74–75; Hawkins and Benson, *Nat King Cole*, 46.

43. Greenland, "Route 66," 73; Krim, "Song Map," 54–55; "Lyric Lingers," 11; Scott and Kelly, *Route 66*, 149; Teague, *Searching*, 231; Troup, conversation, 8 April 1989; Wallis, *Mother Road*, 15.

44. Teague, *Searcing*, 231.

45. "Hollywood Echoes Lots of Good Music," *Down Beat* 13 (February 11, 1946): 3; "Lyric Lingers," 11.

46. Teague, *Searching*, 232.

47. John Houston Hall, ed., *Dictionary of American Regional English*, vol. 4 (Cambridge: Harvard University, 2002), 654; Krim, "Cartography," 18; Krim, "Mapping," 206.

48. Craig M. Carver, *American Regional Dialects* (Ann Arbor: University of Michigan, 1987), 202; William Craige and James R. Hulbert, *A Dictionary of American Regional English*, vol. 4 (Chicago: University of Chicago, 1944), 1980; H. L. Mencken, *The American Language*, supplement 2 (New York: Knopf, 1962), 85; Harold Wentworth, *American Dialect Dictionary* (New York: Thomas Y. Crowell, 1944), 522; Wilbur Zelinsky, "Cultural Geography" in *A Geography of Pennsylvania*, ed. E. W. Miller (College Park: Pennsylvania State University, 1995), 147.

49. Carver, *Dialects*, 48; Arthur Krim, "Right Near Sallisaw," *Steinbeck* 12, no. 1 (1999).

50. Chow, "Our Kicks," 5; *Nat "King" Cole 1946*, Classic Records; Cole and Robinson, *Nat King Cole*, 164; Christina Hopkinson [Capitol Records] to author, 19 May 1989; Troup, interview.

51. Nat King Cole Trio, *Straighten Up and Fly Right*, Vintage Jazz Classics, #1044, LP.

52. Ibid.

53. *Nat "King" Cole 1946*, Classic Records; Cole and Robinson, *Nat King Cole*, 164; Gourse, *Unforgettable*, 267; King Cole Trio, *King Cole Trio V-Disc*, Collector's Choice Music, #MVSCD-56.

54. "Advance Record Releases," *Billboard* 58 (April 27, 1946): 29; Cole and Robinson, *Nat King Cole*, 164; Hopkinson to author; *Nat "King" Cole 1946*, Classic Records.

55. "Records, King Cole Trio," *Down Beat* (May 20, 1946): 16; "Review of New Records," *Billboard* 58 (May 18, 1946): 34.

56. Ulanow, *Cosby*, 312; Georgie Auld, *Georgie Auld and His Orches-*

tra, Discovery Records, #1044; Bing Crosby, *Bing Crosby and the Andrews Sisters*, MCA/Decca, #MVSCD-56; Troup, conversation, 6 December 1998.

57. "Most Played Race Songs," *Billboard* 58 (July 13, 1946): 29; *Nat "King" Cole 1946*, Classic Records.

58. "Music, Fiddlers Three," *Newsweek* (August 18, 1946): 97; Gourse, *Unforgettable*, 67.

59. Bobby Troup, "Route 66!—," song sheet (New York: Burke and Van Husen, 1946).

60. James Ackerman, "Paper Trails," exhibition brochure, Newberry Library, Chicago, 1996; Krim, "Cartography," 16–17; Krim, "Mapping," 206–07; Krim, "Song Map," 58; Scott and Kelly, *Route 66*, 149; Teague, *Searching*, 235–37; Troup, conversation, 20 May 1989; Cynthia Troup, interview with author, Malibu, CA, 23 March 2002; idem, *Route 66 Song Map*, mixed media, 1946, Cynthia Troup Collection, Malibu, CA.

61. Troup, *Song Map*, back label.

62. John H. Finley, *Homer's Odyssey* (Cambridge, MA: Harvard, 1978), 35–36; Melinda Grenier Guiles, "Archeology of the Early Auto Age," *Wall Street Journal*, November 10, 1988; Geoffrey S. Kirk, "The Homeric Epics" in *Encyclopedia Britannica* 20 (Chicago: University of Chicago, 1994), 636; Krim, "Mapping," 206; Krim, "Song Map," 58.

63. "Lyric Lingers," 11.

64. "King Cole Trio Plans Serious Stuff," *Down Beat* (March 25, 1946): 3; Schuller, *Swing*, 824.

65. Cole and Robinson, *Nat King Cole*, 164; Gourse, *Unforgettable*, 79; Haskins and Benson, *Nat King Cole*, 46–47; Larkin, *Guinness*, 292; *Nat "King" Cole 1946*, Classic Records; Nat King Cole, *Nat "King" Cole 1946–1947*, Classic Records, #1005, LP; Schuller, *Swing*, 824.

CHAPTER ELEVEN

1. Patricia Buckley, *Route 66: Remnants* (offprint by the author, 1988), 11–12; Quinta Scott and Susan Croce Kelly, *Route 66: The Highway and Its People* (Norman: University of Oklahoma, 1988), 184; Tom Teague, *Searching for 66* (Springfield, IL: Samizdat House, 1991), 129; Michael Wallis, *Route 66: The Mother Road* (New York: St. Martin's, 1990), 34.

2. Teague, *Searching*, 129.

3. Bosley Crowther, "The Screen in Review: 'The Story of Will Rogers,'" *New York Times*, July 18, 1952; Thomas M. Pryor, "Film Phenomenon: One Picture Actor," *New York Times*, January 25, 1952; Scott and Kelly, *Route 66*, 168–69; Wallis, *Mother Road*, 22–24, 65, 101.

4. Warren J. Belasco, *Americans on the Road: From Auto Camp to Motel* (Cambridge: MIT, 1979), 141; John Jakle, et al., *The Motel in America* (Baltimore: Johns Hopkins University, 1996), 18; Arthur Krim, "Motel Mystery Revealed," *SCA News Journal* 2, no. 1 (1982): 3; Chester Liebs, *Main Street to Miracle Mile* (Boston: New York Graphic Society, 1985), 182.

5. Krim, "Motel Mystery"; Liebs, *Main Street*, 188–89.

6. Arthur Krim, "Pre-War Motel Listings," *SCA News Journal* 11, no. 3 (1990): 19; *Lodging for a Night* (New York: Duncan Hines, 1949), 22, 43, 105, 219, 252.

7. Hal Borland, "From Pup Tents to Motels," *New York Times*, September 16, 1951; Krim, "Motel Mystery"; "Motels Become Big Business," *Business Week* (September 3, 1952); "Motels: Billion Dollar Roadside Business," *Newsweek* (September 29, 1952): 76–77.

8. Jim Edwards and Hal Ottaway, *Vanished Splendor II: A Postcard Album of Oklahoma City* (Oklahoma City: Abalache Book Shop, 1984), nos. 373–84; Michael B. Jackson, "The Curt Teich Postcard Collection," *SCA Journal* 2, no. 6 (1985): 8–9; "Route 66" file listings, Curt Teich Archives, Wauconda, IL.

9. Jerry McClanahan, "Rock, Scissors, Pavement," *Route 66 Maga-*

zine 4, no. 1 (1996): 24–26; Michael Wallis and Suzanne Wallis, *Route 66 Postcards* (New York: St. Martin's, 1993).

10. David Gebhard and Harriette Von Bretton, *L.A. in the 30s* (Layton, UT: Peregrine Smith, 1975), 40–41; Krim, "Mapping Route 66, A Cultural Cartography" in *Roadside America*, ed. J. Jennings (Ames: Iowa State University, 1990), 203; "No Left Turn Here," *Missouri Motor News* (February 1932); Jack Rittenhouse, *A Guide Book to Highway 66* (Albuquerque: University of New Mexico, 1989), 110; Scott and Kelly, *Route 66*, 198–99; John Weiss, *Traveling the New, Historic Route 66 of Illinois* (Frankford, IL: A. O. Motivation Programs, 1997), 13.

11. Buckley, *Remnants*, 37; R. Robinson Rowe, "Red Rock Bridge on U.S. 66," *California Highways and Public Works* 26, no. 7–8 (1947): 20–22; Wallis, *Mother Road*, 207.

12. Donald Jackson, *Great American Bridges and Dams* (Washington, D.C.: Preservation, 1988), 248–49.

13. Scott and Kelly, *Route 66*, 187.

14. "Oklahoma Opens Major Toll Pike," *New York Times*, May 17, 1953; "Oklahoma To Offer Road Bonds," *New York Times*, January 20, 1950.

15. Krim, "Mapping," 204.

16. Scott and Kelly, *Route 66*, 182; Wallis, *Mother Road*, 113.

17. Tom Lewis, *Divided Highways: Building the Interstate Highways* (New York: Viking Penguin, 1997), 43–45, 53–55; Mark Rose, *Interstate Express Highway Politics* (Lawrence: University of Kansas, 1979), 11.

18. Norman Bel Geddes, *Magic Motorways* (New York: Random House, 1940), 4–5.

19. Richard F. Weingroff, "Broader Ribbons Across the Land," *Public Roads*, June 1996, 8.

20. House of Representatives, *Toll Roads and Free Roads*, 76th Congress, House Document 272, 1939, plates 11, 57; Weingroff,

"Broader Ribbons," 9; Lewis, *Divided Highways*, 53–55; FHA, op. cit., 272.

21. *America's Highways, 1776–1976: A History of the Federal-Aid Program* (Washington, D.C.: FHA, 1976), 158–59; Albert C. Rose, *Historic American Roads* (New York: Crown, 1976), 108; M. Rose, *Interstate Politics*, 20–21; Weingroff, "Broader Ribbons," 10–12.

22. "A 37,681-Mile Super Highway System Planned," *Herald Tribune*, August 3, 1947.

23. Weingroff, "Broader Ribbons," 12–16; Lewis, *Divided Highways*, 72, 89–91, 105–13.

24. Weingroff, "Broader Ribbons," 16.

25. Ibid., 32; Lewis, *Divided Highways*, 115–17; Richard F. Weingroff, "When Highways Had Names," *SCA Journal* 14, no. 1 (1996): 32.

26. *America's Highways*, 473–74; Lewis, *Divided Highways*, 121; M. Rose, *Interstate Politics*, 88–89; Weingroff, "Highways," 33–35.

27. Lewis, *Divided Highways*, 125–27, 129–31; Weingroff, *Highways*, 17–18, 36–38.

28. A. E. Johnson to members of AASHO, memorandum, 22 January 1957, NRC.

29. A. E. Johnson, "Committee on U.S. Route Numbering" in *Golden Anniversary*, ed. AASHO staff (Washington, D.C.: AASHO, 1964), 121; idem to members of AASHO, memorandum, 5 March 1957, NRC.

30. A. E. Johnson to members of AASHO, memorandum, 20 June 1957, NRC.

31. A. E. Johnson to C. Bryce Bennet [Idaho State Highway Engineer], 26 August 1957, NRC.

32. *America's Highways*, 277; "Interstate Route Marker Developed," *American Road Builder* (October 1957): 25; "Interstate Route Marker Selected and Numerology Map Approved," *American Highways* 32, no. 4 (1957): 1; A. E. Johnson to B. D. Tallamy [Washington, D.C.

Bureau of Public Roads], 29 August 1957, NRC; idem, "My Years in Washington," *American Highways* (October 1972): 10; Lewis, *Divided Highways*, 130; "Official Route Numbering for the National System of Interstate and Defense Highways," pamphlet, AASHO, Washington, D.C., 1957; Weingroff, "Highways," 37–38.

33. Buckley, *Remnants*, 13; Krim, "Mapping," 204; "Official Route"; Scott and Kelly, *Route 66*, 188; Wallis, *Mother Road*, 26.

34. Buckley, *Remnants*, 12; "Official Route"; Weingroff, "Highways," 43–44.

35. Jack Cutberth to A. E. Johnson [AASHO], 6 September 1926, NRC; A. E. Johnson to members of AASHO, memorandum, 24 September 1957, NRC.

36. A. E. Johnson to Jack Cutberth [U.S. Highway 66 Association, Clinton, Oklahoma] 11 October 1957, NRC.

37. Buckley, *Remnants*, 12–13; Scott and Kelly, *Route 66*, 184.

38. *New Travel Guide Along Route 66* (San Francisco: H. S. Crocker, 1965); Scott and Kelly, *Route 66*, 185.

CHAPTER TWELVE

1. Ann Charters, "Introduction" in *On the Road* by Jack Kerouac (New York: Penguin, 1991), x–xiv; Jack Kerouac, *Visions of Cody* (New York: McGraw-Hill, 1972), 338; Gerald Nicosia, *Memory Babe: A Critical Biography of Jack Kerouac* (New York: Grove, 1983), 84; Steve Turner, *Jack Kerouac: Angelheaded Hipster* (New York: Viking, 1996), 83; Steven Watson, *The Birth of the Beat Generation* (New York: Pantheon, 1995), 22–23.

2. Ann Charters, *Kerouac: A Biography* (San Francisco: Straight Arrow, 1973), 129–30; Nicosia, *Memory*, 343–48; Watson, *Birth*, 136–37.

3. Jack Kerouac, *On the Road* (New York: Viking, 1957), 14–15.

4. Charters, "Introduction," xx–xxi; idem, *Kerouac*, 285; Nicosia, *Memory*, 556–57; Turner, *Hipster*, 119; Watson, *Birth*, 253–56, endmap.

5. Jack Kerouac, *On the Road* (New York: Signet, 1958), back cover.

6. Eric Barnouw, *The Image Empire: A History of Broadcasting in the United States from 1953* (New York: Oxford University, 1970), 24, 80.

7. C. Horace Newcomb, *Encyclopedia of Television*, vol. 2 (Chicago: Fitzroy Dearborn, 1997), 1123–25.

8. Herbert B. Leonard, telephone conversation with author, 30 August 1989; Michael Wallis, *Route 66: The Mother Road* (New York: St. Martin's, 1990), 227; Mel Gussow, "Sterling Silliphant, 78," *New York Times*, April 27, 1996; Newcomb, *Encyclopedia*, 1488–89.

9. Kermit D. Park, "The Original Road Warriors," *Route 66 Magazine* 4, no. 1 (1996): 18–19; Daniel Ross, "Route 66 Episodes," mimeograph, 1990, Cedarville, CA, 1990; Sterling Silliphant to author, 28 July 1989; Newcomb, *Encyclopedia*, 1406; Leonard, conversation; Wallis, *Mother Road*, 227.

10. Barnouw, *Image Empire*, 153; Les Brown, *Encyclopedia of Television*, 3rd ed. (Detroit: Gale Research, 1992); idem, *Television* (New York: Harcourt Brace, 1971), 71; Leonard, conversation; Silliphant to author, 28 July 1989.

11. Michael Seiler, "Route 66: The Highway We All Have Traveled," *Los Angeles Times*, July 24, 1977.

12. Tom Teague, *Searching for Route 66* (Springfield, IL: Samizdat House, 1991), 232; Wallis, *Mother Road*, 15.

13. "Fall Preview, Friday," *TV Guide* 8 (September 24, 1960): 20, 27; Ross, "Episodes."

14. Bob Chandler, review of "Route 66," *Variety* (October 12, 1960): 32.

15. Barnouw, *Image Empire*, 149, 162–69; Brown, *Encyclopedia*, 409; Chandler, review; Park, "Road Warriors," 19; "Nixon-Kennedy Debate," *TV Guide* 8 (October 7, 1960): A65; "Route 66, Adventure: Debut," *TV Guide* 8 (October 7, 1960): A67–68.

16. Wallis, *Mother Road*, 227–29; Ross, "Episodes," 20.

17. Park, "Road Warriors," 18; Daniel Ross to author, June 10, 1990; idem, "Episodes."

18. Park, "Road Warriors," 18.

19. Richard Gehman, "He's Always Racing His Motor: 'Route 66's' George Maharis," *TV Guide* 10 (April 14, 1962): 5–7; "A Knock Develops in 'Route 66,'" *TV Guide* 11 (January 26, 1963): 22–25; Wallis, *Mother Road*, 227.

20. Park, "Road Warriors," 20; Newcomb, *Encyclopedia*, 1407–08; Nelson Riddle, *Route 66 Theme and Other Great TV Themes*, Capitol Records, #1771k, LP; Dan Harlow, "Songs of the Road," *Route 66 Magazine* 5, no. 1 (1998): 24–26.

21. Barnouw, *Image Empire*, 235–38.

22. Jim Dawson and Steve Propes, *What Was the First Rock 'N' Roll Record?* (Boston: Faber and Faber, 1992), xviii, 1–4; Nelson George, *The Death of Rhythm and Blues* (New York: Penguin, 1988), 26–28; Leslie Gourse, *Unforgettable: The Life and Mystique of Nat King Cole* (New York: St. Martin's, 1991); John S. Winslow, *Jazz: The Transition Years* (New York: Appleton Century, 1966). 141.

23. Chuck Berry, *The Autobiography* (New York: Harmony, 1987), 89–90; Robert Christgau, "Chuck Berry" in *The Rolling Stone Illustrated History of Rock and Roll* (New York: Random House, 1976), 58; Brock Herlander, *The Rock Who's Who* (New York: Schrimmer, 1996), 45; Colin Larkin, "Chuck Berry," *The Guinness Encyclopedia of Popular Music* (London: Guiness, 1993), 138; Krista Reese, *Chuck Berry, Mr. Rock 'N' Roll* (London: Proteus, 1982), 19.

24. Berry, *Autobiography*, 89–90; Johnnie Johnson, telephone conversation with author, 20 November 1991; Larkin, "Chuck Berry," 138.

25. Berry, *Autobiography*, 103–07, 154; idem, *Rock & Roll Music/Blue Feeling*, Chess Records, #1671, 45rpm; Christgau, "Chuck Berry," 58–60, 63; John Curtis, *History of Chess Records* (New York: Bloomsbury, 1998), 130–32; Herlander, *Who's Who*, 45; "Honor Roll of Hits," *Billboard* (September 24, 1955): 20; Larkin, "Chuck Berry," 138; Reese, *Mr. Rock 'N' Roll*, 23, 44.

26. Berry, *Autobiography*, 199–207; Christgau, "Chuck Berry," 62; Herlander, *Who's Who*, 46; Reese, *Mr. Rock 'N' Roll*, 49–51.

27. Chuck Berry, *More Rock 'N' Roll Rarities*, Chess Records, #9190, LP.

28. Chuck Berry, *New Juke Box Hits*, Chess Records, #1456, LP.

29. Christgau, "Chuck Berry," 63; Reese, *Who's Who*, 118.

30. Stanley Booth, *Keith* (New York: St. Martin's, 1995), 33–34; Christgau, " Chuck Berry," 58; David Dalton and Mick Farren, eds., *Rolling Stones: In Their Own Words* (London: Omnibus, 1994), 14; Colin Larkin, "Keith Richards," *Guinness*, 959; Keith Richards, interview with Robert Greenfield, in *The Rolling Stone Interviews*, ed. P. Herbst (New York: St. Martin's, 1989), 158.

31. Richards, interview, 159.

32. Booth, *Keith*, 33–34; Dalton and Farren, *Rolling Stones*, 20–21; Larkin, "Keith Richards," 959.

33. Griel Marcus, "The Beatles," in *Illustrated History* (New York: Random House, 1976), 172–74.

34. Martin Elliot, *The Rolling Stones Complete Recording Sessions, 1963–1989* (London: Blanford, 1990), 10–12, 16; Larkin, "Keith Richards," 959.

35. Elliot, *Complete*, 17–18.

36. The Rolling Stones, *Meet Me at the Bottom*, Magic Dwarf Records, #MDR-6, LP.

37. The Rolling Stones, *Radio Rocks*, Starlight Records, #87011, LP; Elliot, *Complete*, 23.

38. Christgau, "Chuck Berry," 185; Elliot, *Complete*, 17–18; Rolling Stones, *England's Newest Hit Makers*, London/Decca Records, #7375.

39. Booth, *Keith*, 57; Elliot, *Complete*, 17–19, 27–33.

40. Brian Hinton, *Celtic Crossroads: The Art of Van Morrison* (London: Unwin, 1997), 56, 64; Griel Marcus, "Van Morrison," *Illustrated History*, 294–96.

41. Elliot, *Complete*, 42.

42. Them, *The Story of Them Featuring Van Morrison*, Deram/Decca Records, #42284, LP.

43. Elliot, *Complete*, 89.

CHAPTER THIRTEEN

1. Kerry Brougher, "Words as Landscape" in *Ed Ruscha*, ed. N. Benezra and K. Brougher (Washington, D.C.: Smithsonian Institution, 2000), 157; idem, *Joe Goode, Edward Ruscha* (Balboa, CA: Fine Arts Patrons of Newport Harbor, 1968), 1; Edward Ruscha, *Edward Ruscha, Young Artist* (Minneapolis: Minneapolis Institute of Art, 1972), 6–7; Henry T. Hopkins, "Director's Foreword" in *The Works of Edward Ruscha*, ed. Henry T. Hopkins (New York: Hudson Hills, 1982), 11; Richard Marshall, *Edward Ruscha, Los Angeles Apartments* (New York: Whitney Museum, 1990), 5; Ralph Rugoff, "The Last Word, Ed Ruscha," *Art News* 88, no. 10 (1989): 123.

2. Joe Goode, telephone conversation with author, 17 June 1999; Dave Hickey, "Available Light," *Works of Edward Ruscha*, 26; Hopkins, *Joe Goode*, 1, 10; Anne Livet, "Chronology," *Works of Edward Ruscha*, 159–60; Edward Ruscha, "Appreciation" in *Joe Goode* (Newport Beach, CA: Orange County Museum of Art, 1996), 1–3; idem, *Edward Ruscha*, 10–11.

3. Goode, conversation; Dave Hickey, "The Work of Ed Ruscha" (lecture, Graduate School of Design, Harvard University, Cambridge, MA, October 27, 1993); Livet, "Chronology," 160; Marshall, *Apartments*, 5; Rugoff, "Last Word," 124–25; Ruscha, *Edward Ruscha*, 7, 12–13; George Wagner, *The Books of Ed Ruscha* (Cambridge: Graduate School of Design, Harvard University, 1993), 3.

4. Marshall, *Apartments*, 5; Jerry McClanahan, "Bypassed Books," *Route 66 Magazine* 4, no. 3 (1997): 41–42; Phyllis Rozenweig, "Sixteen (And Counting): Ed Ruscha's Books," *Ed Ruscha*, 178; Rugoff, "Last Word," 125; Edward Ruscha, *Twentysix Gasoline Stations* (Los Angeles: Heavy Industries, 1963).

5. Arthur Krim, "Mapping Route 66, A Cultural Cartography" in *Roadside America*, ed. J. Jennings (Ames: Iowa State University,

1990), 204–05; McClanahan, "Bypassed," 41.

6. Hopkins, *Joe Goode*, 1968; Lucy R. Lippard, *Pop Art* (London: Thames and Hudson, 1966), 151; Wagner, *Books of Ed*, 1.

7. Rayner Banham, "Under the Hollywood Sign" in *Edward Ruscha, 1962–74*, ed. J. Drew (London: Arts Council of Great Britain, 1975), 3–5; Brougher, "Landscape," 158; Hopkins, "Foreward," 11; Rugoff, "Last Word," 125.

8. David Halberstram, *The Fifties* (New York: Villard, 1993), 268–69; Richard Schickel, *Brando: A Life in Our Times* (New York: Atheneum, 1991), 81–85.

9. Peter Fonda, *Don't Tell Dad* (New York: Hyperion, 1998), 240–44; Lee Hill, *Easy Rider* (London: British Film Institute, 1996), 10–11, 13–14; Dennis Hopper, "Into the Issue of the Good Old Time Movie Versus the Good Old Time," in *Easy Rider: Screenplay* by P. Fonda, et al. (New York: Signet Classics, 1969), 15; idem, *Out of the Sixties* (Pasadena, CA: Twelvetrees, 1986); Mark Singer, "Whose Movie Is This?" *The New Yorker* (June 28, 1998): 113.

10. Peter Biskind, *Easy Riders, Raging Bulls* (New York: Simon and Schuster, 1998), 61–63; Fonda, *Don't Tell*, 246–51; Hill, *Easy Rider*, 14–17, 20; Singer, "Whose Movie," 113.

11. Fonda, *Don't Tell*, 253–55, 259–60; idem, "On the Road Still Riding Solo, Free and Easy," *New York Times*, June 26, 1998; Hill, *Easy Rider*, 20–22, 24; Singer, "Whose Movie," 113.

12. Fonda, *Don't Tell*, 263.

13. *Easy Rider*, VHS, directed by Dennis Hopper (1969; Los Angeles, Columbia Home Video, 1998); Henry Fonda with Howard Teichman, *Fonda: My Life* (New York: New American Library, 1981), 237; Fonda, et al., *Screenplay*, 49–50; Donald C. Jackson, *Great American Bridges and Dams* (Washington, D.C.: Preservation Press, 1988), 249; Arthur Krim, "Dear SCA, 'Easy Rider,'" *SCA News* 6, no. 2 (1998): 6–7.

14. *Easy Rider*, VHS; Fonda, *Don't Tell*, 264–65; Fonda, et al., *Screenplay*, 51–52; Krim, "Dear SCA."

15. Hill, *Easy Rider*, 24–26; Fonda, *Don't Tell*, 256–66, 268, 271.

16. Robert Christgau, "Easy Rider's' Soundtrack," in Fonda, et al., *Screenplay*, 22–25; Hill, *Easy Rider*, 27–28.

17. Fonda, *Don't Tell*, 277–79; Hill, *Easy Rider*, 29.

18. Vincent Canby, film review of *Easy Rider*, *New York Times*, July 15, 1969.

19. Hill, *Easy Rider*, 32–33; Debora Holdstein, "Easy Rider" in *International Dictionary of Films and Filmmakers*, ed. N. Thomas (London: St. James, 1990), 279.

20. "Crazy Like a Fox," *Forbes* (February 1, 1976): 36; Chip Lord, *Automerica* (New York: Dutton, 1976), 133; idem to author, 10 July 1989; Hudson Marquez, telephone conversation with author, 16 July 1989.

21. C. Edson Armi, *The Art of American Car Design* (College Park: Pennsylvania State University, 1988), 75–76; Stephen Bayley, *Design Heroes: Harley Earl* (London: Grafton, 1992), 99–107; Grady Gammage and Stephen L. Jones, "'Orgasm in Chrome': The Rise and Fall of the Automobile Tailfin," *Journal of Popular Culture* 8 (1974): 134–35.

22. Chip Lord and the Ant Farm, "A Backward Look at the Forward Look," *Rolling Stone* 168 (August 29, 1974): 68; Lord, *Automerica*, 124.

23. Lord, et al., "Backward," 68.

24. Gordon Chaplin, "Stanley Marsh Plays with His Money," *Esquire* 82, no. 12 (1974): 168–69, 240; *Forbes*, "Crazy"; "The New Supercollectors," *Newsweek* (August 11, 1975): 68–69; Jepk Thibeau, "The Man Who Cast the Land," *Rolling Stone* 167 (August 13,1974): 36.

25. Chaplin, "Stanley Marsh," 169; Lord, *Automerica*, 124; Lord, conversation; Marquez, conversation.

26. Frank Deford, "A Sight for Tired Eyes," *Sports Illustrated* (April 18, 1977): 94; Lord, *Automerica*, 124; Lord, conversation; Marquez, conversation.

27. Deford, "Tired Eyes," 96; Lord, *Automerica*, 124, 126; Lord, conversation; Marquez, conversation.

28. Chaplin, "Stanley Marsh," 241; Deford, "Tired Eyes," 96; Patton, *Open Road: A Celebration of the American Highway* (New York: Simon and Schuster, 1986), 244.

29. Deford, "Tired Eyes," 96.

30. Chaplin, "Stanley Marsh," 241; Lord, *Automerica*, 127; Lord, conversation.

31. "Supercollectors," 69; "Crazy," 36; Lord, *Automerica*, 128–29; Deford, "Tired Eyes," 98; Patton, *Open Road*, 244.

32. Lord, *Automerica*, cover.

33. Daniel Ichbiah and Susan Knepper, *The Making of Microsoft* (Rocklin, CA: Prima, 1991), 20–21; Stephen Manes and Paul Adres, *Gates: How Microsoft's Mogul Reinvented an Industry* (New York: Simon and Schuster, 1993), 63; Robert Slater, *Portraits in Silicon* (Cambridge: MIT, 1987), 263–65.

34. Manes and Adres, *Gates*, 63–64; "William Gates," *People Magazine* (December 26, 1983): 37.

35. Ichbiah and Knepper, *Making*, 24–25; Manes and Adres, *Gates*, 74; "William Gates," 37.

36. Manes and Adres, *Gates*, 74.

37. Ichbiah and Knepper, *Making*, 25; Manes and Andrews, *Gates*, 75, 79.

38. Ichbiah and Knepper, *Making*, 26; Manes and Andrews, *Gates*, 219, Fig. 26; John Markoff, "A Tale from the Days When It Was Still Micro Soft," *New York Times*, September 18, 2000.

39. Manes and Andrews, *Gates*, 219–28; Markoff, "Tale"; Slater, *Portraits*, 268.

CHAPTER FOURTEEN

1. Patricia Buckley, *Route 66: Remnants* (offprint by the author,

1988), 26; Quinta Scott and Susan Croce Kelly, *Route 66: The Highway and Its People* (Norman: University of Oklahoma, 1988), 187; Richard F. Weingroff, "When Highways Had Names," *SCA Journal* 14, no. 1 (1996): 37.

2. Helen Leavitt, *The Superhighway Hoax* (Garden City, NY: Doubleday, 1970), endmaps; *Rand McNally Road Atlas* (Chicago: Rand McNally, 1969).

3. Scott and Kelly, *Route 66*, 187.

4. J. Dekema, "Cajon Pass," *California Highways and Public Works* 32, no. 5–6 (1953): 7–11.

5. Paul O. Harding, "Southern Freeways," *California Highways and Public Works* 33, no. 1–2 (1954): 9; Arthur Krim, "The Four-Level 'Stack' as Los Angeles Icon," paper given at Society for Commercial Archeology, Los Angeles, April 18, 1996; *Los Angeles and Vicinity Freeway System* (Los Angeles: Automobile Club of Southern California, [1957]).

6. "The 1965 Construction Picture," *California Highways and Public Works* 44, no. 11–12 (1965): 11–17; Laurel Clark [California Department of Transportation] to author, 7 January 1999; Mary Hanel, "Route Numbering Systems Used on California State Highways," 1988, photocopy, CALTRANS Library, Sacramento, CA; E. T. Telford, "District 7 Progress," *California Highways and Public Works* 44, no. 3–4 (1965): 49.

7. Taylor Smith, "California's Interstate 15," *California Highways and Public Works* 44, no. 9–10 (1965): 14–18; Carl B. Wolfram, "Mountain Pass," *California Highways and Public Works* 43, no. 1–2 (1964): 53–56.

8. Clark to author.

9. Roy Fonda, telephone conversation with author, 3 February 1999; Charles McClean, telephone conversation with author, January 17, 1999; James R. Powell, "Route 66 Timeline, With Emphasis on Missouri," *Show Me Route 66* 12, no. 4 (Fall 2001): 13; Michael Wallis, *Route 66: The Mother Road* (New York: St. Martin's, 1990), 30.

10. Michael Seiler, "Route 66: The Highway We All Have Traveled," *Los Angeles Times*, July 24, 1977.

11. Scott and Kelly, *Route 66*, 185.

12. Buckley, *Remnants*, 13; Wallis, *Mother Road*, 113–15.

13. Thomas W. Pew, "Route 66: Ghost Road of the Okies," *American Heritage* 28, no. 5 (1977): 26.

14. John M. Crewdson, "The Interstate's Shadow Is Overtaking Route 66," *New York Times*, July 7, 1981; Don Dedra, "Old U.S. 66," *Arizona Highways* 57, no. 7 (1981): 15.

15. Drew Greenland, "Route 66," *Life* (June 1983): 76.

16. "No More Kicks on Route 66," *San Francisco Chronicle*, October 14, 1984.

17. Jack Freidenrich, "Report of the Special Committee on U.S. Route Numbering," AASHTO meeting, Duluth, MN, June 27, 1985, photocopy, NRC; "The Road Ends for Route 66," *AASHTO News*, June 27, 1985; "Route Numbering Committee Agenda," AASHTO meeting, June 26, 1985, photocopy, NRC.

18. Richard F. Weingroff [FHA] to author, 6 January 1999.

19. "Route Numbering," 29–30.

20. "Final Chapter Is Written for Route 66," *New York Times*, June 29, 1985.

21. Phil Patton, *Open Road: A Celebration of the American Highway* (New York: Simon and Schuster, 1986), 230.

22. *Historic Route 66*, pamphlet, [1998], Historic Route 66 Association of Arizona, Kingman, AZ.

23. "The '89 Fun Run," *Route 66 News* (Arizona), June 1989.

24. Teri A. Cleeland, "US Route 66: Historic Context," 1988, photocopy, Kaibab National Forest Archives, Williams, AZ; Michael B. Jackson, "Route 66 in Arizona Accepted By National Register," *SCA News* 9, no. 2 (1987): 1; Arthur Krim, "Mapping Route 66, A Cultural Cartography," in *Roadside America*, ed. J. Jennings (Ames: Iowa State University, 1990), 205–06.

25. Mary Ann Anders, ed., *Route 66 in Oklahoma: An Historic Preservation Survey* (Stillwater: Oklahoma State University, 1984); Melvina T. Heisch, "Sooners Set Sights on Route 66," *SCA News* 9, no. 1–3 (1987): 4–5; John Conoboy, "Where the Planner Meets the Road: The NPS Route 66 Study," *CRM* 16, no. 6 (1993): 34–35.

26. Scott and Kelly, *Route 66*, xiii–xiv.

27. Ibid., 188–89.

28. Tom Snyder, *The Route 66 Traveler's Guide* (New York: St. Martin's, 1990); Wallis, *Mother Road*.

29. Wallis, *Mother Road*, 1.

30. Jack Rittenhouse, *A Guide Book to Highway 66* (Albuquerque: University of New Mexico, 1989), v–vii.

31. Synder, *Traveler's Guide*, xv.

32. Krim, "Mapping," 206; "Route 66: Auto River of the American West," in *Geographical Snapshots of North America*, ed. D. Janelle (New York: Guilford, 1992), 32.

33. "Clothing and Accessories," *Route 66 Magazine* 4, no. 1 (1996): 17.

Index

About the Author and Editor

ARTHUR KRIM (AUTHOR) was born in 1943 in Cambridge, Massachusetts, and he was raised in the Boston area. He received his B.A. in geography (with honors) from Clark University, his M.A. in geography from the University of Chicago, and his Ph.D. in geography at Clark University. Dr. Krim has taught at Boston University (1980–84), Salve Regina University (1984–91), and the Boston Architectural Center (since 1992), and he has served as a survey consultant with the Cambridge Historical Commission (1971–77) and the Massachusetts Historical Commission (1978–2005), and as a consultant with Sotheby's Photographs Division (since 1997). He is a founding board member of the Society for Commerical Archeology. His research articles on Route 66 have appeared in *Landscape, Journal of Cultural Geography, Journal of Historical Geography, SCA Journal, Steinbeck Newsletter,* and two books: *Roadside America* (Iowa State, 1990) and *Place, Power, Situation and Spectacle* (Rowman and Littlefield, 1994). Dr. Krim resides in Cambridge, Massachusetts.

DENIS WOOD (EDITOR) was born in 1945 in Cleveland, Ohio. He passed his childhood along the Cuyahoga River and his youth in Cleveland Heights. He received a B.A. in English from Western Reserve University and an M.A. and a Ph.D. in geography at Clark University. From 1974 to 1998 he was a professor of design at North Carolina State University where he taught environmental psychology and landscape history. In 1998, Dr. Wood became an independent writer and scholar. His books include *World Geography Today* (Holt, Rinehart, and Winston, 1976; 1980), with Saul Israel and Douglas Johnson; *The Power of Maps* (Guilford, 1992), which was a History Book Club and a Quality Paperback Book Club selection; *Home Rules* (Johns Hopkins, in association with the Center for American Places, 1994), with Robert J. Beck; and *Five Billion Years of Global Change: A History of the Land* (Guilford, 2004), among others. Dr. Wood resides in Raleigh, North Carolina.

CENTER FOR
AMERICAN
PLACES

The Center for American Places is a tax-exempt 501(c)(3) nonprofit organization, founded in 1990, whose educational mission is to enhance the public's understanding of, appreciation for, and affection for the natural and built environment. Underpinning this mission is the belief that books provide an indispensable foundation for comprehending and caring for the places where we live, work, and explore. Books live. Books endure. Books make a difference. Books are gifts to civilization.

With offices in Santa Fe, New Mexico, and Staunton, Virginia, Center editors bring to publication as many as thirty books per year under the Center's own imprint or in association with publishing partners. The Center is also engaged in numerous other programs that emphasize the interpretation of place through art, literature, scholarship, exhibitions, and field research. The Center's Cotton Mather Library in Arthur, Nebraska, its Martha A. Strawn Photographic Library in Davidson, North Carolina, and a ten-acre reserve along the Santa Fe River in Florida are available as retreats upon request. The Center is also affiliated with the Rocky Mountain Land Library in Colorado.

The Center strives every day to make a difference through books, research, and education. For more information, please send inquiries to P.O. Box 23225, Santa Fe, NM 87502, U.S.A., or visit the Center's Website: (www.americanplaces.org).

ABOUT THE BOOK:

The text for *Route 66: Iconography of the American Highway* was set in New Baskerville with Franklin Gothic display. The paper is acid-free Japanese A, 140 gsm weight. The book was printed and bound in China.

FOR THE CENTER FOR AMERICAN PLACES:

George F. Thompson, President and Publisher
Randall B. Jones, Independent Editor
Amber K. Lautigar, Associate Editor
Kendall B. McGhee, Assistant Editor
Ernest L. Toney, Jr., Chelsea Miller Goin Intern
Kristine K. Harmon, Manuscript Editor
Rebecca A. Marks, Production Assistant
David Skolkin, Book Designer and Art Director
Dave Keck, of Global Ink, Inc., Production Coordinator